The Chartered
Institute of Marketing

CIM Companion:

marketing operations

CIM Publishing

CIM Publishing

The Chartered Institute of Marketing
Moor Hall
Cookham
Berkshire
SL6 9QH

www.cim.co.uk

First published 2002
© CIM Publishing 2002

Series Editors: Mark Stuart and John Ling.

Applications for the copyright holder's written permission to reproduce any part of this publication should be addressed to the Editors at the publisher's address.

It is the publisher's policy to use paper manufactured from sustainable forests.

British Library Cataloguing in Publication Data
A CIP catalogue record for this book can be obtained from the British Library.

ISBN 0 902130 94 3

Printed and bound by The Cromwell Press, Trowbridge, Wiltshire.
Cover design by Marie-Claire Bonhommet.

contents

Study guide

This companion is written to complement the recommended core text by Kotler, Armstrong, Saunders and Wong, *Principles of Marketing* (2nd edition, Prentice-Hall, 2000.) It aims to offer you support as either an individual or group learner as you move along the road to becoming a competent and proficient marketer. This is a process of learning that has two important elements:

Understanding marketing concepts and their application

The study text in the following Sessions has been deliberately written to highlight the concepts that you will need to grasp as you start to understand marketing at an operational level, what marketing can achieve, and how it is implemented. The material is described briefly and concisely, to enable you to cover a range of key material at Advanced Certificate level. It does not attempt to be fully comprehensive, and you should read widely from other sources, including the recommended course text (readings are specified for each of the Sessions in this book, and shown in Table 3 which follows), the marketing press and national newspapers, to develop your understanding of the concepts introduced here. More comprehensive marketing textbooks are detailed on the module reading list, provide a wider context for the concepts explained in this Companion, and provide more Case Studies and examples to illustrate marketing in practice.

Developing the skills to implement marketing activity

Equally important in the journey towards marketing excellence is the acquisition, development and refining of a range of skills that are required on a daily basis by marketers across all industries and sectors. These transferable skills hold the key to the effective implementation of the marketing techniques explored in the study text.

Using the Companion

The syllabus for the module has been broken down into fifteen Sessions, each of which covers approximately the same proportion of the content. Every student brings with them to their studies different levels of experience; as a customer, from previous studies, and possibly from working in marketing or sales. You should therefore be aware that, whilst you may need to spend considerable time on an unfamiliar area of the syllabus, you may make up this time when studying another area with which you are more familiar.

Each Session has a series of short Activities, which you should try to complete as you work your way through the text. These will help you to check your understanding of the material. Brief feedback is provided at the end of each Session, so that you can compare your answers.

At the end of each Session there is also a Case Study and a series of related questions. Many of these have been taken from past examination papers, so you can use them to help prepare you for this type of activity within your exam. Try to complete these without reference to your notes, or the Session text, and then compare your answers with some key points that are given at the end of the Companion, in Appendix 1.

Finally, you will see that there is a Past Examination paper in Appendix 3. This can help you with your revision, examination technique, and preparation. Allow time nearer to your actual examination to complete the paper under examination conditions – that is, allow three hours of uninterrupted time, and complete the paper without reference to your notes or the study material. When you have completed the exercise, you can compare your answers to the notes in Appendix 4. If either your approach to the exercise, or the comparison of your answers highlight areas of particular weakness, you should refer back to the text and re-read the relevant Session, together with the chapters of the supporting textbook.

This Companion's structure and content follows the syllabus order, as this module follows a standard 'process' which in itself is logical in its 'flow'. You will note that this is not always the same order as the core textbook. The first part of the Companion covers the general principles that apply to marketing at an operational level, and later Sessions apply and adapt those principles in a number of different contexts, including the marketing of services (7 Ps).

The Advanced Certificate in Marketing allows direct entry to graduates from most disciplines. However, it expects some prior understanding of the basic concepts and 'language' of marketing. Holders of the CIM Certificate in Marketing may find that they are familiar with some of the topics in this companion, as it includes some background to support those who are new to marketing.

One of the syllabus outcomes is that you will be able to 'communicate ideas effectively in a variety of formats; report, article, presentation', and you should expect some examination questions to request that your answer is put into one of these formats. If you are unfamiliar with business formats they are covered in 'Customer Communications' at CIM Certificate level.

Table 1 – Web sites

CIM	
www.connectedinmarketing.com www.cimvirtualinstitute.com	
General Marketing	
www.new-marketing.org	Research updates into new marketing issues, customer segmentation and repercussions for marketing practitioners.
www.royalmail.co.uk	General marketing advice and information.
Advertising	
www.adslogans.co.uk	Online database of advertising slogans enabling marketers to check whether a slogan is already in use.
www.ipa.co.uk	Institute of Practitioners in Advertising.
www.asa.org.uk	Advertising Standards Agency.
Public Relations	
www.prnewswire.co.uk	UK media monitoring service – reviews mentions in all media types (print, online publications and broadcast).
Events	
www.e-bulletin.com	Guide to exhibitions, events and resources.
www.venuefinder.com	International venue and event suppliers directory.
Secondary data sources	
www.keynote.co.uk	Market research reports.
www.verdict.co.uk	Retail research reports.
www.datamonitor.com	Market analysis providing global data collection and in-depth analysis across any industry.
www.mintel.com	Consumer market research.
www.store.eiu.com	Economist Intelligence Unit providing country-specific global business analysis.
General Business News	
www.ft.com	Financial Times online newspaper and archives.
www.afxpress.com	Global business news.

Legislation/Codes of Conduct	
www.europa.eu.int	European Union online.
www.wapforum.org	Industry association responsible for creating the standards for Wireless Application Protocol (WAP).
Business Contexts	
www.startups.co.uk	Small business information.
www.corporate-planning.com	Corporate planning software.
www.corusgroup.com	Industrial/Business to business.
www.oxfam.org.uk	Charity.
www.unilever.com	FMCG organisation.

Table 2 – Background reading

The following references are suggested background readings for each Session. It is suggested that the student undertake this reading before studying the relevant Companion Session.

Session	Reading from core text: Kotler, Armstrong, Saunders and Wong, *Principles of Marketing* – Second European Edition, Prentice-Hall Europe.
Session 1	Chapter 3 (Page 81-110) Strategic Marketing Planning.
Session 2	Chapter 4 – The Marketing Environment.
Session 3	Chapter 3 (Page 111+) Strategic Marketing Planning.
Session 4	Chapter 3 (Page 109, 110 + 113) – Strategic Marketing Planning.
Session 5	Chapter 18 – Integrated Marketing Communication Strategy. Chapter 19 – Mass Communications: Advertising, Sales Promotion and Public Relations. Chapter 22 – Direct and Online marketing.
Session 6	Chapter 16 – Pricing considerations and approaches. Chapter 17 – Pricing strategies.
Session 7	Chapter 13 – Brands, Products, Packaging and Services. Chapter 14 – Product Development and Life-Cycle Strategies.
Session 8	Chapter 21 – Managing Marketing Channels. Chapter 22 – Direct and Online Marketing.
Session 9	Chapter 11 – Building Customer Relationships: Customer Satisfaction, Quality, Value and Service.
Session 10	
Session 11	Chapter 2 – Marketing and Society: Social Responsibility and Marketing Ethics.
Session 12	Chapter 7 – Business Markets and Business Buyer Behaviour.
Session 13	Chapter 15 – Marketing Services.
Session 14	Chapter 1 – Marketing in a Changing World: Satisfying Human Needs (Page 24).
Session 15	Chapter 5 – The Global Marketplace.

Table 3 – Marketing models

The text in the Companion Sessions refer to appropriate models but does not reproduce these, as they can be seen in the core textbooks. The references for these are supplied in the following table. Please note that this does not necessarily represent the full range of models that you will need to study for your exam or assessment.

Session	Marketing Model	Reference: Kotler, Armstrong, Saunders and Wong, *Principles of Marketing* – 2nd European Edition, Prentice-Hall Europe.
Session 1	■ The Planning Process.	■ Page 86.
Session 2	■ Influences on Marketing Strategy.	■ Page 105.
Session 3	■ Product/Market Grid. ■ The BCG Matrix. ■ GE Matrix. ■ The Marketing Mix.	■ Page 103. ■ Page 97. ■ Page 99. ■ Page 110.
Session 4	■ Adoption of Innovations. ■ Elements of the Communication Process.	■ Page 262. ■ Page 759.
Session 5	■ Primary steps in effective selling.	■ Page 865.
Session 6	■ Factors affecting price decisions. ■ Inelastic and elastic demand. ■ Break-even chart. ■ Cost based versus value-based pricing. ■ Price adjustment strategies.	■ Page 682. ■ Page 692. ■ Page 701. ■ Page 704. ■ Page 725.

Session	Marketing Model	Reference: Kotler, Armstrong, Saunders and Wong, *Principles of Marketing* – 2nd European Edition, Prentice-Hall Europe.
Session 7	■ Three levels of product. ■ Major branding decisions. ■ Steps in new product development. ■ The product life – sales and profits ■ Product life cycle – characteristics, objectives and strategies.	■ Page 562. ■ Page 573. ■ Page 607. ■ Page 627. ■ Page 634.
Session 8	■ Consumer and industrial marketing channels. ■ Demographics of Internet Users.	■ Page 898. ■ Page 967.
Session 9	■ The generic value chain.	■ Page 481.
Session 10	■ None.	
Session 11	■ Legal issues facing marketing management.	■ Page 60.
Session 12	■ Business Buying Situations.	■ Page 283.
Session 13	■ Dimensions of perceived service quality.	■ Page 659.
Session 14	■ None.	
Session 15	■ International Planning Model. ■ Five International product and promotion strategies.	■ Page 188. ■ Page 212.

Session 1

The marketing planning process – an overview

Introduction

The Marketing Operations module focuses on the short-term marketing plan and its implementation. The length of time the plan covers at this level varies from company to company, but generally will be between three and twelve months. This is the first of three Sessions on the marketing planning process. This Session looks at an overview of the process, and where it fits in the planning hierarchy.

LEARNING OUTCOMES

At the end of this Session you will be able to:

- List the stages of the marketing planning process.

- Explain the importance of the marketing planning process.

- Explain the difference between corporate planning, marketing planning, operational planning, and tactics.

The Marketing Planning Process

The marketing planning process requires the organisation to assess and evaluate the current marketing and positioning and the external marketplace so that new plans can be developed. This activity may happen every year in-line with budgets and the organisation's financial year-end. Marketing plans may also be required for new product introduction as a separate activity.

The process stages are as follows:

- Overview and context.
- The marketing audit –   Analysis of the external marketplace and business environment. (PEST – presenting Political, Economic, Social and Technological opportunities and threats). Internal analysis of the current marketing activities and brand image. (Strengths and weaknesses). Analysis of the competitive position.

- Segmentation and target markets, customer relationships and buying behaviour.

- Marketing objectives.

- Strategic choices for products and markets.

- Marketing Mix – 7 Ps.

- Action planning for implementation.

- Control and budgets.

A review of the recent successes and failures of the organisation helps to provide a context for the planning process. A SWOT analysis can help to provide a framework to review the organisation's strengths and weaknesses and external factors affecting planning decisions. Changes in the marketplace such as major political initiatives may have an impact on the organisation. Government funding might be withdrawn or new legislation may force changes in the way the organisation is structured.

Environmental factors such as climate changes or economic downturns will require new thinking and ideas so that revenues remain stable and profits can be developed. The competition change their product, pricing, promotion and distribution on a regular basis and up to date information will support targeting and positioning decisions. We will look further at this part of the process, referred to as the marketing audit, in the next Session. There are various models that can assist the collection and analysis of external factors at this stage of the planning process.

As sales decline in certain product areas new products are sought to take place of the lost revenue. An evaluation of the product portfolio is essential to track changes in profits across the range and to set priorities for the future marketing efforts. The Boston Matrix can be used here to review the product portfolio. Targeting customer groups to improve sales requires a thorough knowledge of buying habits so that promotions can be designed to maximise return on investment.

The marketing mix

The marketing mix of 7 Ps is used for each range or product area, describing the major priorities likely to bring the best profit margins. The major budgetary spend needs to be focused on new emerging products and markets that can provide long-term sales. Products that are established in the marketplace need wider distribution opportunities. The Ansoff matrix helps to define the strategic choices of the product/market match at this stage of planning.

Action plans need to be developed with timescales, costs and responsibilities. At this stage of the planning process it becomes clear how realistic the plan is and whether there are sufficient financial and human resources to implement the ideas.

The marketing objectives are the main control mechanism and these need to link closely with the budgets and timeframes. Systems for recording marketing activities and the resulting successes need to be kept so that a review process guides all future planning activities.

There are a number of tools and models that can assist decision-making during the planning process.

Activity 1.1

Develop a PowerPoint presentation detailing the various stages of the planning process, explaining where you would obtain the relevant information for each stage.

Marketing planning

Marketing planning is a systematic process that assesses market potential and the capacity of the organisation to expand to take advantage of emerging opportunities. A key output from the process is a document called the marketing plan. This acts as a 'road map' for the organisation and in particular the marketing department. It articulates priorities and provides a schedule of work for the forthcoming year or particular planning cycle.

Marketing managers need to orchestrate and control the appropriate mix of activities that will satisfy the target markets needs, profitably. The marketing environment is in constant flux and decisions become more complex to determine the best mix of products and markets to sustain and develop activities.

A business organisation relies on a clear statement of its purpose and long-term goals to be commercially successful. Profits are essential for economic growth and without them the culture of the organisation will stagnate and die. Organisations cannot afford to stand still and must plan for evolution and growth.

Whether the organisation is not-for-profit, a multinational or a small business, funds are still required for growth. Customers are ever more demanding and new products and improved processes are expected to meet changing desires and preferences. Popular music highlights the constant demand from fans for new albums and hit records. Bands that do not maintain a presence in the charts are quickly forgotten and replaced by more energetic newcomers.

It's important to be articulate about the organisation's core activities. For example Virgin Trains is in the transport business, and this helps them identify their customer priorities – safety and reliability. Organisations that continue to add products and services to their range without checking back to their main purpose will dilute their message to the customer and make marketing more difficult and expensive.

The marketing planning process is responsible for creating a strategy that will sustain the organisation's activities and improve the quality of life for all the key stakeholders. Shareholders desire improved profits, employees want improved conditions and increases in pay and customers want new and improved products. The planning process requires a review of the organisation's activities, which helps to re-define the main purpose of the business providing an overall framework for the decisions about which products and markets to provide.

The marketing planning process allows the decision makers to reflect on current activities in order to improve and eliminate waste. The allocation of resources to planning activities is related to expected performance and likely outcomes. The marketing plan should specify expected results. This is so that the monitoring of activities can flag up key milestones where new decisions need to be made, if profits are falling and new actions are required.

Activity 1.2

Working with a colleague, discuss the problems and opportunities within your own job that would benefit from having a marketing plan that provided a framework for improved decision-making.

The roles of different types of plans

As we saw in the last section, organisations use strategic marketing planning to guide the decision-making process so that they can choose the most appropriate mix of products and services to serve their target markets.

The product life cycle assists organisations to review their product portfolios on a regular basis so that new and modified products can be introduced to boost diminishing sales. The marketplace never stands still and a combination of external factors and competition means that organisations have to evaluate their effectiveness on a regular basis, changing not only their mix of products and services but also their operational processes and marketing tactics.

Corporate planning views the organisation's activities over a longer period of time than operational planning. The corporate planning process reviews the whole organisation and asks the question, 'Where do we want to be in 5-10 years time?' The vision of the senior management may be to expand exponentially, or to build up the corporate assets and sell or merge the organisation in partnership with other similar organisations, to form either vertical or horizontal integration. The planning required for these ambitious ideas is often concerned with new financial structures including borrowing, capital expenditure on premises and equipment. At this level of planning the people play a major role and succession planning and human resource development is key to ensuring sustainable growth.

Big ideas drive organisations forward. Marketing planning assesses the major goals and develops a mix of products and services to meet the target market needs and wants, according to the financial targets set by the corporate plan. Revenue budgets are agreed at senior level and marketing supports sales to achieve targets through leading the organisation to prioritise the emphasis of marketing different products to specific market segments. The Boston Matrix is a useful tool to help analyse the current and future market share of the product portfolio. Priorities can then be decided on the basis of expected revenues from each product type. Market segmentation is often the strategy chosen to target specific buying groups who have particular needs not currently served by the competition.

Operational planning takes the marketing objectives and puts them into practice. The marketing department needs to be organised to fulfil expectations and comprehensive plans need to be agreed. The 7 Ps (Product, Price, Promotion, Place, People, Process, Physical Evidence) can be used as a model to formulate the mix of key variables that make up the marketing mix used to launch products and services into the marketplace. This stage of planning needs to draw on external research about the competition, the financial environment and the customer segments' buying behaviour. The marketing mix planning process is key to fulfilling financial revenue targets and maintaining the marketing budget within available resources.

Once the marketing budget has been agreed the tactical planning process can begin. Marketing activities are designed to give the best return on investment and the mix of tactics appropriate for the given target market. Smaller organisations have less opportunity to use the full range of media available due to limited budgets and innovative ideas are sought to stretch the budget. External agencies can be used for various parts of the tactical mix such as advertising or PR agencies. Specialists are often expensive, however their expertise in their particular disciplines can often improve the return on the marketing investment due to their contacts and buying power.

Activity 1.3

How do the 7 P s assist the planning process?

Develop a real or fictitious marketing programme that describes the range of decisions that might be used for each of the 7 Ps. Show your answer in a table.

Case Study – Leading the way

The creation of a successful marketed organisation can only be driven from the top, says Professor Malcolm McDonald.

Business leaders are under intense pressure to deliver against stakeholder expectations. Customers are demanding greater levels of customisation, access, service and value. Shareholders are expecting to see continuous growth in earnings per share and in the capital value of shares. Pressure groups are demanding exemplary corporate citizenship.

Meanwhile, the rules of competition have changed. The make/sell model has been killed off by a new wave of entrepreneurial, technology-enabled competitors, unfettered by the baggage of legal bureaucracy, assets, cultures and behaviours. The processing of information about products has been separated from the products themselves and customers can now search for and evaluate them independently of those who have a vested interest in selling them. Customers have as much information about suppliers as they traditionally accumulated about them, which has created a new dimension of competition based on who most effectively acts in the customers' interests.

On top of all of these pressures, a new wave of business metrics such as EVA (Economic Value Added) and Balanced Scorecards has emerged. These, together with pressure from institutional shareholders to report meaningful facts about corporate performance rather than the turgid, near-useless financial dross that appears every year in corporate accounts, are forcing business leaders to re-examine tired corporate behaviours such as cost cutting, mergers and downsizing as a route to profitability.

Gross ignorance

This surge in customer power has exposed the irrelevance of traditional views of marketing and the gross ignorance about its role in business. What is most worrying about the flurry of articles and reports over recent years claiming that marketing has failed, is the evident confusion about the marketing concept and the marketing function. The marketing function (or department) never has been and never will be effective in an organisation with a technical, product, operations or financial orientation. Such enterprises adopted the vocabulary of marketing a long time ago and applied a veneer of marketing techniques.

Many of the high street banks have spent fortunes on hiring marketing people, often from Fast-Moving Consumer Goods (FMCG) companies, producing expensive television commercials and creating a multiplicity of products, brochures and leaflets. But most customers still cannot distinguish between the major players, so what competitive advantage have any of these organisations gained? Is this marketing in the sense of understanding and meeting customers' needs better than the competition, or is it old-fashioned selling with the name changed, where we try to persuade customers to buy what we want to sell them, how, when and where we want to sell it?

Generally, marketing departments never have, nor ever will, actually do marketing. The reasons are obvious. If the term 'marketing' embraces all those activities related to creating and satisfying demand and the associated intelligence, then it is clear that most marketing takes place during the delivery of the service and during contact with customers. While marketing supports and reflects this process, it is not the sole preserve of those in the organisation who happen to work in the marketing department. It is equally absurd to suggest that personnel issues are the sole preserve of the HR department, as though nobody else in the organisation need concern themselves with people.

Flourish

For marketing to work, it must flourish at three different levels in the enterprise. The board of directors must understand and enthusiastically embrace the notion that creating and maintaining customer satisfaction is the only route to long-term

15

profitable success. Only when the top management team share this common vision is there any chance of inculcating an organisation-wide marketing culture where everyone believes in and practises the concepts of superior customer service. This corporate top-down driven vision of what marketing is, can create significant and sustainable success, as companies like General Electric, 3M and Unilever have demonstrated.

The business strategies of the company must start with and be evaluated against what the market wants. Unless marketing has a strategic input in order to ensure the future of the company is planned from the marketplace inwards, then any subsequent marketing activity is likely to be unsuccessful. This is the role of marketing as a function. Tactical marketing activities must be implemented within the context of the market-led strategies. They must meet high professional standards across the spectrum of functions such as market research, product development, pricing, distribution, advertising, promotion and selling.

Specialist function

Fundamentally, marketing is simply a process, with a set of underlying tools and techniques, for understanding markets and for quantifying the present and future value required by the different groups of customers within these markets – what marketers refer to as segments. It is a strictly specialist function, just like accountancy or engineering.

In Creating a Company for Customers, this process is called 'The Market Understanding Process'. It is important that business leaders understand how this process, whilst being led by marketing professionals, must involve all other relevant customer-impacting functions in order to gain buy-in and to ensure subsequent delivery of the value required by customers. The most important person in the process is the CEO. He or she has ultimate responsibility for guiding the processes that will:

- Position and brand the organisation in the market.

- Create superior value for the chosen customer groups by meeting their needs better than competitors.

- Create excellent profits (sustainable competitive advantage).

- Create the requisite stakeholder value for groups other than shareholders, such as employees, suppliers and influence groups such as local and international communities, governments and the like.

There could be other processes, depending on organisational circumstances, but these are the ones that have been observed in dealings with thousands of world-class companies each year. The business leader's role is to drive key processes that are designed to position and brand the organisation, create a customer value and create shareholder (hence stakeholder) value. This is what leading-edge organisations are doing to create sustainable competitive advantage. There is no other way to cope with the uncertainty and increased competition in the new millennium.

Source: 'Leading the Way', extract from *Marketing Business*, December/January 2001.

Questions

1. From the article, identify three examples of ways in which strategic and tactical marketing are differentiated.

2. List three stakeholder groups that companies are expected to satisfy, and make brief notes about the prime focus of each.

3. What activities can be found in the article that constitute 'marketing'?

SUMMARY OF KEY POINTS

In this Session, we have introduced the marketing planning process, and covered the following key points:

- The marketing planning process has various advantages, and follows a structure that includes analysis, development of a plan, implementation, and control mechanisms.

- The marketing mix, made up of 7 Ps – Product, Price, Promotion, Place, People, Process and Physical Evidence – plays an important role in operational marketing.

- There is a planning hierarchy, with objectives and plans cascading down from corporate objectives, strategic marketing objectives, operational marketing objectives, and promotional objectives.

Improving and developing own learning

The following projects are designed to help you develop your knowledge and skills further by carrying out some research yourself. Feedback is not provided for this type of learning because there are no 'answers' to be found, but you may wish to discuss your findings with colleagues and fellow students.

Project A

Look at the following web sites, and see what evidence you can find of marketing and customer focus.

www.unilever.com

www.corusgroup.com

www.oxfam.org.uk

Project B

Identify one of your organisation's products or services, and see if you can identify the elements of its marketing mix. Talk to your colleagues to identify how well they think the elements of the mix integrate.

Project C

Talk to others in your marketing department and identify your corporate objectives, your strategic marketing objectives, and your operational marketing objectives, noting how they interconnect.

Feedback to activities

Activity 1.1

- Overview – annual report.

- Analysis of the external marketplace and business environment – desk research.

- Internal analysis of the current marketing activities and brand image – review of current activities and customer surveys.

- Analysis of the competitive position – feedback from the sales department and field research.

- Segmentation and target markets – field research, market research reports.

- Marketing objectives – derived from the Business and Sales plan.

- Strategic choices for products and markets – priorities to meet sales and profit objectives.

- Marketing Mix – 7 Ps – new ideas for an integrated campaign.

- Action planning for implementation – schedule of work activities.

- Control and budgets – financial costs of campaigns and systems for collecting success.

Activity 1.2

Plans and frameworks provide clear boundaries aiding decision-making. Each person's job scope is different but the following tasks would be generic to most marketing executive/management roles.

- Setting and managing marketing budgets.

- Deciding on the range of marketing activities to support a campaign.

- Prioritising product campaigns.

- Using positioning messages in briefs to advertising agencies.

- Commissioning competitor and customer research.

- New product launches.

- Setting objectives for target markets.

Activity 1.3

The 7 Ps are used to decide on the operational marketing mix, which launches a product into the marketplace and describes the various integrated activities used to manage the process effectively. They help direct important decisions about key integrating marketing programme factors such as deciding which products should make up the future product portfolio.

Product	New or modified products. Product portfolio.
Price	Strategic pricing decisions e.g. premium pricing, competitive pricing etc.
Promotion	Choosing the appropriate mix of media for promoting the product e.g. advertising, PR, online media etc.
Place	What distribution network to use, where to sell the product e.g. mail order, retail, resellers etc.
Process	What new processes will be needed; for example if selling online how will the orders to be taken? Will there be an online order form? How many days before despatch etc.?
People	Target audience. Are you selling to a niche market? How will you target their specific buying behaviour?
Physical Evidence	Packaging and image. Will you use corporate or product branding? How will you differentiate your products from the competition?

Session 2

The marketing audit

Introduction

In this Session we move on from the overview of marketing planning introduced in the last Session, and look in more detail at the marketing audit, which entails a full analysis of an organisation's situation at a point in time. It looks internally and externally at an organisation's environment to identify factors that will impact on both the way in which it operates, and the way in which it carries out its marketing plan. Session 3 concludes coverage of the planning process.

LEARNING OUTCOMES

At the end of this Session you will be able to:

- Explain the role and constituents of a basic Marketing Audit.
- Analyse internal and external factors.
- Conduct an environmental analysis.

The marketing audit

The marketing audit is the systematic and critical review and appraisal of the external business environment and the internal operating environment. The information is used to identify the opportunities and threats on which the marketing strategies are based, taking into consideration the organisation's current strengths and weaknesses.

The marketing audit results in a re-evaluation of objectives, strategies and tactics with a view to preparing a plan for the subsequent year. From time to time a longer, broader, more comprehensive plan may be required if a company is considering re-structuring.

The external audit includes:

- Macro environmental analysis
- Industry analysis   )
- Competitor analysis   ) referred to as micro environmental audit.
- Market and customer analysis   )

These external factors often cannot be controlled, however threats can be minimised and opportunities can be exploited.

The internal audit includes:

- Organisational capabilities and resources.
- Marketing systems.
- Marketing structure and organisation.
- Marketing orientation.
- Marketing mix audit.

Internal strengths and weaknesses highlight the likely barriers to implementation and give opportunities to control organisational variables.

Audits are often carried out by marketing personnel in-house or may be supplemented by research undertaken by external agencies. Occasionally external consultants are used to carry out a complete investigation and this is often the case when a major growth initiative is planned.

Research methods used will probably be a combination of desk research, surveys, talking to leading experts in the industry sector and meeting with internal specialists. Objectivity needs to be built into the process so control measures for evaluating internal activities are an important element of the marketing information system.

The external factors can be assessed through a combination of reading the current press, looking at economic predictors, obtaining forecasts from the bank, and researching sector specific reports or commissioning field research. The competitor information can also be supplemented by sales force feedback from customer contact.

Internal data can be obtained from both the marketing and management information systems. What marketing activities were carried out last year and how successful were they? Detailed reports are needed on success against specific campaigns, customer profiles, product profiles, pricing strategies and distribution activity.

Information needs to be up-to date and reliable. Assumptions my be made about the likelihood of change to certain external factors; however minimising risk is important and often requires quite detailed business cases to be developed.

The objective of the audit is to answer the question 'Where is the company now?' and to show the possibilities for the future corporate plan.

The marketing audit is the basis for marketing planning. Marketing audits can be carried out throughout the year, ideally seen as part of the planning cycle. The audit builds on customer information, which is used to make strategic, operational and tactical decisions.

Activity 2.1

Write a memo to a new member of your marketing team, outlining the stages of the marketing audit and explaining its importance to marketing planning.

Analysing internal and external factors

The SWOT (Strengths, Weakness, Opportunities and Threats) or situation analysis is the most commonly used framework used to make sense of internal and external factors affecting marketing decisions. Meaningful recommendations can be drawn from the process of analysing the strengths and weaknesses of internal marketing orientation and resource capabilities, helping focus on the issues where action is needed. The external opportunities and threats are derived from analysing market trends, competitor activity and customer demands.

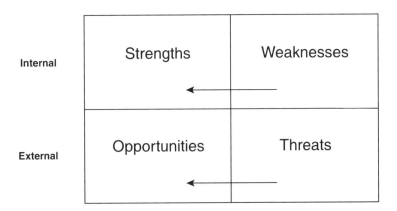

The SWOT framework helps you to visualise a situation. Issues are not listed in any order nor do they denote importance. The process is a kind of brainstorm exercise where internal organisational factors are listed under strengths and weaknesses. These factors are in the control of the organisation and can be used to determine objectives and priorities for planning, turning weaknesses into strengths. For example a weakness might be a product that has caused a lot of customer complaints, which could be divested, or more resources could be diverted to modify it and improve performance.

The main factors assessed for the internal SWOT are:

- The financial health of the organisation:
  - Cash flow.
  - Profit.
  - Capitalisation.
  - Investment.

- Management structure and culture:
  - The skills of senior management.
  - Overall morale and motivation.
  - Skills and knowledge of the workforce.
  - Recruitment and succession planning.
  - Training and development programme.

- Marketing strategies and tactics:
  - Marketing orientation and customer satisfaction.
  - Marketing mix, successes and failures.
  - Budgets and resources.
  - Image and perception of the brand(s).

- Customer service:
  - Production and customer expectations.
  - Product portfolio.
  - Distribution and accessibility of products.
  - Customer facing systems and procedures.

Obviously if you are using this framework for a particular market or product some of the factors will become more detailed and specific. Note that in one instance something that might be seen as strength, for example a wide product range, may also be a weakness if the company has to market too many line items.

The main factors assessed for the external SWOT are:

- Market trend analysis:
    - Competitor activities.
    - Sector structures.
    - Financial health of the sector.

- Customer trends:
    - Buying behaviour.
    - Brand loyalties.
    - Complementary product analysis.

- External business analysis:
    - Benchmarking with other sectors.
    - Profit trends.
    - Financial predictions.

A SWOT can be used for each market segment, and each product or used to develop a concise overview of the organisation's activities.

Various models exist to provide a framework for external environmental analysis. These include PEST (Political, Economic, Social and Technological), SLEPT (the same variables with the addition of 'legal'), and PLEESTIC (Political, Legal, Environmental, Economic, Social, Technological, International and Competition). This analysis feeds into the overall process of analysis and is distilled into opportunities and threats. In this module we will focus on the PLEESTIC model, breaking down the influences on the organisation as far as we can.

> **Activity 2.2**
>
> Prepare a short report explaining the benefits of using a SWOT as an analytical tool and how it helps to focus the planning function.

Analysing the external environment

The macro environment provides the organisation with opportunities and threats for growth. The growing demands of customers and shortening of product life cycles has put pressure on organisations to predict sales and growth patterns with more accuracy than in the past. Profitability is more difficult to manage and competitor activity is unpredictable, and the more there is opening of international boundaries, so markets become more complex. The Internet has provided the opportunity for any company to become international/global overnight. Information opportunities have exploded.

As mentioned earlier, macro environmental factors fall into the following categories, covered by the PLEESTIC acronym:

P – Political
L – Legal
E – Environmental
E – Economic
S – Social/Cultural
T – Technological
I – International
C – Competition

P – Political

National and local government changes, policies, laws, regulatory bodies and pressure groups have a major impact on marketing. Cross border trade, tariffs, and quotas put pressure on profitability. As barriers to trade come down, opportunities present themselves.

L – Legal

Legal restrictions and legislation can either cause a reduction in profits or present an opportunity. Many companies have made millions as a result of new laws such as the enforcement of wearing seat belts for automotive manufacturers. Other legislation such as increased health and safety requirements have put some small restaurants out of business.

E – Environmental

There have been growing concerns about global warming and diminishing natural resources that have affected the way we do business. The 'green' movement is highly active and constantly putting government and organisations under pressure to improve practices in waste management, pollution and energy use.

E – Economic

The financial health of the economy, interest rates, inflation, investments and exchange rates has an affect on disposable income and patterns of spending. The cost of borrowing and bank rates can have a major impact on business, and in a recession banks are less enthusiastic about lending funds and are more enquiring about future growth and financial management.

S – Social/Cultural

Buying trends and behaviour are difficult to measure and are particular to a society. Language, family, religion, attitudes, perceptions, education, health and recreation can affect the marketing mix programme. Recently we have seen the change to out of town shopping following the trends in the USA. This has put the local shop owner under threat and in many towns and villages the local butchers, bakers and greengrocers have disappeared.

T – Technological

Technological changes provide both threats and opportunities. Organisations are expected to keep up-to-date with changes and new equipment is costly and puts additional pressure on profits. The introduction of the Internet, mobile phones, laptops, and new software programmes have revolutionised the way we do business. More people work from home than ever before and communication has got faster and harder in the process.

I – International

The introduction of the Euro will change the way we do business with most of Europe. New systems and procedures will need to be developed to deal with currency conversions. Opportunities may present themselves and organisations will have to quote in two currencies. The flow of goods overseas has increased and this has brought new challenges, not least language barriers.

C – Competition

New competitors enter the market and their strategies can affect our market share. Mergers and acquisitions, knocking out smaller companies out of business, can affect the whole structure of a market.

The external marketing audit can be distilled into a SWOT analysis, providing direction for the marketing planning process.

Activity 2.3

Prepare a presentation, taking each factor from the PLEESTIC analytical tool and using a product of your choice.

Detail the external environment now, and any likely changes in 2-5 years' time.

Case Study – The BBC goes digital

The British Broadcasting Corporation (BBC) is the UK's main public service broadcaster providing TV, radio and online services to listeners and viewers at home and around the world. A Royal Charter and Agreement governs its constitution, finances and obligations. The Corporation is financed by a licence fee paid by viewers, plus the commercial revenues from its BBC Worldwide operations. The BBC provides a range of domestic broadcast services including BBC 1 and BBC 2 TV channels, and BBC Network Radio Channels 1, 2, 3, 4, and 5 Live. In addition BBC Worldwide is a major international broadcaster which operates the BBC World and Prime Channels and acts as a publishing house for BBC publications of magazines, books, video and audio recordings, and CD-ROMs. The BBC also operates an online channel accessed via the Internet and has a small portfolio of existing digital channels, which includes BBC Choice and BBC Knowledge. The BBC World Service supplies free radio broadcasts to millions of people throughout the world.

As part of its current mission "to meet its public service obligations and operate effectively in a competitive market" the BBC recently announced that it was going to spend more than £300 million on new digital TV and radio channels. Digital represents the latest technology and is regarded as superior to the existing analogue broadcasting systems, enabling better quality sound and vision and the availability of additional channels. As a result of its largest ever public consultation exercise which involved nearly 7,000 responses via its web site and Freepost address, and 1,000 interviews undertaken by the independent research agency BMRB, the Corporation claimed that its plans for the introduction of new digital channels had wide public support.

The BBC made a formal application to the UK Government in January 2001 to replace its existing digital TV channels with four new digital TV services to be launched over the next two years. One of the new TV channels, BBC3, is aimed at 16 to 34 year olds and will focus "exclusively on the young and young at heart". Another channel, BBC4, is aimed at "everyone interested in culture, arts and ideas". A further TV channel (provisionally called Playbox*) is aimed at pre-school children and will be mostly educational. The fourth, which has the working title Children's B**, is for 6-13 year olds and will have an interactive element. The Corporation also wants to launch five digital radio services including a music station aimed at a young black audience, a speech radio station, an Asian network, a station focusing on music from the 1970s to the 1990s, and a sports network provisionally titled Five Live Sports Plus.

The BBC Director General, Greg Dyke, said viewers and listeners would get "imaginative and distinctive services". The proposal is designed to raise the take-up of digital television and radio. Without a wide choice of free-to-air channels on digital platforms, many viewers may not give up their existing analogue services. The UK Government wants to switch off analogue services between 2006 and 2010, but there are signs that insufficient viewers will have gone over to digital to allow the switch in that period. The BBC's commercial rivals aim to lobby hard against the plans, particularly the proposals for the two children's channels. They believe that the BBC should not spend licence fees on services already provided elsewhere.

* Note – since this Case Study was produced, Playbox has been named Cbeebies and Children'sB has been named CBBC. Both have been launched.

Source: From *Marketing Operations* Examination Paper, December 2001.

Questions

1. Identify the main challenges in the political and legal environment that are likely to affect the BBC.

2. Identify the main challenges in the social environment that are likely to affect the BBC.

3. Identify the main challenges in the technological environment that are likely to affect the BBC.

SUMMARY OF KEY POINTS

In this Session, we have introduced the marketing audit, and covered the following key points:

- The marketing audit is essential to the survival of organisations, and to help them make the best of opportunities presented to them.

- The audit involves a review of the internal and external environment (the micro environment and macro environment).

- Factors to be considered during internal analysis include:
  - The financial health of the organisation.
  - Management structure and culture.
  - Marketing strategies and tactics.
  - Customer Service.

- A useful framework to help analyse the external environment is PLEESTIC (Political, Legal, Economic, Environmental, Social, Technological, International and Competition).

Improving and developing own learning

The following projects are designed to help you develop your knowledge and skills further by carrying out some research yourself. Feedback is not provided for this type of learning because there are no 'answers' to be found, but you may wish to discuss your findings with colleagues and fellow students.

Project A

Talk to colleagues in your organisation's marketing department and establish to what extent a marketing audit is undertaken, and how often.

Project B

Carry out a PLEESTIC analysis for your own organisation or one you know well.

What key opportunities and threats can you identify?

Project C

Carry out a SWOT analysis for your own organisation or one you know well. Discuss this with colleagues in your marketing department. Is their perception of what constitute threats and opportunities to the organisation the same as yours? What are the differences?

Feedback to activities

Activity 2.1

CUSTOMER CARE CORP.

Memorandum

To: Jennie Brown Marketing Executive	Date: 12th September, 200X
From: Geoff Black Marketing Analyst	

Subject: The Marketing Audit

Welcome to the team! Jan has asked me to send you the following brief notes on how we use a marketing audit in our planning process, and what the stages of the audit are in outline.

It is essential that we monitor our environment on an ongoing basis so that we are in a position to take advantage of any opportunities that it offers to us, and, at the same time, to avoid any threats. We need to maintain a competitive edge to achieve our objectives, and keeping in touch with our customers, our competitor activity, and our own strengths and relative weaknesses, helps us to do this.

A full marketing audit includes a review of both our internal and external environments, and the stages involved are as follows:

The external audit:

- Macro environmental analysis.
- Industry analysis.
- Competitor analysis.
- Market and customer analysis.

The internal audit:

- Organisational capabilities and resources.
- Marketing systems.
- Marketing structure and organisation.
- Marketing orientation.
- Marketing mix audit.

I hope this helps.

Regards,

Activity 2.2

The value of the SWOT planning tool is that you can take the internal strengths and weaknesses of an organisation and using the key points enter them into the SWOT matrix, plus the major external threats and opportunities derived from the PLEESTIC.

These factors then become the focus for strategic and operational objective setting. Using weaknesses and changing them to strengths and eliminating obstacles to success. With external opportunities, plans can be made to take advantage of emerging markets and threats can be avoided by long-term thinking and action planning.

Activity 2.3

Strategic long-term planning requires assumptions to be made about external factors and how the changes may affect marketing strategy. Risk analysis can be used to project likely changes into the future, giving each factor a numerical value and rating possible threats to sustainable growth. For example, for the NHS, if there is a change in government will all the policies now in place be changed? Will they have the time to implement all the changes now in process?

The following table uses Pension Plans as an example:

External Factor	Situation Now	Likely situation in the future
Political	Government encouraging personal pensions.	Government may make personal pension contributions compulsory because of changing nature of demographic environment.
Legal	Legislation impacts on the amount of contribution that can be made, the taxation situation, and the way pensions are sold.	Limits on contributions may be lifted, and tax benefits taken away.
Environmental	No real impact.	Customer preferences may lead to an increase in investment in 'ethical' funds.
Economic	Stability of economic situation has an impact on investment funds.	Future budgets may impact on products.
Social/Cultural	Lots of discussion about the ageing population, and changes being made to company pension schemes.	Working population could be smaller than the retired population, thus straining state pension arrangements.

External Factor	Situation Now	Likely situation in the future
Technological	Information about products available on the Internet – easier to compare products.	Little change envisaged.
International	Investments tend to be in UK companies, but may be international funds, which are impacted upon by the global economic situation.	Little change envisaged – the same will apply in respect of the global economic situation.
Competition	A contracting market, but still very competitive.	Little change envisaged – other than competition may be even more fierce.

Session 3

Marketing planning at an operational level

Introduction

In previous Sessions we have looked at the marketing planning process, and the value of the marketing audit. In this Session we will consider the process as it applies at an operational level, with specific reference to setting objectives and implementing marketing strategy. This Session concludes the section on marketing planning.

LEARNING OUTCOMES

At the end of this Session you will be able to:

- Understand the process of marketing planning at an operational level.

- Develop marketing objectives at an operational level.

- Develop marketing strategies at an operational level.

- Explain the role of gap analysis.

The operational planning process

The marketing planning process is continuous throughout the year; however, depending on your organisation's year end, a marketing plan is often finalised at the end of a year to guide the marketing activities over the next 12 months.

A complete marketing plan is the result of considerable analysis and decision-making and follows this simple cycle shown below:

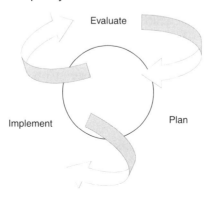

Evaluate

Implement

Plan

Evaluate

New opportunities may be recognised in the external environment such as new technology and possible threats through new legislation – whatever the driving issues, these key factors are often the starting point of the planning process. As we saw in the last Session, this is referred to as the **marketing audit**.

Internal issues need to be investigated so an internal marketing audit needs to be organised to establish strengths and weaknesses and likely obstacles to implementation of the marketing plan. Often customer research feeds into the process, highlighting attitudes towards the products and brands.

Current marketing activities are reviewed and there may be a continuation of successful tactics and the planning of new promotions and communications.

Plan

There is no linear starting point for the planning process. Decision-making rests on the current market situation and assumptions about any likely changes; for example new competitors and major economic shifts plus internal imperatives such as launching new products.

Objectives are agreed, taking into consideration the external environment, opportunities and threats and the planned product portfolio. Often a planning tool referred to as Ansoff's Matrix can be helpful at this stage to assist decisions about product and market priorities.

Implement

The 7 Ps marketing programme will give clear guidance for implementation. Action plans need to be developed showing detailed budgets, with time-scaled and detailed milestones. The action plan helps to guide practical activities and tasks and gives a direct course of action to follow.

The following questions help the planning process:

1.   What significant changes are taking place in the marketplace?

2.   How successful has our marketing been in the past – what worked well and what needs to be changed?

3.   What do we want to achieve in the future?

4. Which products/market mix will help us achieve our profit and revenue targets?

5. What combination of the 7 P marketing programme will help us achieve these goals and objectives?

6. What resources do we need to achieve our plan?

7. How will we organise our resources, time, people, money and information, to achieve our plan?

The marketing planning process may be a combination of research and analysis and decision-making at a number of levels within the organisation. For example tactical planning – deciding on the media to use for promotions – may be actioned by marketing executives, whilst the decision to prioritise one product promotion over another will usually be made by the marketing manager. The operational organisation of the plan as a whole will often be the manager's role. External agencies may also be used to research the market or propose a media campaign.

Activity 3.1

Discuss with a colleague the answers to the questions concerning marketing planning above, using your own organisation or one you are familiar with.

The role of gap analysis

Gap analysis is an essential planning approach used to evaluate success against objectives. Conditions change both internally and externally and these can affect achievement of specified objectives. Performance needs to be measured regularly, and variances investigated so that remedial action can be taken to remedy any shortfalls immediately.

The sales forecast is based on historical figures, assumptions about market growth or decline and new product/market introduction. Ideally the sales forecast is a product of both market research and internal decision-making. Sales forecasting is an art, not a science, but analytical techniques such as time-series analysis, moving averages and exponential smoothing can be used as predictive techniques.

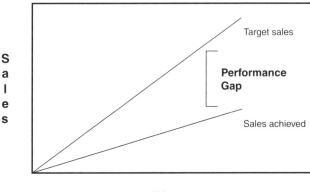

T i m e

The variance between expected sales and forecast sales has a major implication for business. It's not just the cash flow that is affected by falling sales but also the implications for profit and business sustainability. If there is a sales forecast for £10 million a year which equates to £833,333 per month, then if there are two slow months in the summer or over Christmas, it means that in fact, sales need to be over £1,200,000 per month to cover expected overheads and profit margins. If sales are slow for longer than two months then the rest of the year is under further pressure to achieve higher sales.

Organisations have a sum of working capital, somewhat like a float, which can be drawn on to pay immediate commitments. In time of poor cash flow that capital is used up, leaving businesses unable to meet commitments to suppliers. Further sums then need to be borrowed from the bank incurring additional interest rates and hence diminished profit margins. This causes internal stress, poor morale and poor relations with suppliers, which in turn reduces likely discounts and profit opportunities.

If debtors, i.e. customers, do not pay on time then additional working capital has to be sought from the bank, putting a further strain on the cash flow, as the debt becomes an increased overhead.

This 'see-saw' relationship, adding and contracting, has to be managed by the accounts department. However it is the responsibility of Marketing to organise campaigns and marketing support so as to minimise the gap in performance to create a financially healthy environment.

The marketing budget is also part of this picture. If marketing spend is all bundled in the first half of the year when the company is already feeling the strain from a quiet new year, then it may cause cash flow problems. Marketing need to work with Accounts to improve the finances of an organisation and plan their activities to help boost sales when income is needed the most.

This is an area most often overlooked by marketing staff. Reaching marketing objectives for the sake of generating materials and awareness is only half the picture. Marketing supports Sales, to assist in generating profits.

Businesses are organised to satisfy a number of stakeholder needs. Shareholders are looking for a return on their investment of capital, which comes from profits. If this is not forthcoming support may be withdrawn and this has major financial implications. Poor profits inhibit investment and growth, without which organisations atrophy and die.

Operational marketing objectives

Having identified the 'gap' that marketing will help to fill, clear objectives need to be set.

Objectives are the main mechanism for controlling marketing and therefore need to be measurable. Objectives need to be unambiguous and specific to the area of marketing that needs to be evaluated, whether it's strategic, operational or tactical.

The strategic plan articulates the long-term vision for market expansion, which may include mergers and acquisitions to grow market share and re-position the organisation. The operational plan translates the strategic vision into action and uses the product portfolio to satisfy customer demand whilst making a profit.

All objectives need to be **SMART**: Specific, Measurable, Achievable, Relevant and Timed.

At an operational level the 4 Ps or 7 Ps give a framework for objective setting and control to achieve the strategic objectives.

Product

Judgments are made as to the product portfolio mix that will support the strategic objectives, divesting those that make little profit and supporting others which maintain and build market share. The planning tool the Boston Matrix is often used to assess the current and future position of the products.

Product objectives may include:

- Product market share.
- Product positioning.
- Product image.

E.g. To increase market share for X product in Europe to 25% by the end of 2003.

Promotion

The promotional mix is designed to create synergy and media is chosen that reinforces different aspects of product campaigns. For example a promotion on the Internet will also use off-line media such as advertising to drive 'traffic' to the site.

The promotional objectives that drive such campaigns could be any of the following:

- Brand awareness.
- Re-positioning.
- Brand loyalty.

E.g. To improve unprompted awareness of Brand Z in the South-east region from 10% to 15% by the end of the campaign (December 2003).

Place

Channels of distribution and physical distribution management are a major aspect of marketing operations. At a strategic level it will be decided as to whether product will be sold directly or indirectly to customers. When selling indirectly a distribution network needs to be managed and supported with pricing structures and marketing activities to promote their efforts.

Objectives for distribution will often be evaluated through sales achievement and customer service. For example:

- Customer service complaints.
- Stock levels per distributor.
- Number and size of distributors and geographical location.

E.g. To reduce the number of customer complaints received in a 3 month period (to September 2003) from 25 to 20.

Price

Pricing takes into account external factors such as competitor activity, economic indicators and internal needs such as cash flow, stock levels, and revenue targets.

The major pricing objectives are:

- Maximising profits.
- Maximising revenue.
- Maintaining market leadership.
- Cost recovery.

E.g. To achieve 20% gross profit on sales of product Y in the financial year ending April 2004.

Marketing objectives are developed through reviewing past history, assessing current resources, planning for survival and growth, and forecasting success. To ensure that objectives are achievable, scenario planning needs to be researched so that likely estimates of success can be forecast. A system for controlling marketing spend must be in place to review variances and regular evaluations needs to take place so that plans can be adjusted.

Activity 3.2

Choose a promotional campaign that you are familiar with and research all the media used. Decide what you think the likely objectives were for the campaign.

How might a different mix of media have achieved a different set of objectives? List a selection of media types and the objectives that might be achieved by using them as part of a promotional campaign.

Marketing strategy at operational level

At an operational level, marketing strategy translates the strategic objectives into a workable marketing plan. Segmentation, positioning and differential advantage are decided at a strategic level within the organisation and at operational level translated into the marketing programme.

At operational level, using Ansoff's growth matrix may provide a framework to analyse the products and markets that need to be prioritised. For example:

Products

	Existing Products	New Products
M a r k e t s		
	New Markets	Diversification

Ansoff's Matrix (Adapted from Ansoff).

Existing products (market penetration)

Prioritising marketing activities often causes tension when there are limited resources. Concentrating on launching new products means that less time, money and energy are spent marketing the existing portfolio. Distribution can often be a key strategy here and developing new channels of distribution plus the export market can help organisations to expand their market.

New markets (market development)

Segmenting the market and developing new markets is essential for growth and maintaining market share. Inevitably, customers migrate to different brands and market expansion in new geographical areas such as overseas and adding new segments to the marketing mix are important. For example, the mobile phone market has extended the use of hand-held units to shops, airports and other sectors who need to communicate internally with their staff.

New products (product development)

Extending the life of existing products by re-packaging, adding value and new features or entirely new product development is necessary to maintain market share. The Product Life Cycle highlights the need to continually update products in the marketplace as sales start to diminish over time, eroded by the competition and new technologies. The couturier Jean Paul Gaultier has captivated the perfume market by creating limited edition perfumes for every occasion, which means he sells the same perfume packaged differently two or three times a year. The bottles and packaging have become collector's items in a similar way as the Swatch watches.

Diversification (new products for new markets)

In the 1980s diversification was a popular strategy and pioneers like Richard Branson developed products for completely new markets such as his cosmetic company Virgin Vie. These ventures were often not successful as lessons learnt from one sector are not always directly transferable to another. Customer service is not enough to win the hearts and minds of the target audience. Many organisations have sold their additional businesses and gone back to their core competence – it's hard to concentrate on too many market variables at once.

Using the above framework, strategic alternatives are decided and priorities translated into objectives. For example, the first half of the year may be focused on gaining distribution channels both in the UK and overseas whilst in the second half of the year a new product launch is planned.

At an operational level Marketing need to translate these strategies into reality by developing the marketing programme that will allocate tasks and responsibilities to make this happen. Organising internal staff to take responsibility for either certain product or market areas so that the whole product portfolio can be prioritised and marketed seamlessly.

Once the main strategies have been decided upon, then attention at strategic level will turn to segmentation, targeting and positioning.

Methods of segmenting markets are covered in depth in the recommended text for this module, and the key methods for consideration include:

Geographic segmentation – by county, region, or country.

Demographic segmentation – by factors such as age, gender, income, education, family life cycle stage.

Geodemographic segmentation – a combination of geographic and demographic segmentation methods.

Psychographic segmentation – by lifestyles or personality.

Behavioural segmentation – by factors such as customer attitudes towards the product, how frequently they buy it, what benefits they are seeking from it, and whether they are new or existing buyers or users.

Bases for segmenting industrial or business-to-business markets are covered in Session 12.

Implementing the marketing plan

At an operational level marketing needs to translate strategies mentioned above into reality by developing the marketing programme that will allocate tasks and responsibilities to make this happen.

The implementation stage is not easy, and there are many potential barriers that can get in the way. It involves all staff within an organisation working together with the needs of the customer at the centre of their actions. Barriers include:

Organisational culture – true marketing needs strong and visible support from senior management.

Organisational structure – organisations can be structured in a number of ways, and when senior management teams are looking to improve the level of customer focus within their organisation, some restructuring is often necessary. Methods include:

By function – This type of structure is suited to organisations where the management of marketing is centralised. Advertising, research, product development, sales and customer service are all seen as separate functions, and careful co-ordination is necessary.

By product – An organisation that produces several different ranges of products will often manage by product group, which allows for different marketing mixes to be developed for each.

By region – This structure is most common with organisations that market internationally, or have regional variations to their product portfolio. It is also common where personal selling plays a large part in the communication mix, as it allows the company to respond quickly to competitor activity on a regional basis.

By type of customer – This might be involved where different segments are targeted, all with very different needs.

Relationships with other departments/divisions – management of the marketing mix relies on other departments within the organisation. For example, a well structured and scheduled promotional campaign, designed with the objective of increasing orders, will soon turn negatively if production are unable to keep pace with orders. Two-way communication is needed ahead of launch, so that production know what is expected and can give advance warning of any potential pitfalls. It needs to continue throughout the campaign, so that both sides are informed about progress, and are able to make any adjustments.

Lack of communication – the above example highlights the need for excellent communication, both with internal divisions, and with external agencies and suppliers. This is covered in more depth in Sessions 9 and 10.

Activity 3.3

Taking a portfolio of products of your choice, work with a colleague to decide on product objectives for each range.

Develop an action plan based on the 4 Ps for each product.

Case Study – Derby Cycle Corporation

The Derby Cycle Corporation (DCC) is a bicycle designer and manufacturer which holds the leading market share in Canada, Ireland, the Netherlands and the UK, and is a top supplier in the US. Formed in 1986 to acquire Raleigh, Gazelle, and Sturmey-Archer from TI Group, the company markets under those brands and others, including Derby, Nishiki, Univega and Diamondback. DCC has manufacturing operations in five countries and produces mountain, city, hybrid, British Motorcross (BMX) and racing bicycles. The company plans to expand through acquisitions in the US and Europe and by offering accessories and apparel.

The UK bicycle market has seen the rise of global brands and competition on the back of different bicycle types targeted at different market sectors. In the 1980s mountain bikes from US manufacturers became popular and Raleigh became a follower rather than leader with such products. Despite Raleigh's 98% brand recall scores with UK consumers, the popular mountain bikes have US heritage and today's parents are not necessarily buying Raleigh for themselves and their children. In addition, as the mountain bike market matures a wider product range is available, with some bikes selling for as little as £99 (40% of the mountain bike sector is below £120). Own label bikes are available from retailers, mail order and the Internet.

The Diamondback brand was acquired by DCC in 1999, and the UK bicycle manufacturer Raleigh was later appointed as the distributor for UK and Ireland. This was significant for Raleigh as Diamondback was a global brand with consistent West Coast USA youth imagery. This gave it credibility in the product sectors of BMX and mountain bikes where Raleigh's older, British and family oriented brand equity was less appropriate.

With both brands, Raleigh needed to establish distinct positions in the market. This would have an impact on new product development, pricing, distribution and communication activities. Focus groups were conducted in the USA and UK with male/female, urban/rural and serious/leisure cyclists in order to develop a detailed understanding of both the Raleigh and Diamondback brand essence and values. This would form a blueprint for all communication agency briefings in order to provide consistency and focus.

The results of this research follow:

Brand Essence/Raleigh

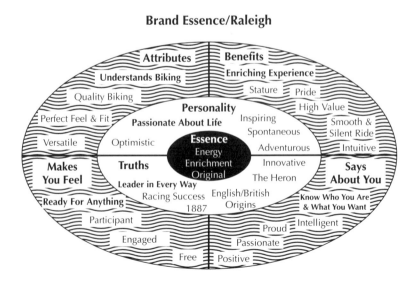

Brand Essence/Diamondback

Source: *Marketing Operations* Examination Paper, June 2001.

Questions

1. Outline the stages in an operational marketing plan.

2. Write two SMART objectives for each of the brands mentioned in the Case Study.

3. Outline a marketing mix for one of the products identified, and a specific target audience.

SUMMARY OF KEY POINTS

In this Session, we have introduced marketing planning as it applies at an operational level, and covered the following key points:

- The three main stages involved in planning are 'evaluate', 'plan', and 'implement'.

- The operational marketing plan exists to carry out the strategy in the longer-term marketing plan.

- SMART objectives are set for each element of the marketing mix.

- Gap analysis is a useful planning tool, helping establish what needs to be done to meet objectives.

Improving and developing own learning

The following projects are designed to help you develop your knowledge and skills further by carrying out some research yourself. Feedback is not provided for this type of learning because there are no 'answers' to be found, but you may wish to discuss your findings with colleagues and fellow students.

Project A

Talk to colleagues in your marketing department and identify the planning framework that is used in your organisation.

Project B

Identify two objectives in your marketing plan, and how they are used to measure progress to the plan.

Project C

Taking any budget for which you are completely or partially responsible plot actual spend against forecast spend month by month.

Prepare a cash flow for the rest of the year using either monthly budget figures or tactical activities such as particular campaigns to show peaks in spend.

If possible discuss the implications with your manager, Sales and the Accounts department.

Feedback to activities

Activity 3.1

1. What significant changes are taking place in the marketplace? This may be a major new competitor, economic changes such as recession, or vertical/horizontal integration.

2. How successful has our marketing been in the past – what worked well and what needs to be changed? Some of the marketing activities such as promotions or advertising campaigns may not have brought the revenue expected.

3. What do we want to achieve in the future? This may be both quantitative in terms of profits and qualitative such as attitude changes, brand loyalty etc.

4. Which products/market mix will help us achieve our profit and revenue targets? Products and markets need to be prioritised so that the optimum revenue and profit targets are reached.

5. What combination of the 7 P marketing programme will help us achieve these goals and objectives? The integration of the 7 Ps is a powerful coherent strategy, ensuring a consistent approach. The whole is greater than the sum of the parts.

6. What resources do we need to achieve our plan? Financial budgets, human resources, timeframes and information enable the success of implementation of the marketing plan.

7. How will we organise our resources, time, people, money and information, to achieve our plan? Organising the marketing team to implement the activities, the MkIS system, budgets and cash flows are all part of the operational organisation of marketing.

Activity 3.2

Choosing the right mix of media to achieve campaign objectives depends on the product, market and segment you are promoting to. For example, business to business and not-for-profit would require a different approach to consumer products.

The buying cycle in simple terms needs to create Awareness, Interest, Desire and Action (AIDA). Promotional campaigns need to take customers through the buying cycle, each media activity building on the next to ultimately create sales.

Promotional Media	Possible Objectives
TV Advertising	Mass market awareness
Sales Promotions	Increased sales
Direct Mail	Segmented sales
Public Relations	Third party credibility
Sponsorship	Brand association, profile, image
Exhibitions	Contacts, sales leads, profile within the industry
Presentations	Awareness, informing, networking

Activity 3.3

This activity highlights the differences between marketing one product alongside another and the complex task of differing segments and therefore promotional needs. Your answer will depend on the products you selected. The following table shows an example using two of Sony's contrasting products.

Product	Price	Place	Promotion
Sony Walkman	£60	Electronic cataloguesHigh Street electronic stores	Photographs Catalogues In-store displays Packaging
Sony widescreen TV	£1,500	High Street stores	TV advertising Retail sales training After sales service

Session 4

The promotional mix

Introduction

This Session is the first of five that look at the marketing mix (4Ps). Marketing communications form an important tool of the overall marketing mix. Products may be ideal for customer needs, priced appropriately and widely available, but unless consumers are aware of them, customers are unlikely to buy the products. In this Session we will look at the way in which marketing communication serves to inform the general public and more specifically the target audience about the existence of the products. Session 5 will take a further look at Promotions at an operational level.

LEARNING OUTCOMES

At the end of this Session you will be able to:

- Understand the need to integrate promotional mix tools.

- Explain various theories of communication.

- Identify the role advertising plays in the promotional mix.

- Understand the importance of communicating a suitable message.

Integrating the promotional mix tools

Marketing communication can be expensive and ineffective communication is therefore a waste of time and money. It is essential that the marketer understand the process of marketing communication, the wide range of promotional tools available and how to plan promotion to give the greatest impact for a given level of expenditure. The ultimate effectiveness of marketing communication is determined by the degree to which it affects product adoption amongst potential buyers, or increases the frequency of current buyers' purchases.

Adoption models

The product adoption process is usually divided into five stages and there are effective promotional tools associated with each stage:

- Awareness: mass communication sources, such as TV, magazines, Internet.

- Interest: mass communication as above, but with different message.

- Evaluation: personal sources such as friends and family.

- Trial: personal sources as above, plus salespeople.

- Adoption: personal sources, plus mass communication for reassurance and reduction of cognitive dissonance (i.e. doubts that might be in the purchaser's mind about whether they made a correct purchase decision).

The promotional mix

Promotional tools include:

- Advertising, either to the trade, to consumers or to other organisations.

- Personal selling, including face-to-face contact, technical sales and retail.

- Sales promotion, such as coupons, special offers, discounts and incentives.

- Publicity and public relations such as press releases, third party endorsements and sponsorship.

- Direct and interactive marketing, such as direct mail, telesales, database marketing and web sites.

Planning promotional campaigns

There are several key steps in planning a promotional campaign:

Identify target audience

These are usually the target market in terms of potential customers. Audiences can also be the general public and other stakeholders such as employees. The marketer must define the target market precisely using segmentation by socio-economic characteristics, usage levels or customer attitudes/personality. Identification and profiling of the target audience is essential for marketing communications.

Set promotional objectives

These can be the results that the marketer wants to achieve in terms of increased sales and profit levels. Objectives can also be communication tasks that the promotional activities are trying to fulfil. These tasks include:

- Category need: The consumer must perceive a need for a particular type of product in order to be motivated even to consider it, especially if the product is new and innovative.

- Brand awareness: The consumer must be able to recognise a company's brand within the category in sufficient detail to make a purchase. The promotional activity must be distinctive so that consumers are aware of the brand features and benefits.

- Brand attitude: The consumers will form an overall impression of the brand based on their own values and beliefs. This attitude will influence the consumers' choice of brand.

- Brand purchase intention: Once a consumer has established a category need, is aware of the brand and has a favourable attitude towards it, then they may decide to purchase.

- Purchase facilitation: The marketer has to ensure that the consumer knows where he can readily obtain the brand, once the decision to purchase has been made.

Once objectives have been agreed, the marketer must determine the message (see next section) and select the channels. Examples of media channels include: television, radio, cinema, newspapers, magazines and posters. These should be chosen with the target audience in mind, to maximise coverage or reach, i.e. the number of consumers, and frequency, i.e. the number of 'opportunities to see'.

Setting the promotional budget

There are four common methods for setting the budget:

- Affordability: how much money is allocated for marketing communications is often related to the target profit level.

- Percentage of sales revenue: some organisations allow a certain percentage of total sales revenue for promotional expenditure.

- Competitive parity: companies benchmark with competitor organisations and match their expenditure.

- Objective and task: the most logical way to set a promotional budget is to establish specific communication objectives, establish the tasks required to achieve these objectives and then estimate the total cost of these tasks.

Measure and control effectiveness

As with all marketing activities, it is important to measure the impact of promotional campaigns on sales and profit. There may be other objectives, such as brand awareness, that also need to be monitored before, during and after any promotional campaign.

Activity 4.1

Prepare a short report for the marketing manager in your organisation with recommendations on the process for selecting promotional tools, based on some of the factors mentioned above.

Compare your recommendations with the promotional mix already in place.

Theories of communication

Communication can be defined as an exchange of information. This incorporates all forms of marketing communication from the one-way process that marketers send out with mass advertising, to the more complex and interactive dialogue that occurs between marketer and customers via the Internet or personal selling.

Process of communication

In virtually all types of communication and certainly in all marketing communications, the following elements are present:

The sender (source, transmitter)

All communication needs someone who generates the messages contained in communications. This could be an organisation, a marketer or an agency.

The receiver (audience)

There also needs to be the person(s) with whom the sender organisation or individual wants to communicate. Unless the audience receives the message there is no possibility of effective communication. In marketing communications the target audience is usually the customer or potential customer. Other target audiences could be individuals or organisations who may influence the customer's buying decision-making process, e.g. regulators; or who are important to the company, e.g. competitors.

The channel (media)

Once a sender and receiver have been established, there needs to be a method of communication from one to the other. There are many methods of communication and therefore many types of channel, from personal to impersonal, broad to narrow, written and spoken. Media selection and planning is one of the most important areas in marketing communications.

In addition to these three basic elements, there are a number of technical issues that are involved in the communication process:

Encoding

In order to transmit messages and share information, the sender must translate the message using a variety of signs and symbols appropriate for both the channel and the receiver. The signs and symbols used in encoding the message must be clearly interpreted, understood, and familiar to the receiver. Similarly, the message needs to be relevant to the target audience, and this may relate to the benefits of using the product. For example, a marketing communication for a kitchen towel needs to be simple enough for anyone to understand – i.e. it absorbs spills. Many classic mistakes have been made in marketing communications over the years at this stage of encoding messages. For example, the Vauxhall Nova was not successful in Spain, as Nova literally translated as 'no go', and who wants a car that doesn't go? This risk of misunderstanding is even more complex in international marketing, with differences in language and culture.

Decoding

At the receiver's end of the communication process, there is a need for decoding of the encoded message. The target audience tries to interpret and make sense of the messages that are being transmitted. Very often in the decoding process the intended message can become changed or distorted as a result of the receiver's own perceptions and beliefs.

Noise

Any disturbance in the communication process can be called noise. One source of noise could be the perceptions and beliefs mentioned previously. More commonly, noise is created by the vast volume of information created and channelled through communication systems. Every day, you are subjected to a barrage of selling and promotional messages, competing for attention. Or there may be actual interference in the communication process caused by the media, e.g. poor reception or breakdown in radio, TV or telephone signals. Information transmitted may be lost on the way and so marketers have to plan communication processes carefully to minimise these losses.

Feedback

Information which is sent by the receiver as a result of the original communication completes the loop. This means that the communication process is rarely one-way and is usually a circular system.

A single step communication model assumes that the sender is active, the receiver is fairly passive and that communication is one-way. A two-step communication process assumes that the messages are sent out to key opinion leaders who filter the information and pass it on to other receivers. A multi-step communication model acknowledges that communication is a complex, multi-directional process. Opinion leaders talk to each other as well as other receivers. All receivers then communicate with each other. Once the elements of feedback and noise are added into this process, it becomes even more complex and difficult to manage. An understanding of this multi-step process is important for marketers to communicate directly to mass audiences and indirectly through opinion leaders, style leaders, innovators, early adopters, influential individuals and opinion formers.

Activity 4.2

In this exercise, you will be using the example of one of the most recently developed and rapidly adopted channels of communication: the mobile phone.

Through discussion with some of your colleagues, what 'noise' could interfere with the transmission of spoken messages and text messages (e.g. CU L8R) from the sender to the receiver (and in the feedback)?

The role of advertising in the promotional mix

Advertising can be defined as a 'paid for' type of marketing that is non-personal, aimed at a specific target audience through a mass media channel.

Trade advertising is usually aimed at the intermediary market, such as wholesalers or distributors. Some trade advertising is related to b2b markets, e.g., a medical device manufacturer may advertise its products in specialist magazines for surgeons. Corporate advertising is often used to increase public awareness of a company name and the products or people associated with that company.

The most common form of advertising is that targeted at consumers. This is all around us, from television advertisements to the posters seen on the street or the sides of buses.

Advertising is effective where the marketer wants to reach many customers who are widely scattered. Mass communication techniques are usually more appropriate for low cost products, used by many different people (i.e. consumers) for personal or domestic use. Advertising is useful when marketers need to inform the public quickly. It is also essential for markets where the end-users are remote from manufacturers, where many people are involved in the decision-making process, e.g. b2b, or where potential users are not easily identified. Advertising is most valuable where the product is simple to explain and no discussion is needed between marketer and consumer.

Advertising can be used to influence people at all stages of the product adoption process, from creating brand awareness to reassuring consumers in the post-purchase stage.

Advertising can be used to announce new products, help expand existing markets or enter new markets. It can also educate the market or help salespeople to achieve their objectives. Finally it can help a company to create and sustain an image around a product, or to offset competitor advertising.

Advantages

- Advertising has a potentially low cost per target audience.
- It allows repetition of messages, which helps with brand retention and loyalty.
- It enables dramatisation of the company and products, which can impact on the visual and other sensory perceptions of the customer.
- Advertising can be used to build up a long-term image of the organisation or the products.

Disadvantages

- This form of marketing communication has relatively high levels of absolute cost.
- It is often very difficult to evaluate the effectiveness of advertising.
- The persuasive value of advertising may be less than the more personal methods of promotion, such as face-to-face selling or direct mail.
- Because advertising is a mass communication method, it is not easy to get feedback and if feedback is obtained, it is often delayed.

Advertising techniques

Most large companies use advertising agencies to help with campaign planning. An agency will usually undertake three key roles:

- Account handling: liaison with the client to set and track objectives.
- Creative work: developing the actual advertisements.
- Media buying: negotiating rates on behalf of the client.

Together with the agency, marketers will develop a creative brief, which will include:

- Current situation.
- Objectives: quantitative or qualitative.
- Strategy: how to achieve the objectives.
- Tactics: detailed action plans.
- Target market.
- Budget.
- Timescale and deadlines.
- Human resources.
- Measurement.

Evaluation

Three are several ways to assess the effectiveness of advertising, including:

- Measuring achievement of advertising objectives.

- Gauging effectiveness of copy, illustrations or layout.
- Assessing certain media.

Pre-testing

Evaluations done before the advertising campaign attempt to assess one or more elements of the message, using consumer focus groups. One method is to show a commercial in storyboard format to a sample of the main target audience.

Testing during campaign

To measure advertising effectiveness during an advertising campaign, marketers or their agents can use feedback mechanisms such as response coupons or freephone numbers to compare different advertisements.

Post-testing

Once the campaign is over, advertisers can use focus groups or in-depth interviews for qualitative research into customer perceptions, to see if these have changed in response to the advertising. Many advertisers evaluate print and television advertising according to the degree of consumer recall. Various tests are used to measure this ability to remember advertisements, such as recognition tests, spontaneous and prompted recall tests.

Activity 4.3

Write a short creative brief for an advertising campaign for one of your organisation's products.

The importance of communicating a suitable message

For all promotional media, but especially for advertising, designing the appropriate messages for the target audience is crucial. As well as the more obvious principles, such as avoiding ambiguity, there are more specific tasks that the advertising message must achieve. To examine these tasks, we can use the process that the consumer follows when making a purchasing decision (AIDA):

Awareness

Messages need to be striking and unusual enough, to gain the attention of the potential buyer. The creativity of the copywriter or advertising agency is very important here.

Interest

After the message has 'grabbed' the initial attention of the target audience, it must then hold their interest long enough to persuade them to read on. This stage depends on a good appreciation of the results of marketing research into the values and beliefs of the target market.

Desire

The message has to explain the product and its benefits in such a way that the target audience can understand and appreciate them. The marketer or agency will need the research results, plus good copywriting skills.

Action

The message needs to persuade readers to adopt a positive attitude towards the product and to want to go out and buy it. Once again, the advertising team will use creative copywriting and artwork to portray a positive image of the product.

Message content

The main message will usually be based on a specific benefit that the advertiser has identified as the main advantage that the product offers over its competitors.

This may not be the main benefit that the buyer will receive from the product, which may be common to all the products in that category. The advertiser has to find a USP (Unique Selling Proposition) that is an important feature, unique to that brand. An effective advertisement should only contain one USP. Complicating advertisements by adding further messages will generally dilute the main message and reduce the overall impact.

For example, the main USP in a John Smiths beer advertising campaign was related to the 'widget' in the beer can that claims to give the beer its frothy head. Sometimes a USP is based upon a psychological appeal or a negative emotion, such as fear or guilt, e.g. the 'speed kills' campaign. Other messages can appeal to positive emotions such as love, e.g. Nescafé Gold Blend, or use humour, e.g. Budweiser.

Message consistency

Each successive campaign should fit well with its predecessors. Advertising messages do not usually stand alone and often build on previous marketing communication. All marketers should note the history of products and ensure that due consideration is taken of all past advertising when creating new programmes.

What the marketer wants to achieve with the message will determine not just the content, but also the medium that conveys it. Effective posters or short broadcast communication require simple concise messages. Printed advertisements in newspapers or web sites that can be read at the reader's own pace can include more detailed and lengthy explanations.

Believability

The message has to be credible enough for the potential buyer to be moved to action, i.e. purchase the product. However, the benefits delivered by the product once it has been purchased must match the claims made for it in the advertising.

Advertisements normally contain copy and artwork. Copy is the verbal portion, including headlines, body copy and the signature (usually product or company name). Often, this text moves the reader through a persuasive sequence that corresponds to the AIDA process mentioned above. Body copy normally consists of an introductory statement, several explanatory paragraphs and a closing paragraph.

The guidelines for preparing copy are as follows:

1. Identify a specific customer problem, e.g. do you like the taste of fresh coffee but don't have the time to make it?

2. Suggest the product that solves the problem, e.g. instant coffee brand A.

3. State the features and benefits of the product, e.g. quick and convenient.

4. Indicate why the product is best for the customer's particular situation (USP), e.g. better taste than other brands.

5. Substantiate the benefit claims, e.g. in customer taste tests, x% preferred brand A to other brands.

6. Ask the buyer for action, e.g. try brand A today!

Artwork

This part of the advertisement includes the illustrations, which can be photographs, images, drawings, charts or tables. The layout is the physical arrangement of the illustrations, headline, copy and signature.

Case Study – Café Direct

Café Direct holds approximately 3% of the UK fresh ground and freeze-dried coffee markets, despite very little marketing spend. The company began trading in 1991 as a non-profit joint venture involving the following ethical trading organisations: Equal Exchange, Oxfam Trading, Traidcraft and Twin Trade.

Cutting out the middlemen is key to the organisation's success. The company buys coffee beans directly from small co-operatives in Latin and Central America and Africa. Café Direct guarantees an agreed trade price for the coffee beans which means they have occasionally paid suppliers more than twice the normal market rate. If the international coffee price rises above the agreed trade price, they pay the international price plus a ten percent 'social premium' which the co-operatives distribute as they see fit. Café Direct also provide an upfront subsidy of up to sixty per cent of the value of one contract. It also provides regular updates on world coffee prices. This is important because the fourteen co-operatives who supply the company only sell a quarter to one half of their beans to Café Direct.

What does all this ethical trading mean for the consumer? The recommended retail price for a 227 gram jar of roast or ground Café Direct is £2.09. A jar of the leading brand Kenco costs £1.99. Café Direct's 100 gram freeze?dried product retails at £2.39; Nestle Gold Blend sells for £2.19. The UK supermarkets have maintained their profit margins and have passed on the cost of ethical business practices to the consumer, a number of whom are clearly willing to pay a slight premium if they believe the company behind the brand is operating ethically.

The issue of ethical trading has been driven by publicity about poor working conditions in factories and plantations in some developing countries. A recent documentary focused on the relationship between a major supermarket chain, and one of its larger suppliers of peas in Zimbabwe where it revealed that out of the retail price of a 99p pack of peas, the pickers got less than 1p. Supermarkets have been prompted to initiate audits of their supply and production lines and make public statements about their commitment to ethical trading. For example, Tesco recently set up a team of ethical advisors to help monitor the goods it sells in its stores and develop an ethical trading policy. Other major chains, such as the Co-operative, have signed up to participate in a project with the Fair Trade Foundation to investigate the mechanics of implementing independent auditing procedures to meet international ethical trading standards. These include agreements to negotiate with independent worker organisations and to honour or better any locally agreed minimum wage.

As the profile of ethical trading increases, the retailers' position that consumers will have to pay a premium may become untenable – especially if one of the supermarket chains takes a more definite ethical stance to distinguish itself from the other companies.

Source: From *Marketing Operations* Examination Paper, December 1998.

Questions

1. What is Café Direct's USP?

2. Recommend an outline promotional campaign for a supermarket that has decided to take a similar stance to Tesco and the Co-operative in adopting ethical trading to differentiate itself from its competitors.

3. Write 150-200 words of copy for a press release introducing the supermarket's new ethical stance on trading.

SUMMARY OF KEY POINTS

In this Session, we have introduced the communications process and the role of advertising in the promotional mix, and covered the following key points:

- The promotional mix consists of five elements:
  - Advertising.
  - Sales Promotion.
  - Public Relations.
  - Personal Selling.
  - Direct and Interactive marketing.
- In planning a promotional campaign, the target audience needs to be considered, and promotional objectives set, that can be measured for effectiveness.
- Theories of communication can help us shape appropriate promotional messages.
- Advertising has advantages and disadvantages, and needs to be consistent with other promotional activities.

Improving and developing own learning

The following projects are designed to help you develop your knowledge and skills further by carrying out some research yourself. Feedback is not provided for this type of learning because there are no 'answers' to be found, but you may wish to discuss your findings with colleagues and fellow students.

Project A

Talk to your marketing manager or colleagues within the marketing department, and identify a promotional campaign that has been carried out recently.

Identify the objectives, the media used, the message communicated, and how the campaign was evaluated.

Project B

Look at a number of advertisements in magazines, newspapers or on the TV.

Identify the target audience, and the message that is being communicated.

Project C

Using PowerPoint, or other presentation or graphics software, prepare a short message or 'mini ad', which clearly demonstrates the USP for your organisation's product.

Feedback to activities

Activity 4.1

Your answer will depend on the promotional mix you are evaluating. Ensure that you use the points in the text to compare your recommendations with the promotional mix already in place.

Activity 4.2

In addition to the internal 'noise' that the two parties in a mobile phone conversation may create when they use their own perceptions to interpret the other person's messages, external noise could include:

- Interference due to poor signal strength.

- Distraction of the listener, e.g. driving.

- Background noise, e.g. music.

- Symbols or abbreviations used in text messaging that may not be understood.

Activity 4.3

Ensure that you have covered all elements of the brief:

- Current situation.

- Objectives: quantitative or qualitative.

- Strategy: how to achieve the objectives.

- Tactics: detailed action plans.

- Target market.

- Budget.

- Timescale and deadlines.

- Human resources.

- Measurement.

Session 5

Promotional operations

Introduction

In the last Session, we considered the role of advertising in the promotional mix, and highlighted the fact that it needs to be consistent with other promotional tools. This Session looks at the advantages and disadvantages of the other promotional tools, and how they are used. It is the first of four Sessions looking at the traditional 4 Ps of the marketing mix from an operational perspective.

LEARNING OUTCOMES

At the end of this Session you will be able to:

- Explain the role of sales promotion and how it can be evaluated.

- Explain the role of PR and how it can be evaluated.

- Explain the role of personal selling and how it can be evaluated.

- Explain the roles of Direct and Interactive promotional tools and how they can be evaluated.

- Select an appropriate promotional mix for a particular marketing context.

Sales promotion – its role and how it can be evaluated

Sales promotion has been one of the fastest growing areas of marketing communication. The definition of sales promotion is an intermittent and/or short-term incentive designed to encourage purchase or sales of a product or service. It is usually impersonal in nature and non-media based.

This category encompasses a wide range of activities aimed at the trade and intermediaries such as distributors, and directly at consumers, as well as incentives for the sales force.

Examples of sales promotions targeted at wholesalers or distributors are discounts and buy-back allowances, usually based on quantity of product purchased.

Customer promotions include premiums, coupons, offers and giveaways. Objectives of this type of promotion can be to encourage trial purchase, gain extra sales volume from new customers or repeat business, or to create point of sale impact. Premiums encourage customers to buy a product by offering another product at a reduced price or even free, e.g. meal deals that offer a sandwich, soft drink and packet of crisps at a set price. Customers may collect coupons from a magazine and use them to gain a discount on a particular product. Some products include a 'giveaway', e.g. collectible items included inside cereal packets.

Loyalty programmes are used by several retail organisations to encourage regular and ongoing purchases, usually with a card that stores transaction information, e.g. Homebase Spend & Save card. After a certain amount has been spent, the customer receives gift vouchers to use in the store. Data captured by the organisation when customers apply for store cards can be used for direct mail and other forms of promotion. Many supermarkets in the UK now use this form of sales promotion. Other examples include air miles, where points that can be exchanged for flights can be collected when buying fuel, using credit cards, and many other purchases.

Some promotions are intended to stimulate sales using in-house resources. Sales contests, prizes and incentive schemes are designed by marketers to encourage the sales of particular products at different times and to change the focus between product ranges, especially at different stages in the products' life cycles.

Advantages

- Sales volume increase: the main short-term benefit.

- Defined target audience: can be targeted at specific groups, especially selected retailers and their customers, using POS coupons.

- Defined role: can be used to achieve specific objectives, such as increasing repeat purchase, again using POS dispensers and coupons.

- Indirect role: can also be used to achieve secondary objectives such as widening distribution channels.

- More easily evaluated - EPOS.

Disadvantages

- Short term: almost all effect is immediate.

- Hidden costs: management and sales force's time and effort.

- Confusion: promotions may conflict with main brand messaged.

- Price cutting: may damage quality image and persuade users to expect lower prices in the future.

- Lack of effectiveness: possible increase in revenue but loss of profit.

Evaluation of sales promotion

Unlike other forms of promotion that can be considered to have a cumulative long-term effect, most sales promotions are almost always developed to have a direct and an immediate effect. Additional sales should always result from the promotion. Therefore each promotion should have specific performance objectives and performance should be monitored to ensure that these objectives are attained. The marketer can then decide whether to use similar promotional tools in the future.

It is relatively easy to monitor the results of a coupon campaign, where the coupons are returned to the organisation or its agent for counting. However the effects of giveaways, discounts or special offer pricing is more difficult to measure, and may have undesirable effects on profit levels.

Activity 5.1

Look through any magazine or trade journal, (paper copy or online) and at least one supermarket web site, to find 3 different types of promotional offers. List the types of sales promotions you have identified, against their sources. How do these differ?

PR – its role and how it can be evaluated

The promotional tool that has become more professionally and successfully managed in recent years is that of publicity and public relations.

Publicity is any type of news story and information about an organisation and/or its products transmitted at no charge through a mass medium.

Public relations are activities designed to create understanding and goodwill between an organisation and its publics/stakeholders.

These activities are often planned together, frequently using the services of a specialist publicity and PR agency, and may include the following:

- Press releases, where information about key events is sent to newspapers or trade journals. For example, a marketer would send an article about a new type of razor blade to a selection of men's magazines.

- Company open days, where the public is invited to visit the head office or to tour the manufacturing plant.

- Press conferences, where the organisation gathers together TV or newspaper journalists to make a statement about a particular incident or topical situation. For example, a company might want to comment on a current political issue that directly affects the organisation or its products.

- Third party endorsements are used where celebrities or other famous and respected members of society are shown to be using the organisation's products.

- Sponsorship is common practice for sporting events, where company names appear all over the sports players' clothing and their surroundings, e.g. football kit and stadium. Sometimes, it is used by companies who have limited access to other forms of media or promotional tools, e.g. tobacco companies.

- Exhibitions are useful where the physical display and demonstration of products is important. Exhibitions are used to promote the company and its products to the target audience, which could be other organisations, or intermediaries such as wholesalers. The entrance to top fashion shows is usually restricted to professional buyers, although the public may have the opportunity to view on an allocated day. Some exhibitions are designed primarily for the general public, but organisations also attend to see what their competitors are doing.

Word of mouth and personal recommendation is an additional source of communication, which, like other forms of publicity, cannot be directly controlled, but can be influenced by promotional activities.

Publicity and PR can be used by companies to lobby influential organisations such as government departments or regulatory bodies.

Crisis management has become a more developed skill in large organisations which need to have contingency marketing communication plans in place, to offset any adverse publicity.

The influence of public relations reaches beyond product marketing and into corporate strategy, particularly where long term decisions and social responsibility issues are involved.

Advantages

Publicity or public relations can be used to promote the entire company, including the whole range of products. Publicity, especially if reported in the quality press, is often perceived by potential customers as being less biased than other 'paid for' forms of communication such as advertising. Finally, it can be a relatively low cost method of communicating with potential customers.

Disadvantages

It may be difficult to control media comments or reactions to publicity and public relations. Certain stories may produce unexpected results. Moreover it is almost impossible to assess the impact of PR on sales and profit levels. Therefore it is hard to evaluate the cost effectiveness of a PR campaign.

Some PR activities such as sponsorship, third party endorsement and exhibitions can be extremely costly and are only viable for large organisations with large marketing budgets.

It is not easy to control the content and the timing of communication. The marketer or his agent may submit a relevant and well-written article to a journal at an appropriate time in advance of publication. However, the journal editor may cut down the article to a meaningless paragraph, or even more frustratingly, the article may be published late, or even not at all.

Evaluation

To be most effective, PR needs to be a continuous activity, with carefully planned, well-timed events. It is imperative that the organisation establishes the target audience or stakeholders. Free publicity, news coverage or editorial can be measured in column inches, airtime or number of references made to a particular organisation or product. More qualitative feedback can be gauged through market research of attitudes and opinions about a company's public image.

Activity 5.2

Draft a short press release about a product that has recently been launched by your organisation (or one that you know well), which would gain the interest of the target audience.

Personal selling – its role, and how it can be evaluated

Personal selling can be defined as a paid for type of marketing communication that normally requires personal and face-to-face contact between the marketer and the customer. Personal selling includes telephone selling (telesales or telemarketing), technical or field selling, missionary or pioneer selling and retail selling.

Face to face selling by trained salespeople is used in b2b markets e.g. companies selling industrial components, where lengthy technical selling is needed. It is also used in b2c markets, for example in department stores where retail assistants can advise on available sizes or colours. Telemarketing can be used to sell simple products or services over the telephone, or more usually, to set up appointments for field salespeople to visit potential customers.

Advantages

Personal selling offers a two-way communication between the marketer and the target audience. This allows an effective dialogue, which ensures that the customers' needs are clearly understood by the salesperson. In turn, it is also more likely that the customer receives the appropriate marketing messages.

It also means that the salesperson receives immediate feedback on their efforts and less time is wasted on unproductive calls. Personal selling is more flexible than many other forms of communication and it allows the salesperson to respond to each customer's personal needs, sometimes even with a slightly amended product offering (customisation).

Finally, personal selling allows the development of long-term customer relationships, which can promote customer loyalty and repeat business.

Disadvantages

It is more difficult to alter spending levels in the short-term, versus other promotional tools. For example, it is easy to suspend advertising for several weeks, but not so easy to reduce the number of salespeople or to postpone their activity temporarily.

The cost per customer contact can be relatively high, especially if the selling process is a long one, as is typical in a technical sales situation.

This type of selling relies on the human factor and the ability of the salespeople to build relationships with their customers. Therefore the consistency and quality of the communication may be variable and is highly dependent on the level of training received by the salespeople.

Evaluation

In many organisations, the main marketing resource is the sales force. As a promotional tool, it is different from many other forms of marketing communication in that it depends on relationships between individuals. The effectiveness of personal selling is usually measured via the performance of individual salespeople (or a sales team) and the territories or accounts they manage. Short-term performance measures might be the number of sales calls made per week, the number of orders gained per week or the average size of an order. Longer-term performance measurements include annual sales volume, revenue and profitability of their territories against annual forecasts. Other measurement criteria may be the number of new accounts opened, customer retention or repeat business. Salespeople may also be evaluated against more qualitative measurements, such as their personal development or team working skills. The effectiveness of the sales team will also depend on the training and coaching that they receive from their management.

Activity 5.3

In discussion with your colleagues, think of at least three recent examples, either as a consumer or in business, where you have received marketing communication in the form of personal selling.

How effective were these communications?

Direct and interactive promotional tools – their role and evaluation

Direct marketing has developed significantly in recent years as an important promotional tool. Direct marketing can be defined as an interactive system of marketing that uses one or more advertising media to affect a measurable response or transaction.

The trend towards direct marketing is in-line with marketers changing from treating their customers as a homogenous mass, to addressing them as individuals. The key to success in direct marketing is the availability of detailed information about individual customers.

The increased use and sophistication of technology has allowed the development of marketing databases that can process and manage customer information. This data is collected through various sources, such as primary market research, secondary research, e.g. generally available market reports, in-house computer systems and other transactional data, e.g. EPOS and EFTPOS.

Database marketing is also made possible by the availability of media that can deliver messages to tightly defined target audiences, e.g. specialist magazines.

Direct mail

This form of direct marketing is used in both consumer and industrial marketing. Response rates range from 1% for mass mailings, to 10% for more carefully targeted campaigns. For b2b markets, it is often used to create prospects for follow up by a field salesperson.

Advantages
- Specific targeting: it can be directed exactly at the specific individual customer.

- Personalisation: it can be directly tailored to customer needs.

- Optimisation: because of its direct response nature, it can be tested and altered to obtain the optimal results.

- Accumulation: responses can be added to the database, allowing future mailings to be even more targeted.

- Flexibility: a direct mail campaign can be mounted quickly on a wide variety of topics within an overall campaign.

Disadvantages
- Cost per thousand will be higher than almost any other form of promotion, although the wastage rate may be lower.

- Poor quality lists: externally sourced lists may be of initially poor quality, with duplications, 'gone-aways', etc. It is expensive to clean mailing lists and unwanted mail. Mail addressed to dead people, for example, can cause upset.

- Relative lack of development: the techniques of direct mail are as yet relatively unsophisticated and the medium is probably not being used to its full potential.

- Poor image: many people still view unsolicited mail as 'junk mail', especially if it is badly targeted and presented.

Telemarketing/telesales

This form of marketing falls somewhere in between direct mail and face-to-face personal selling. It is more personal and interactive than direct mail. It also has a greater success rate, especially when the objective of the call is to move the potential customer along the buying decision process, by inviting them to a seminar to learn more, or making an appointment for a field salesperson to visit. The advantage over face-to-face selling is the large number of calls that can be made in one day.

Disadvantages of telesales

- Calls tend to be much shorter than face-to-face selling and relationships are more difficult to establish.

- Lack of visual stimuli means that body language signals cannot be used to gauge customer response.

- More expensive than direct mail.

Many organisations are now using specialist telesales agencies or call centres to handle their outgoing telemarketing efforts. Outsourced customer service centres are also being used to manage in-coming calls, such as order placing, enquiries and complaints.

E-marketing

The latest promotional tool that organisations can use to inform their target audience about products is e-marketing, using new media such as the Internet and digital TV. This area is evolving quickly and as technologies converge, it is not obvious which media will become the most dominant. Many dot.coms were set up to trade solely over the Internet, e.g. Amazon. Some traditional organisations have started to trade over the Internet (e-commerce) via their web sites, e.g. Tesco.

Most companies simply use their web site as an online catalogue, but others are now building more interactive features and feedback mechanisms into their web sites. Email and newsgroups are also used for marketing communication aimed at registered members, usually linked to a web site.

Evaluation

Direct and interactive promotional tools are much more easily evaluated as the feedback is often immediate and can be measured.

Activity 5.4

Look at the following web sites to see how they are interacting with customers:

www.amazon.co.uk

www.WHSmith.co.uk   Make notes on your findings.

Select an appropriate promotional mix for a particular marketing context

Marketers must allocate limited marketing budgets between the different elements of the promotional mix, i.e. personal selling, advertising, sales promotion, publicity, public relations and the more interactive tools such as e-marketing.

The ideal promotional mix will be specific to an individual product or service and to the marketing objectives that have been set for it. In deciding that optimal mix, a number of general factors can be considered:

- The organisation's resources, objectives and policies.

- Characteristics of the target market.

- Characteristics of the product.

- Cost and availability of promotional tools.

Resources, objectives and policies

In many organisations, there are several products which all need marketing support and sometimes more than one marketer who is fighting for the resources to carry out all their marketing strategies. The marketing budget may be shared across the product range.

The size of the budget will depend on the type of organisation, with a large corporation more likely to make investment in marketing communication than a small company. Unless the available budget is well into six or seven figures, television advertising will be out of the question. Limited budgets of below 100,000 Euros may mean that advertising is restricted to the specialist press.

Different marketing and sales strategies will also influence the type of promotional tools used. 'Push strategies', where companies direct their promotional efforts towards the distribution chain will require different tools to 'Pull strategies' which are used to persuade end-users to buy the products from the retailers or distributors. Some organisations use a combination of both strategies, e.g. pharmaceutical sales.

Characteristics of target market

Market size and location will influence the choice of promotional tools. If the target audience is widespread, then TV or Internet advertising is appropriate. If the market is more niche-based or narrow, then direct mail or specialist press may be sufficient.

The type of customer in the target audience is relevant to the choice of promotional tool. In industrial markets, personal selling techniques based on relationship marketing are expected and therefore necessary. In consumer markets, less personal contact, such as direct mail and advertising has become acceptable and online activity is increasing.

All marketers need to take account of what their competitors are doing. If the competitors are using high profile TV or national press advertising, then marketers need to decide whether to copy them or become more targeted in their approach.

Characteristics of product

Complexity of the product or service has a considerable effect on the promotional tools that are used. If a product needs a lengthy explanation or demonstration, then face-to-face or interactive methods are the most suitable as they allow potential customers to ask questions.

The **product life cycle** stage is also relevant to the choice of promotional activity. In the introduction phase, building awareness is key and new products are likely to require heavy promotion to ensure market penetration and early success. At the growth stage, companies will want to persuade customers to switch brands. To encourage customer retention in the maturity phase, more personal and targeted promotional methods may be used.

Characteristics and cost effectiveness of each promotional tool

The promotional message will usually determine the media channels used. For example, product demonstration requires face-to-face selling whereas advertising and sales promotion require the press or television.

The availability of promotional tools may dictate which methods are used and when. In certain countries, the media may be restricted, which can limit the use of advertising. Customer data is more freely available in certain markets that would support the use of direct mail.

Ultimately, the promotional mix must fit with the overall marketing mix: product, price, place (plus the extended mix of people, processes and physical evidence).

Successful marketing is where individual elements of the marketing mix are co-ordinated and combined to give a consistent and planned approach to the market. Each element of the marketing mix requires wide-ranging and complex decisions and it is important that each of the **7 Ps** is considered together with the others. Effective marketing planning requires that all activities that impinge on the satisfaction of customer needs must be harmonised. This will ensure full consistency between the elements of the marketing mix and ideally a high level of synergy.

Activity 5.5

Prepare a one-page report, making recommendations about the appropriate mix of marketing communication for your organisation or a specific product or range that you are familiar with.

If possible, estimate a budget expenditure for each promotional tool specified in the report.

Case Study – Derby Cycle Corporation

This Case Study was used at the end of Session 3, when we looked generally at the issues in marketing planning. This time, we focus on promotional activity, and extend the work you have done previously.

The Derby Cycle Corporation PCC) is a bicycle designer and manufacturer which holds the leading market share in Canada, Ireland, the Netherlands and the UK and is a top supplier in the US. Formed in 1986 to acquire Raleigh, Gazelle, and Sturmey-Archer from TI Group, the company markets under those brands and others, including Derby, Nishiki, Univega and Diamondback. DCC has manufacturing operations in five countries and produces mountain, city, hybrid,

British Motorcross (BMX) and racing bicycles. The company plans to expand through acquisitions in the US and Europe and by offering accessories and apparel.

The UK bicycle market has seen the rise of global brands and competition on the back of different bicycle types targeted at different market sectors. In the 1980s mountain bikes from US manufacturers became popular and Raleigh became a follower rather than leader with such products. Despite Raleigh's 98% brand recall scores with UK consumers, the popular mountain bikes have US heritage and today's parents are not necessarily buying Raleigh for themselves and their children. In addition, as the mountain bike market matures a wider product range is available, with some bikes selling for as little as £99 (40% of the mountain bike sector is below £120). Own label bikes are available from retailers, mail order and the Internet.

The Diamondback brand was acquired by DCC in 1999, and the UK bicycle manufacturer Raleigh was later appointed as the distributor for UK and Ireland. This was significant for Raleigh as Diamondback was a global brand with consistent West Coast USA youth imagery. This gave it credibility in the product sectors of BMX and mountain bikes where Raleigh's older, British and family oriented brand equity was less appropriate.

With both brands, Raleigh needed to establish distinct positions in the market. This would have an impact on new product development, pricing, distribution and communication activities. Focus groups were conducted in the USA and UK with male/female, urban/rural and serious/leisure cyclists in order to develop a detailed understanding of both the Raleigh and Diamondback brand essence and values. This would form a blueprint for all communication agency briefings in order to provide consistency and focus.

The results of this research follow:

Brand Essence/Raleigh

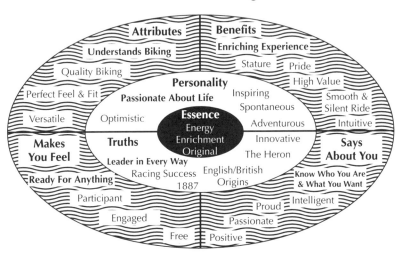

Brand Essence/Diamondback

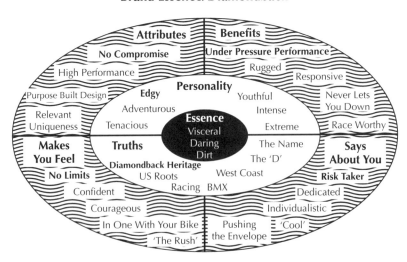

Source: From *Marketing Operations* Examination Paper, June 2001.

Questions

1. You are looking to launch the Diamondback mountain bike. Set some media objectives for the launch.

2. Identify the promotional tools you will use within the launch campaign. Justify your answer.

3. Explain why you have chosen not to select other promotional tools.

SUMMARY OF KEY POINTS

In this Session, we have introduced the elements of the promotional mix (with the exception of advertising, covered in the last Session), and covered the following key points:

- Sales promotions can be run for consumers, for the trade and for the sales force, and are used to increase sales in the short term.

- Public relations needs to be planned, and is used to enhance relationships between the organisation and its stakeholders.

- Personal selling is useful when products or services are complex in nature, and is often used in business-to-business promotional mixes.

- It is important that all messages communicated within any single campaign are consistent and do not confuse the customer.

Improving and developing own learning

The following projects are designed to help you develop your knowledge and skills further by carrying out some research yourself. Feedback is not provided for this type of learning because there are no 'answers' to be found, but you may wish to discuss your findings with colleagues and fellow students.

Project A

Talk to colleagues within the marketing department and identify whether your organisation uses sales promotion within its promotional mix.

In which of the following situations are the following used?

Consumer promotions.
Trade promotions.
Sales force promotions.

Project B

Visit the 'press' or 'media' pages of the following web sites and read examples of public relations activities or releases.

www.comicrelief.com
www.unilever.com
www.heinekencorp.com

Project C

Talk to a member of your sales force, or to someone you know who works in selling.

How well is information communicated to them about other promotional activity?

What improvements might you suggest in this respect?

Feedback to activities

Activity 5.1

It is likely that you will have found coupons in the magazines offering discounts or even free products available for the first to call a certain telephone number. On a supermarket web site or in the store itself, you will find 'buy one, get one free' offers, free gifts and special offer prices for a limited period of time.

Activity 5.2

As with all marketing communication, the message needs to be interesting and relevant to the target audience or potential customer, but also 'newsworthy'. An appropriate structure and style for press releases is covered in Customer Communications at CIM Certificate level. Compare your press release with those in the 'News' sections of corporate web sites.

Activity 5.3

As a consumer, you may have been approached by a shop assistant wanting to help. Many organisations are now contacting people over the telephone or calling at the house to encourage consumers to switch gas or electricity supply. In a business setting, you may receive several calls from potential suppliers or meet with a sales representative from another company.

Activity 5.4

These companies are encouraging their customers to register with them, so that they can capture relevant information and make their marketing communication more relevant and personal.

Activity 5.5

Compare your recommendations with the promotional plan that your organisation is currently adopting for the particular product(s). How is it different or similar? If your organisation does not have a promotional plan in place, talk to colleagues and see how appropriate they feel your plan would be.

Session 6

Pricing operations

Introduction

This Session looks at the 'price' P of the marketing mix and considers some of the aspects of pricing that it is useful for the marketer to understand. Often, financial specialists within the organisation determine price. However, the marketer may take a different view on what is appropriate, and an understanding of these aspects will help discussions on price setting.

LEARNING OUTCOMES

At the end of this Session you will be able to:

- Explain the importance of price and its determinants.
- Explain various pricing objectives and methods.
- Explain the role of pricing within the marketing mix.

Price can be regarded as the customer's buying power for satisfaction or utility. It is the monetary value placed on a product by the marketer, which must be paid in order to acquire the product. It may take several forms, based on the type of product or service that is being purchased and who is the vendor. The most common form is financial price, which usually relates directly to the price paid to obtain a product. Other terms used for price include: fee, commission, rent, interest and tax.

Importance of price

Price is the major basis for generating revenue and profits in an organisation. Total revenue derived from a product equals the price of product multiplied by the quantity of product sold. Total profit from a product equals total revenue less total costs associated with the product. Therefore the revenue and profitability from a product is directly related to the price charged. Price also has an indirect effect on the cost of the product and the quantity sold. Change in price can have a huge effect on profitability.

Other roles of price

Prices connect customers and suppliers at the point of exchange. Prices send signals to customers about factors such as product quality, exclusiveness, etc. There are powerful psychological and behavioural aspects to the price element. Price can be used as a powerful competitive weapon in markets, to drive other competitors out of the market, prevent new ones entering and forcing others to follow similar marketing strategies. Price is often the only variable in the marketing mix that can be adjusted quickly and easily in response to changes in the external environment.

Price competition

Suppliers of commodity goods mostly use price to gain business. Examples of such products include own-brand frozen vegetables and utilities. Many other companies use strong branding to differentiate their products and win business based on non-price competition, i.e. related to product benefits, value added elements and promotion.

Enduring customer loyalty can be achieved from differentiation based on unique selling propositions and branding, not from pricing levels. Most companies aim to differentiate their products in order to achieve premium pricing.

Pricing theories and definitions

Most pricing theory is based on economics. Demand is the quantity of a product that buyers wish to purchase at each conceivable price. Normally, as the price of a product increases, demand will fall. Supply is the quantity of a good that sellers wish to sell at each conceivable price. Supply of the product is expected to increase as price increases, as manufacturers enter the market. If prices fall, supply will also decrease as the market becomes less attractive. If the two curves of supply and demand are overlaid, then the equilibrium price can be established, at which the quantity demanded equals the quantity for sale.

Price elasticity

The degree to which demand is sensitive to changes in price is called the price elasticity of demand. The formula used is the percentage change in demand quantity divided by the percentage change in price. Products are said to be relatively price inelastic where demand does not change much in-line with price increases or decreases. Examples are essential items such as petrol, for which there are few or no substitutes.

Products where demand is price elastic show a significant change in quantity demanded as a result of a small rise or fall in prices. Examples of elastic demand can be seen in goods where substitutes are more readily available, such as soft drinks.

Price elasticity of demand is heavily influenced by the characteristics of the industry. Perfect competition means that there are unlimited numbers of competitors, homogenous products and perfect market information. This would tend to result in price elasticity. The other extreme would be a monopoly situation where there is only one supplier and almost no substitutes. This would result in price inelasticity, as the consumer has little choice but to pay the increased price for the same amount. More usually, industries will tend to fall somewhere in between, i.e. oligopoly (where there are some, but not many, competitors in the market) or monopolistic competition, with varying degrees of product differentiation and therefore price elasticity.

Key influences on pricing can be summarised by the 4 Cs:

- Costs.

- Customers/markets.

- Competitors.

- Corporate strategy.

Activity 6.1

Through discussion with colleagues in the Marketing (and Accounting) department, find out whether the products sold by your organisation have elastic or inelastic demand.

Various pricing methods

Some organisations use a structured approach to determining price levels. One suggested process for setting prices is as follows:

Select pricing objectives

These are the overall goals for the pricing policy for a product or range of products. Sometime short-term profit goals need to be balanced with longer-term strategic goals. There may be different objectives for each market segment or product range.

Examples of objectives include:

- Long-term business survival.

- Increase in sales revenue/volume, especially related to economies of scale.

- Improved profitability: maximisation is the ideal but satisfactory levels are frequently accepted.

- Good return on investment: increased shareholder value.

- Increase in market share.

- Improved cash flow: often indicates a high price, especially related to payback periods for projects such as new product development where research and development costs must be recovered.

- Maintain status quo: to support a stable and predictable marketplace.

- Assess the target market's evaluation of price and its ability to buy:
  - Use market research to establish the target market's perception of value for money, based on the type of product, target consumer and purchase situation.

- Determine demand levels:
  - Determine demand levels using economic theory mentioned earlier.
  - Establish price elasticity of demand.

- Analyse demand, cost and profit relationships:
  - Fixed costs are those expenses that do not change in-line with volume, such as rent and equipment depreciation.
  - Variable costs are dependent on the volume produced.
  - Contribution equals the price per unit less the variable cost per unit, i.e. the product 'contribution' towards fixed costs.
  - Break-even quantity equals the total fixed costs divided by the contribution per unit.
  - Marginal cost is the additional cost of producing an extra item of product.
  - Most profitable level of production is the quantity where marginal revenue equals marginal cost.

- Evaluate competitor prices:
  - Benchmark through market research.

Select a pricing policy

- Price skimming (premium price) is generally used where there are few or no competitors, high barriers to entry, a new or innovative product, price inelastic demand and no substantial scale economies. Examples are luxury goods such as a perfume or a new electronic gadget.

- Penetration pricing is used to gain rapid market share, in competitive sectors with few barriers to entry, 'me too' products and price elastic demand. Examples are commodity goods such as sugar or cinema tickets.

Develop a pricing method

- Cost plus: The marketer takes the total cost of the product and adds a percentage mark-up to arrive at the price.

- Target pricing: usually based on a required level of profitability or return on investment.

- Marginal costing: the marketer attempts to cover variable costs, but this can lead to prices that are lower than full cost.

- Profit maximisation: where marginal revenue equals marginal cost.

- Break-even pricing: based on the equilibrium between revenue and fixed costs.

Most cost-based pricing polices are inward looking, inflexible, do not reflect market demand and therefore can result in missed opportunities. Therefore it is worth considering demand based pricing, such as:

- Market pricing: based on what the market will bear, often known as the 'going rate'.

- Psychological pricing: price is used as an indicator of quality, where high prices can mean prestige. 'Odd' pricing, e.g. £9.99 is still common, although some quality manufacturers, such as Marks and Spencer, have decided that even pricing, e.g. £10.00, portrays a better image.

- Competitive pricing: prevalent in oligopolistic markets, where one company is the price leader and others follow. It is often better for all competitors in a particular market to follow a similar pricing strategy to avoid a price war that can lead to a vicious downward spiral in price.

Determine specific price within range established:

- Set within range established by previous steps in process.
- Influenced by other elements of the marketing mix.

Activity 6.2

You are developing a marketing plan to launch a new restaurant in a city centre. You have the task of determining the pricing policy for the restaurant. Write the section of the marketing plan which outlines the factors you need to take into consideration when setting the price and your preferred pricing approach.

Importance of pricing in the marketing mix

Price is a key element in the marketing mix because it relates directly to the generation of revenue. All other elements of the marketing mix (product, promotion and place) are only indirectly related to revenue. Price can also affect other variables of the marketing mix, as they are all interrelated.

Perceived value pricing

All elements of the marketing mix are used to build up the perceived value of the product in the mind of the customer. Price is then set to reflect this value. Customers tend to balance the price demanded against the anticipated level of use and satisfaction to be gained from buying and using the product. Customers are influenced by their previous experience, perceived quality, brand image, purpose, anticipated usage, overall appeal and the nature of competing offers.

Portfolio or range pricing

Different pricing policies can be used across a product line to balance premium priced products against the budget priced products. For example, many supermarkets now offer own brand economy products with basic packaging and often large sizes, e.g. Tesco's 'Economy' range. These may be sold alongside own brand premium products, usually in special packs, e.g. Tesco's 'Finest' range.

Product life cycle

Stage of life cycle may have an impact on pricing policy, with skimming prices used in the introductory stage to capitalise on the uniqueness of the product. Later in the life cycle, penetration pricing may be used, because lower prices may be more suitable to maximise market share. In the maturity and decline stage, prices may rise again to 'milk' the product.

Segmentation and positioning

To reduce price pressures, an organisation may choose to operate in carefully segmented markets with precisely targeted products that can command premium prices.

Branding

The ultimate goal of developing a strongly differentiated brand is to create a virtual monopoly, where consumers will not choose any other product even if their preferred brand were not available.

Place

The marketer needs to consider the channels of distribution and their required profit levels. If an appropriate market price to the end user has been decided, then the producer will ensure that their price to the next level in the value chain, e.g. the wholesaler or distributor price, is sufficient to allow that company to make their profit margin.

Distribution methods also depend on the type of product and its price. Premium priced products may only be available through selective channels. For example, high quality furniture brands, e.g. Ducal, are only sold in high-class department stores, such as Selfridges.

Promotion

There are strong links between price and marketing communications, especially in connection with the brand image that the company is trying to portray. It does not make sense to use expensive promotional techniques and then price the products at a low level. Advertisements for top of the range items are unlikely to mention the price, whereas advertisements for cheaper products may include the price in the copy. Very cheap products will make the price the prominent part of the copy – sometimes even the only copy. Premium priced products are more likely to be sold personally, face-to-face, rather than using mass communication methods, especially where the customer expects enhanced levels of service, for example from a BMW car dealer or a jeweller.

Price discrimination

Discriminatory pricing exists when the supplier of a product offers different prices to different market segments. Examples of this can be seen frequently in the service industry, e.g. entrance fees to the cinema are different for adults, children and senior citizens. It may also relate to different levels of service, e.g. first class travel or different times of the day, e.g. off-peak fares. Pricing can also be different for new customers compared to those paid by existing customers, to encourage switching (e.g. mortgage rates) or conversely to reward loyalty (e.g. car insurance renewal).

Adapting prices

Prices can be amended according to different circumstances and in-line with short-term promotional tactics:

- Trade discounts: members of the distribution chain take a percentage for their part in the sale.

- Quantity discounts: incentives given to the trade and to consumers, to encourage greater quantities to be bought.

- Cash discounts: reductions on price given for payment in cash or in advance.

- Allowances: offering a trade-in value for an old product against a new one.

- Promotional pricing: special offers, package deals, etc.

Activity 6.3

Check out the prices of digital cameras on the Internet, and compare these to prices in retail stores. Use the four Cs to consider ways in which the Internet has impacted upon the way prices are set for goods such as digital cameras or home computers.

Case Study – Values for your money

"Even when your product is not that different, better or special, it's the job of the marketer to make people think it's different, better and special." When Sergio Zyman, the former chief marketing officer of the greatest icon brand of all time – Coca-Cola – says something like this, we know how tight a grip 'confusion marketing' has got on the profession.

Sergio Zyman may be a marketing genius, but on this subject, marketers need his advice like they need a hole in the head. Confusion marketing has been investigated in several issues of *Marketing Business*, and this quote from Zyman is a perfect example of the phenomenon: "When you can't genuinely add value for your customer (compared to what your competitors are offering), pull the wool over their eyes instead."

It's easy to get preachy and say 'attitudes like that give marketing a bad name'. But actually, confusion marketing is a product of a confusion that runs deep in marketing itself between two roles of creating value for, and realising value from, the customer.

Distribution strategies

Generating customer insight that leads to the development of genuinely new products and services; marketing communications that make consumers aware of new products and offers and that facilitate choice; distribution strategies that make for easy access and availability. These are all examples of marketing as an integral part of a process that adds tremendous value for consumers.

But sometimes the go-to-market, 'realise value from the market' aspect of marketing gets separated out and begins to take precedence. We're all familiar with the results. When NPD retreats from the attempt to create genuinely New! Improved! products and services and degenerates into a desperate search for some way to pretend to be different. When companies resort to image and 'emotional added value-driven' communications strategies simply as an excuse to justify a price premium for parity products. Pricing strategies designed to make comparisons impossible. Small print designed to make finding the best deal so time-consuming that buyers simply opt for what's being offered. Distribution strategies designed to maximise the costs of 'shopping around' and put obstacles in the way of choice.

When Levi's says it wants to restrict distribution of its jeans in certain approved outlets, for example, is it doing this to ensure maximum service and best advice for jeans buyers, or is it merely doing this to ramp up the prices it charges for them? Ditto with car manufacturers and their tied dealerships. We all know the tricks and the debates. And the dilemmas.

There's an irony here. As soon as we accept a division of labour between 'making' and 'marketing' – and accept that it's the company's products and services that add value for the consumer and that it's marketing's job to realise this value – marketing becomes the only profession that's immune from its own precept of 'look at what you do through the eyes of your customer'. In these circumstances, marketers never have to consider whether the things they do add value for customers in their own right.

Marketing is a source of customer value in its own right: this just happens to be the territory upon which many of tomorrow's biggest battles for market superiority will be fought. Here's the issue in a nutshell. Consumers pay for every penny that companies spend on their marketing in the final prices they pay for goods and services. So, by rights, marketing should be a service to the consumer, whereas confusion marketing, Zyman style, is a positive disservice. And a very expensive disservice to boot.

Worth buying

Companies can get away with marketing as a disservice only to the degree that consumers lack power in the marketplace: through a weak bargaining position or lack of information. Today, however, all the key trends point in the opposite direction, towards the easing – or even the eradication – of these imbalances of power between buyers and sellers. In such a world, successful companies will be those that use their marketing skills and resources to add as much value for their customers as possible: to use their marketing to help buyers buy, as well as help sellers sell.

Marketing as a consumer service in its own right – as a 'service worth buying' – is fast becoming the new consumer expectation. It will be soon be as natural for marketers to judge the value of their own activities through the eyes of their target customers, as they do their products and services. And quotes like those from Zyman will become quaint hangovers from marketing's history.

Source: *Marketing Business*, May 2001.

Questions

1. Confusion marketing involves the use of any marketing tool. How does the article state that pricing is used in confusion marketing?

2. The article describes the way that confusion marketing can be used to achieve a premium price. Explain the term 'premium price' and how this type of pricing is usually achieved.

3. 'Marketing is a source of customer value in its own right'. Briefly explain two ways that this might be the case.

SUMMARY OF KEY POINTS

In this Session, we have introduced the 'price' element of the marketing mix, and covered the following key points:

- Marketers need to understand the relationship between price and profitability.
- Price contributes to the customer's perception of the product or service.
- Key influences on pricing are costs, customers/markets, competitors and corporate strategy.
- There are several methods of determining prices that do not consider market demand.
- There are many marketing related uses of pricing – for example, to help position a product in a particular way.

Improving and developing own learning

The following projects are designed to help you develop your knowledge and skills further by carrying out some research yourself. Feedback is not provided for this type of learning because there are no 'answers' to be found, but you may wish to discuss your findings with colleagues and fellow students.

Project A

Talk to colleagues in your marketing department and establish on what basis prices for various products or services are set within your own organisation.

Project B

Write a short report for your own organisation recommending the appropriate pricing strategies according to the current marketing and product mix.

Project C

Produce a table comparing your organisation's prices with those of two or three of your main competitors.

What other differences are there between the products or services you compared? How are these differences reflected in the prices?

Feedback to activities

Activity 6.1

You may have needed to look at historical patterns of demand, or deduced the nature of demand by reference to the type of industry in which your organisation operates.

Activity 6.2

Marketing Plan for Restaurant Launch Factors that Affect Pricing Factors that Affect Pricing Decisions

Organisational and Marketing Strategy.
Pricing Objectives.
Costs.
Other Marketing Mix Variables.
Pricing Decisions.
Buyers' Perception.
Competition.
Legal and Regulatory Issues.

Also other factors to consider:

Product mix issues (one/two/three courses, lunch and evening menus), optional products (side orders), captive pricing (wine). Price adjustments (times of day and year) and promotional pricing (loyalty scheme with discounts?)

Possible pricing approaches and choice

We could adopt a cost, demand or competitive oriented pricing approach. Options include:

- Cost-plus.

- Break-even.
- Profit.
- Market share or price penetration.
- Value-based.
- Price skimming.
- Going rate or competitive pricing.

Preferred approach would be: value-based.

Activity 6.3

The Internet has made information about such products, and the products themselves, much more accessible.

Costs	Selling through the Internet has lower overheads than a retail store.
Customers/markets	Customers using the Internet are often said to be 'cash rich and time poor – this might indicate the potential to charge more. However, prices are often lower. Customers visiting a 'bricks and mortar' store are able to ask questions and gain advice, as well as handling the camera. This attracts a premium.
Competitors	The fact that customers are able to compare prices more easily through Internet sites is bringing prices down in both stores and through the web.
Corporate strategy	This will vary from company to company. Some have opted for web only, some store only, and some a combination of both.

Session 7

Product operations

Introduction

This Session looks at the role of the 'product' within the marketing mix, and considers the need for new product development. It also introduces the concept of the product life cycle and the way the phases within it impact on the marketing mix as a whole. Finally, the important role that branding plays is considered.

LEARNING OUTCOMES

At the end of this Session you will be able to:

- Explain the role of the product within the marketing mix.
- Explain the impact of the product life cycle on the marketing mix.
- Explain the importance of NPD.
- Explain the importance of branding.

The role of the product within the marketing mix

As part of the marketing planning process, the marketing audit will include an analysis of customers, markets and the organisation's current product portfolio.

The marketing strategies subsequently developed will include the traditional four 'hard' Ps of the marketing mix: Product, Price, Place and Promotion.

An organisation's product mix consists of all the products or services offered to the customer. The length of the product mix is the total number of individual products in the entire mix. The breadth of the product mix is the number of product lines that a company offers.

For example, a household detergent supplier may offer three product lines: laundry detergent, dishwasher detergent and surface cleaners. The depth of the product mix means the number of products in each product line. Using the detergent supplier example, there may be several different types of detergent within the laundry product line: powder, liquid and tablets.

Portfolio analysis

The role of the marketer is to manage the product portfolio, to maximise revenue and profit. Product policies include decisions to delete or modify single products or entire lines, rationalisation of product lines and the addition of line extensions. Marketers also need to decide how much to customise products to clients' individual needs (e.g. new BMW cars), rather than offer standard items from stock.

BCG matrix

An organisation will aim to achieve a balanced portfolio of products, over time, to optimise cash flow and sales growth, and to offset any risk.

The technique of portfolio analysis pioneered by the Boston Consulting Group can be used to achieve the desired balance. The vertical axis measures market growth in percentage, which is an important indicator of the sector's future potential. The horizontal axis measures relative market share versus the company's closest competitor. Market share is an indication of the profitability of that product group, assuming that the market leaders gain advantages of scale and experience from the strong competitive position.

After plotting the key SBUs or product groups on to the matrix (as circles representing their revenue contribution), the marketer can see where action is needed to redress any imbalance. Stars (products with high market share in a high growth sector) are usually generating revenue but also require continued investment. Cash cows, in low growth markets, but with high market share, no longer need investment but generate revenue, which can support other product groups. Question marks (sometimes called problem children or wild cats) are those products that have not achieved a high level of market share and are not yet generating significant revenue.

Products in the 'dog' quadrant show no growth potential and have low market share and therefore should be phased out if they are not generating any positive income.

The most useful application of the BCG matrix is to monitor product groups over time, plotting the current position against the historical situation to show trends and movements. Product strategies can then be developed that move products around the matrix. For example, star products can become cash cows as the market growth slows and less investment is needed. Revenue generated from stars and cash cows can be invested in question mark products to increase market share and move them into the star category.

GE screening matrix

Another tool for portfolio analysis is the GE matrix. It is more complex than the BCG matrix, using several criteria to rank the SBUs according to market attractiveness and business strengths – the one quoted is Abell and Hammond.

Market attractiveness (low, medium, high) is plotted on the vertical axis and considers criteria such as:

- Size.
- Growth rate.
- Competitive structure.
- Historical profit margin.
- Technological requirements.
- Social, environmental and legal impact.
- Energy requirements.

Business strengths (strong, medium, weak) are plotted on the horizontal axis and assess the criteria such as:

- Market share.
- Share growth rate.
- Product quality.
- Brand reputation.
- Distribution network.
- Promotional effectiveness.
- Productive capacity and efficiency.
- Unit costs.
- Research and development performance.
- Managerial personnel.

Three broad strategies can then be applied to the SBUs according to their position on the matrix. Those products that score high or medium on competitive position and market attractiveness should be targets for investment and growth. Those products that rank low or medium in both categories should be considered for divestment.

Products that fall in between should be examined to see if selective investment could improve their position.

Activity 7.1

Prepare a short memo to the marketing manager recommending the use of portfolio analysis, comparing the BCG matrix and the GE matrix, giving pros and cons of each.

The Product Life Cycle (PLC)

The product life cycle concept is used to plan the introduction of a new product and to manage existing products. It assumes that each product has a limited life span and goes through several distinct phases from Development and Introduction ('birth') to Decline ('death').

Plotted on a graph, sales revenue for a new product will normally increase through Introduction and Growth, plateau through Maturity and start to fall into the Decline phase. Correspondingly, profit levels follow a similar curve but usually peak later than revenue, and start to fall in the decline phase.

Stages of the product life cycle

Development

This phase is usually a time of heavy investment in marketing research, to test product acceptance. It can be accompanied by heavy promotion to alert the public about the forthcoming product or heavy secrecy to prevent competitors learning about the product (especially if it is innovative).

Introduction

The product is launched, usually amidst heavy advertising, to create public awareness. Advertising tends to be informative, communicating the product benefits to customers. Special sales promotions to the trade may be important to secure distribution channels. If the product is particularly innovative, the company may use selective distribution and skimming pricing strategies. If the company wants to ensure a rapid entry into the market, they can use blanket distribution and penetration pricing strategies. The profit/loss situation is still likely to reflect a negative position, as development costs need to be recovered.

Growth

As sales volume increases, profit margins will improve as the marketing expenditure becomes spread more thinly across the revenue. As other competitive products enter the market, the innovativeness or distinctiveness of the product may be eroded. The organisation may decide to extend the product range or add special features to the product to maintain customer interest. The company may change the promotional messages from generic product benefits to specific brand benefits in order to establish brand superiority. Product prices can often be reduced as the sales grow, where companies decide to pass on the economies of scale to their customer.

Maturity/saturation

In this stage, market shares of different products tend to stabilise and the hierarchy of the various competitors will probably become established. This is the stage where most products are situated. Sales continue to grow but at a much slower rate. Marketers will attempt to differentiate their brands and may continue to modify products or add line extensions. Promotion is usually designed to encourage customer retention through brand loyalty. Price wars may start to erode the profitability of the products. As markets become saturated, some manufacturers may be forced to leave the market due to the intense competition and falling margins.

Decline

Markets fall into decline for a number of reasons. The most common is changing customer preferences, especially in today's fast moving society. Usually new, more innovative products have displaced the existing ones. Price cutting becomes intensified and many suppliers decide to abandon the market. For the companies that remain, it can be worthwhile to milk the product in this phase. This usually means reducing promotional expenditure, eliminating expensive 'above-the-line' promotion and relying on sales promotion to retain loyal customers. Companies may phase out unprofitable distribution channels and look for other ways to cut costs and squeeze profit out of the brand.

Application of the theory

If a marketer knows at what stage their product lies on the life cycle, he or she can develop and implement appropriate marketing strategies. Therefore the key skill is to develop effective marketing research to help identify the stage, and the transitions from one stage to another.

Constraints of the theory

The appropriate marketing strategies mentioned above for each life cycle stage are guidelines, but not set in stone. Other factors may dramatically change the product position, especially those related to the external environment and in particular, competitors. Markets are dynamic not static, so ongoing research should be used to monitor any fluctuations in the market that may affect the product life cycle. The conventional bell shape (when the product life cycle is shown graphically) does not always apply to certain products, whose revenue line may rise, then fall, then rise again, several times. Different stages can last for different lengths of time, depending on the nature of the product and the target markets. For example, Heinz baked beans have an extraordinarily long product life cycle and are still in the mature stage, as a result of customer loyalty to the strong original brand, several line extensions (beans with sausages, curried beans, etc.) and minimal advertising.

Activity 7.2

For your organisation or one that you know well, select a product that has been in the market for at least two years.

Plot the annual revenue since launch using a spreadsheet/graph.

Can you see what stage of the product life cycle it has reached?

Developing new products

In order to survive, most organisations need to increase revenue and profit. There are a number of 'strategic options' possible, which enable an organisation to grow successfully. One of these is to develop and introduce new products (refer to the Ansoff matrix and the BCG matrix, discussed earlier). It may be less risky to develop new products for existing markets rather than entering new markets with existing products and it is certainly safer than full diversification.

Marketers must design New Product Development (NPD) strategies that maximise revenue and profit for the product range, whilst minimising the risks associated with the NPD process.

Types of New Products

- Innovative products: technological breakthroughs.

- Replacements: product refinements.

- Imitations: 'me-too' products.

- Re-launched products: different marketing strategy.

Stages of NPD

Idea generation

Ideas can emerge from formal Research & Development departments or from production departments, who can identify ways of improving the product. The market research process will also highlight areas for further investigation. Importantly, the departments and individuals who have regular contact with customers, such as Sales and Customer Service, can provide the best ideas. This stage can be relatively inexpensive where in-house resources are used to generate ideas, for example via suggestion boxes. Senior management should encourage an innovative and collaborative environment where product ideas can be readily formulated and submitted for evaluation.

Idea screening

At this stage, several basic questions will determine if the ideas are worth considering further:

- Is there a real customer need?

- Does the company have the resources to make and market the product?

- Is the potential market large enough to generate the expected revenue and profit?

If the answer to any of the questions is 'no', then the idea should be rejected.

Concept testing

Using a small sample of potential buyers, an organisation can test one or several versions of the idea, to determine customer attitudes and initial reactions. Product ideas may be presented as written descriptions or in visual form, as drawings or computer generated images. The company can then use the results to understand which product features and benefits are most important to potential customers.

Business analysis

For each potentially worthwhile idea, a business case is drawn up which includes all the essential financial information, based on forecast sales. All costs, including marketing expenditure, are considered, in order to calculate cash flow and profitability. Again, if the business case is not strong enough in financial terms, the idea should be discarded.

Product development

During this stage, it is likely that costs start to escalate, as prototype products are developed in order to gauge potential customers' reactions. Prototypes need to be as close to the envisaged production model as possible, but this may be difficult as they are often handmade, with preliminary packaging and graphics. As customers provide feedback, small changes can be made to the product to more closely match the needs of the target market. If market reaction is negative, then the product should be abandoned. If limited market tests with the prototypes are successful, then the company may decide to proceed to full production and launch. Some industrial companies, with fewer customers, may rely on their feedback as sufficient to commence full-scale production, without further testing.

Test marketing

For many FMCG companies, this stage allows them to try out the marketing mix and acts as a final check to make sure the product will be successful in the marketplace. Test marketing operates in a geographically controlled situation, usually determined by Independent Television areas. Companies use test marketing to investigate the appropriateness of a proposed marketing strategy. Companies can then refine the strategies and predict their effects in terms of market potential. The chosen area for a test market should be as closely representative of the final total market as possible, which will allow the company to extrapolate the results more confidently. Sometimes, a company will run more than one test market simultaneously, with slightly different marketing mixes, in order to find the optimum balance.

Launch and commercialisation

The final stage in the NPD process is the launch of the product to all the target markets, using appropriate marketing strategies. If all the previous stages of the NPD process have been rigorously followed, then the risk of product failure at this stage is much reduced, but success is not always guaranteed. Less than 10% of new product projects actually reach the commercialisation stage and many of these will be withdrawn during the first year.

Products stand a better chance of survival if they are differentiated in some way from those of competitors, and the next section covers an important concept in achieving this.

Branding

One of the key tools for product differentiation is that of Branding. The product is given an image, a character, or sometimes even a personality. Branding is based on a name, and other factors affecting a product's image, such as packaging and advertising. A product has tangible attributes such as design or performance that make up its core benefit, plus intangible aspects such as brand image. These elements, together with support services, such as delivery and customer service, can be considered collectively as a 'brand'.

Definitions

A brand is a name, symbol, design or particular feature that distinguishes a company's product from another similar product. The brand name is the part of the brand that is usually written or spoken, e.g. BMW 3 Series. The brand mark is the element of a brand that is usually represented by a symbol or design, e.g. the blue and white BMW symbol. A trademark is a legal designation indicating that the owner has exclusive use of the brand and that others are prohibited from using it, often depicted by: ™. A trade name is the legal name of an organisation, e.g. BMW Ltd.

Why use branding?

The use of brands helps organisations to build customer loyalty towards the brand, which encourages repeat purchase of the product and the development of long-term relationships between the organisation and the customers.

Three levels of brand loyalty exist:

- Brand recognition: where the customer is familiar with the brand and may buy it if their preferred brand is not available.

- Brand preference: where the customer prefers the brand to all others and will always purchase it, if available.

- Brand insistence: where the customers will only buy that brand and no other.

Brand equity

There can be a high degree of value associated with a brand. Firstly, in the mind of the customer, where the brand represents a guaranteed level of quality. Secondly, the financial value of the brand is related to the brand's strength in the marketplace and represents the value of the brand to the organisation.

Types of brands

Manufacturer brands are those brands where the producers are involved throughout the chain of distribution and control the marketing mix. An example would be Kellogg's. Own label brands are made for wholesalers and retailers by manufacturers who are not identified on the products. Many producers supply supermarkets with products that are sold under the supermarket's own store label, e.g. Asda. These retailers control the marketing mix for the brand. Generic brands are sold under defined product categories, but without clear reference to the supplier's name or other distinguishing features, and usually at a lower price than branded items. They have become less common in recent years, but still exist in some markets, e.g. generic packs of paracetamol tablets are available at most pharmacies.

Brand strategy

Organisations can use branding in several ways:

- Corporate (sometimes called overall family) branding, where the company name is used on all products, e.g. Heinz.

- Range (or line family) branding, where all products within a single line have the same name, e.g. Cadbury's.

- Individual brand brands used for a single product or limited range, e.g. Rolex.

- Combination brands, e.g. Sony Walkman.

Choosing a brand

There are many ways of selecting an appropriate brand for a new product. Some brands may result from internal brainstorming amongst the new product development team. Others are created after careful research and analysis by consultants. Many large organisations will tend to use both methods. Other companies may simply rely on the senior manager's preference. Whatever the method used, the resulting brand needs to be distinctive, memorable and appropriate to the product and the target market.

Packaging

The development of a container and label for a brand is very important. Firstly, for protection of the contents, a product needs an appropriate primary package (tin, carton, etc.). This primary packaging should allow for easy display and storage at the point of sale. Strong secondary packaging may be needed to avoid any damage during transportation. Packaging should allow the product to be easily identified and enhance the brand image. Clear labelling of the product is necessary for promotional, informational and legal purposes.

Using an example, a Chanel perfume will have a glass bottle that protects the contents and portrays a quality image, through shape and colour. Each Chanel brand is packaged to differentiate the fragrances from each other and from competitors' brands. The outer box gives additional protection to the bottle and contains more brand reinforcement through the images, colours and typeface used.

Activity 7.3

Using the Internet or other forms of advertising media, find an example of a product that uses:

The corporate brand;
A family or range brand;
An individual brand;
A combination brand.

Case Study – Marketing magic

The Harry Potter series was launched in 1997 with a 500 print run of *Harry Potter and the Philosopher's Stone*. Three years and three titles later, the initial print run for *Harry Potter and the Goblet of Fire* was 1.5 million copies, 30% of which were sold on the day of publication. Worldwide sales of the series now top 113 million copies, words invented by JK Rowling are in common usage and first editions of her books are sought after.

The UK children's book market is worth £140 million per annum and represents 23.6% of the general retail market. When the first book, one in a series of seven, was launched in 1997 competition was tough. It was entering a market crowded with 10,000 new children's titles every year.

Marketing in the book publishing industry is not as scientific as in many other FMCG categories, says Rosamund de la Hey, Bloomsbury's head of children's sales and marketing. There are no hard and fast rules – it's a lot more instinctive. There is little research you can undertake – you don't add up numbers and then get a novel written to fit particular criteria. You buy the book and then market it. 'No brainers' – books by authors who are not well-known and whose next books are therefore not eagerly awaited – pose particular marketing challenges. "In these cases," de la Hey says, "the market is bookshop led. In-store marketing is essential to success. Around 70% of people buy a book because they saw it in a shop."

Effectively, according to de la Hey, any book has to be sold three times. The agent has to sell it to the publishers, then the editor sells it to the internal sales team and then finally it moves out into the consumer market. It's a gradual process and each stage is as important as the next," she says. "It's also a very personal business. Several publishers turned down *Harry Potter and the Philosopher's Stone*, but it's far from unusual for that to have happened to an eventual best-seller.

"Harry went through all those processes and the in-house buzz the book created was incredible. We had a gut instinct that this was going to be bigger than anything we'd ever done before. That feeling was transmitted beyond the company to the key influencers – the reviewers, booksellers and librarians. They all fed into the groundswell of noise. The first Harry Potter book had to find its way with little money but plenty of word-of-mouth.

"The playground market was also obviously important, but this is always difficult to harness. It helped that *Philosopher's Stone* won the Smarties Book Prize in 1997, which is judged by children. Word-of-mouth marketing cannot be underestimated.

De la Hey adds that one major benefit of the children's book market is that it is constantly refreshing, as children move up an age bracket.

Brand personality

The Harry Potter books proved to be a tremendous success story with distribution quickly spreading from bookshops to supermarkets, service stations and corner shops.

Harry Potter and the Philosopher's Stone was followed by *Harry Potter and the Chamber of Secrets, Harry Potter and the Prisoner of Azkaban* and, most recently, *Harry Potter and the Goblet of Fire*. The books have been welcomed by booksellers and the general public for their readability and high standard of writing and storytelling. They have also been credited with revolutionising the reading habits of a nation – Bloomsbury's key brand proposition.

According to de la Hey, the book jacket design was key to creating a brand personality. "The jacket is the shop window, how you create your brand," she says. "We opted for a very distinct artistic style, with Harry Potter in big type and the words of the title in smaller type below. They are instantly recognisable. "Interestingly, we used three different illustrators, but this hasn't altered the brand perception at all because the blocking is so clear."

Gaining competitive advantage

Bloomsbury had several competitive advantages to exploit – aside from having won the approval of all the key influencers! As a single mother, writing in cafés because she was too poor to afford home heating, there was an excellent publicity angle to the JK Rowling story. The press were quick to pick up on it.

"Compared to most products in the FMCG category, books are able to generate a huge amount of coverage in the press. The Harry Potter series got a huge share from the very beginning," says de la Hey.

As the prizes rolled in, Bloomsbury also recognised that a substantial part of the market included adult readers, but that adults were embarrassed to be seen reading a children's book. The publishers capitalised on the opportunity by re-jacketing them for this audience. "This was a first for the industry," says de la Hey. "It was the same easily recognisable brand, with a different take."

Bloomsbury also decided to publish cloth-bound editions for collectors and boxed sets of paperbacks and hardbacks, all of which have proved very popular.

Advertising and promotion

To date, marketing budgets have been allocated to stunts such as a promotional train, publicity tours, in-store merchandising/point of sale and outdoor and press advertising. In 2000, £400,000 was spent on advertising and promotion.

Apart from major press and outdoor advertising, the most successful campaigning has involved "denial marketing". *Harry Potter and the Prisoner of Azakaban* went on sale at precisely 3.45pm on July 8th, a time dreamed up to prevent children playing truant.

For *Harry Potter and the Goblet of Fire*, the technique was taken still further. A teaser campaign flagged "Harry's Back" and there was a countdown to publication, but the title of the book was not revealed until a week before publication. "A textbook example of classic PR strategy in action," says de la Hey.

The book went on sale at midnight on 8th July 2000. Queues had started forming for hours beforehand and some children had won tickets for special slumber parties inside the bookshops.

To launch the book to the world's press, Bloomsbury hired a steam train, painted it in the colours of The Hogwarts Express – the train from the stories – and stationed it at King's Cross, London. After the launch, it travelled around the country, making eight stops and meeting thousands of fans along the way. JK Rowling signed thousands of books and the stunt received coverage all over the world and across all media. The result was "the fastest selling book in history" (Newsweek).

Measuring effectiveness

Harry Potter and the Goblet of Fire has exceeded its target sales and the series now accounts for 19.1 % of total children's book sales, compared to 3.9% for the next best-selling series.

E-marketing prospects

Bloomsbury recognised that e-marketing represented opportunities for its Harry Potter series and created a web site and online Harry Potter club. However, although the web has spawned many Harry Potter web sites, Bloomsbury's activities in this area have been limited for copyright reasons. Warner controls the digital rights to the series.

Moving on...

It is widely recognised that JK Rowling has changed the shape of publishing. "While most novelists take 15 to 20 years to build a career, she became a household name almost overnight and made reading a cool thing to do," says de la Hey. "There is nothing to rival Harry. Other publishers avoid a July publishing date like the plague."

The Harry Potter phenomenon has reverberated around the world and the books have dominated the best-seller charts internationally, causing both the New York Times and the Sunday Times to alter their format and exclude children's books, which had regularly been taking up the top four places because of Harry.

The paperback mass-market edition of *Harry Potter and the Goblet of Fire* was published on 6th July 2001 and the Warner Brothers film of the book led to a range of 20 stationery items to tie in with the release of the film. Mattel signed a huge toy licensing deal for the film.

Next book due in 2002

The next Harry Potter book is due in July 2002 and Bloomsbury says it is mulling over promotional ideas and looking to create more dramatic stunts. "We will be continuing the existing brand format, drawing inspiration from the book itself," says de la Hey. That's all we're prepared to say," she concludes, "all ideas are under wraps!"

Source: *Marketing Business*, November 2001.

Questions

1. List three ways in which books differ from straightforward products for marketing purposes, according to the article.

2. Identify one way that the product was adapted to attract more customers.

3. How does the article describe the development of a 'brand personality'?

SUMMARY OF KEY POINTS

In this Session, we have introduced the product element of the marketing mix, and covered the following key points:

- An organisation's product mix usually consists of different product lines that are said to make up the product portfolio.

- Marketers need to manage this portfolio, maintaining a balance of products that bring in profit and volume sales. The BCG Matrix and GE Screening Matrix provide tools for undertaking this analysis.

- Products are said to go through a product life cycle – introduction, growth, maturity and decline – each of which requires an adaptation of the marketing mix.

- In order to survive, organisations need to innovate and develop new products to keep up with customers' changing needs.

- The new product development process consists of several stages – idea generation, idea screening, concept testing, business analysis, product development, test marketing, launch and commercialisation.

- Branding is an important way of differentiating your products from those of a competitor. It is a complex process.

Improving and developing own learning

The following projects are designed to help you develop your knowledge and skills further by carrying out some research yourself. Feedback is not provided for this type of learning because there are no 'answers' to be found, but you may wish to discuss your findings with colleagues and fellow students.

Project A

Examine the range of products offered by your organisation, or one you know well.

How long has each been in existence?

Which are the most profitable?

Which sell in the highest volume?

Which sell best to which target group of customers?

Project B

For one of the products that you selected above, identify which stage of the product life cycle has been reached.

Does its current marketing mix reflect that stage?

Project C

Talk to colleagues in your marketing department about the latest product to be launched.

Can you identify the stages of the new product development process as they are described in the text of this Session?

Feedback to activities

Activity 7.1

Either model can help marketing managers to consider the strategic alternatives, showing key data about SBUs/product groups relative to each other and therefore facilitate decision making about the product portfolio.

Both the BCG matrix and the GE model require a great deal of accurate market information before they can be used as meaningful management tools.

The BCG matrix may be easier to apply than the GE matrix, but the latter uses several dimensions in the analysis of product and markets, and could be considered a more thorough approach.

Activity 7.2

You may not always be able to say what stage the product has reached, especially if the curve does not appear to be following the classic bell shape. However, if the product has been in the market for some time, it is likely that it has reached the maturity stage, which can last for several years.

Activity 7.3

More examples:
Corporate branding: Coca-cola.
Family or combination brand: Ford Mondeo.
Individual branding: Snickers.

Session 8

Place operations

Introduction

This Session considers the role of 'place' or distribution in the marketing mix. It looks at the elements that make up the place mix, and considers the role of the various channel members. Finally, it identifies criteria for selection of suitable channels to market.

LEARNING OUTCOMES

At the end of this Session you will be able to:

- Explain the role of the distribution chain within the marketing mix.

- Outline the elements of the distribution mix.

- Describe the roles of various channel members.

- Identify criteria by which a channel to market might be selected.

The role of distribution (place) in the marketing mix

The channel that an organisation uses to get its products to its customers is an important part of the marketing mix, and can contribute to the customer's perception of the quality and value that the product provides.

For some organisations a direct route to the customer is appropriate – for example, mail order catalogues or sales via their web site. However, most manufacturers use intermediaries to help them, and in doing so, achieve 'economy of effort'. Think about your own shopping trips to buy clothes, for example. You do not have to visit the shoe manufacturer, the suit manufacturer, the shirt manufacturer, the accessory manufacturer, etc., but probably visit a department store or a store that focuses on womenswear or menswear. This saves you the effort of visiting many different locations, and also saves the various manufacturers targeting you as an individual – the promotional activity may be carried out by the retail outlet on their behalf.

Intermediaries take several forms. They may be distributors, agents, wholesalers or retailers, and they take on a variety of functions on behalf of the producers. These include the breaking down of stock into smaller quantities, feeding back market and competitor information to the manufacturer, and helping to promote products (including personal selling to customers that they have identified and will negotiate with). They may also contribute to the cost of moving the goods, as well as arranging to transport and store them on a long-term basis.

Companies within a distribution chain are dependent on each other in meeting their organisational objectives. The supply chain works in such a way that each 'link' in the chain performs its own specialist function, and, ideally all work together and co-operate with the aim of providing an efficient service that satisfies customer needs. Unfortunately this is not always the case, as channel members are more likely to focus on their individual short-term goals. Disagreements arise about who does what and who earns what from the process – this is referred to as channel conflict.

Such conflict often has a negative impact on overall service to the customer, and this has led to the formation of vertical marketing systems, in an attempt to manage the likelihood of conflict arising, and improve operations.

A vertical marketing system is a channel within which manufacturers, intermediaries and retailers all work together as one. One member of the system controls the activity, either through ownership of the others, or through contracts with them, or because their size gives them power over the others. Examples of vertical marketing systems include:

Supermarket chains – who own food-manufacturing companies (ownership or corporate vertical marketing system).

Buying groups such as Spar, where independent retailers band together under contract with a wholesaler (contractual vertical marketing system).

Kellogg's, the cereal manufacturer, takes decisions over its channel members because of the power it holds through its size (administered vertical marketing system).

Activity 8.1

Write notes for your Marketing Manager, justifying the switch from a traditional distribution channel to a vertical marketing system.

Elements of the distribution mix

There are many factors that contribute to channel design, and the nature of both the product and the buyer are contributing factors to the decision. Consumer and business-to-business channels therefore differ, although one company may be involved in serving several target segments that cross this divide.

Let's consider the example of a supplier of stationery products.

1. Consumer segment A – buys products in small quantities through catalogues sent direct to their homes.

2. Consumer segment B – buys from retailers such as Staples, or Office World.

3. Business-to-business segment A – buys large quantities, at discount prices, from a salesperson who calls on their company.

4. Business-to-business segment B – buys small quantities from local stationery stores, who in turn purchase from wholesalers.

In the final part of this Session we look at the fact that consumer products demand different quality retail outlets depending on whether they are convenience goods, shopping goods, or speciality goods. For similar reasons, it is unlikely that business-to-business markets will be supplied through retail outlets, although there will again be some crossover for the smaller business that might want more personal advice when purchasing equipment or computers, for example.

Generally, consumer markets are served via direct marketing (catalogues, telesales, Internet, etc.), retail outlets, and personal selling.

Generally, business-to-business markets are served via agents, distributors, direct marketing (catalogues, telesales, Internet, etc.), wholesalers and personal selling.

There is increasing use of e-commerce in supplying both consumer and business-to-business markets through the Internet. Consumer goods still tend to be low value goods such as books, music, DVDs, etc. However, business-to-business buyers who are re-ordering goods with which they are satisfied, from a supplier that they know, are receiving improved service from companies who set up Extranets (password protected extensions of their web sites) to facilitate the order process.

Considerations for companies moving into e-commerce include efficient ways to fulfil orders, and so their focus shifts to physical distribution of their goods, and logistics issues.

Activity 8.2

As a consumer, visit www.amazon.com, and then compare this site with www.pcwbd.com, PC World's Business site.

Make notes comparing the ease of access to information about products, how easy it appears to be to order goods, and the product ranges available.

The role of various channel members

The members of the distribution channel fulfil various roles in getting the product to the customer, and each can add value to the transaction. There are two main types of channel member – those who take ownership of (or title to) the goods on the way to the customer, and those who do not.

Whether or not they buy products for re-sale (to retailers or to consumers), or whether they just play a role in moving goods through the chain for their own reward, they can play a part in the overall marketing process.

Marketing Planning – intermediaries can play a part in conducting marketing research and feeding back market intelligence, setting objectives, planning marketing programmes, and resourcing, both financially as well as through their own work force.

Product – intermediaries can break down volumes of stock into sizes that are more suitable to the end consumer. They can also help by preparing or refining products to get them ready for customers.

Promotion – channel intermediaries can take on a whole range of promotional activities. Full campaigns can be planned to meet promotional objectives, and these will include advertising, sales promotion, personal selling, PR, sponsorship, direct mailings and packaging.

Place – the focus here is on physical distribution of products. Intermediaries often provide warehousing/storage facilities including stock control, onward transportation, and materials handling.

After-sales service – this can include the provision of helplines, technical support, training, installation and warranties.

Relationship marketing – intermediaries can help by developing relationships with other intermediaries, suppliers and customers. If levels of service, relationships, or communication fail at any part of the distribution channel, then it will be difficult to maintain customer loyalty.

Price – Intermediaries can play a role in setting pricing policies, terms and conditions of sales, and provision of financial services and credit facilities.

Customers and producers often take a view that intermediaries add cost to a product on its route to the customer, and push prices up. With recent technological developments, in particular databases and the Internet, there has been a move to direct marketing, cutting out intermediaries from the channel to market. Selling direct to customers via the Internet, and replacing an existing distribution channel, is referred to as **disintermediation**.

Companies that take this view have to be very careful. Cutting the cost of getting the product to the customer in one way has three possible outcomes:

1. The cost of using the intermediary is cut, but the costs in getting goods to many separate customers may be higher in the long term.

2. The cost of using the intermediary is cut, but so are the services that the intermediary adds to the process in return for that cost. Someone has to provide those services, or the customer will move to a competitor who does, and the provision of services will cost the manufacturer money.

3. The nature of the product may mean that costs can be cut by replacing the intermediary by an alternative method of physical distribution. This is the only case when disintermediation should be considered.

Activity 8.3

Your organisation, which currently supplies torches through wholesalers to retailers to consumers, is considering adding an e-commerce facility to its web site with the aim of switching solely to direct distribution in three years' time.

Write a memo to your Marketing Manager, explaining the implications of such a move.

Criteria for selection of a channel to market

There are many considerations when designing appropriate channels to market.

The stages of design include defining customer needs, setting distribution objectives (and recognising organisational constraints), identifying alternative options, and evaluating and selecting an appropriate option.

The key issues to be taken into account are:

Corporate objectives and constraints – is the organisation looking to grow market share, increase profit levels or improve customer service? Each of these objectives will influence the shape of the distribution channels used. For example, cutting back on the number of intermediaries used may improve profits in the short term by cutting costs, but will not help grow market share by moving into new markets. Organisational constraints will also impact on these decisions. Smaller firms may rely on intermediaries for transportation of goods, whereas organisations with stronger financial resources may be able to run their own fleet of delivery vehicles.

Customer characteristics – buyer behaviour is an important consideration when selecting the distribution channel. The way that consumers, in particular, perceive your products will be influenced to some extent by the 'physical evidence' or 'ambience' of the outlet where they buy the product. This is related to the nature of the product, details of which are shown below.

There are obvious differences between consumer and business-to-business buyers, but companies also need to consider targeting different segments through different channels, as mentioned above.

Competitor activity – It is important to be aware of competitor activity. Channels may be designed to ensure that your goods are displayed wherever your competitors are. In other cases, you may be able to differentiate the way you operate from your competitors by using an alternative channel. Directline Insurance services did this effectively at their launch, as all other insurance services involved a more complex channel.

Nature of the product – For example, with convenience products such as bread, newspapers, etc. availability of the product is more important than the environment in which it is purchased. Distribution of such products is described as intensive distribution, where products are sold through as many outlets as possible.

Shopping products, which include electrical goods, furniture, and some fashion goods, involve the customer in slightly more complex decisions and may therefore involve an element of customer service through a more specialised retail outlet. Distribution of these goods is described as selective distribution, where stores are selected for the level of value they will add through the service they offer.

Finally, speciality goods such as designer fashions, jewellery, etc. are bought at premium prices that demand special attention for the customer. The distribution of these goods is described as exclusive distribution, and the environment in which they are bought is often as important to the customer as the item purchased.

The above covers consumer goods, but business-to-business goods are usually bulky or complex. For example, construction materials or photocopiers are not usually bought via retail outlets. They demand different channel decisions to those for consumer markets.

External environmental forces – monitoring the external environment is important for all aspects of marketing, and distribution is no exception. There are legal issues which impact on selection of channel – for example, competition legislation stops channels being created that would effectively form a monopoly situation. When considering distribution into international markets, then trade barriers need to be taken into account, as well as the economic conditions that exist.

Relationships and conflicts – once the marketer has set objectives for its channel, it can then set about the actual design, and decide what specific 'place mix' it will use, linking its decision back to overall decisions about segmentation and target markets. At this stage, considerations about whether to go direct, use the sales force or contract out to a field marketing force, or whether to use intermediaries are made. If the channel will involve intermediaries, then the type of intermediaries needs to be decided upon, bearing in mind the functions they will be expected to perform. Finally, decisions need to be made about which intermediary firms will be the most suitable to serve customer needs in order to maintain or win a competitive advantage.

Case Study – Evolving the supply chain

Life in the manufacturing sector has never been easy. But in the last 15 years, globalisation has brought intense competition and increased buyer power, driving commoditisation and margin pressure on new equipment sales. Many companies have responded by restructuring, merging or accelerating incremental improvements to the product itself. However, the most innovative organisations have begun what the *Harvard Business Review* describes as a move downstream in the value chain away from the shop floor and towards the customer ('Moving downstream, the new profit imperative in manufacturing', September/October 1999).

The traditional focus on incremental improvements in the upstream supply chain has prevented many manufacturers from seeing this downstream opportunity. Jim Kilpatrick, global head of Deloitte Consulting's Supply Chain practice, commented in a recent report that, "Today's manufacturing executives were raised in a product-centric era in which competitive advantage was achieved through product branding, quality and cost. Improving supply chain performance with a focus on the supplier is more natural for them because that is what they know. However, in this Internet era the power has shifted dramatically to the customer, and those companies that are able to integrate their supply chain and their customer strategies will achieve breakthrough performance."

The future of many manufacturers will depend upon how their marketers react to this new situation, for it is marketing that is the owner of this newly dynamic customer relationship. However, the majority of reference points are modelled on high-volume, low value products where the sale marks the end of the process. In low-volume, high-value markets such as Aerospace, High-Tech, Automotive and Telecommunications, the initial sale is only the start of an ongoing relationship or aftermarket, where maintenance and support significantly impact on customer satisfaction and their overall lifetime value.

Where the money is

When manufacturers start selling new products there are no existing customers. How many cars were there before Ford? Or how many aircraft were there before Boeing? At the start of the product life cycle there is no aftermarket, but today there are 13 cars on the road for every new one sold and 150 planes already in service for every new unit delivered. This installed base offers a tremendous revenue opportunity, and the manufacturer has an inbuilt advantage. The customer is dependent upon the original manufacturer for ongoing maintenance and support to keep the product working over a life cycle of anything from 5 to 35 years.

The car makers show that this advantage is not permanent as few people continue to use main dealer services and original spare parts after the three-year warranty lapses. However, in many other sectors the inherent advantage remains; the official dealer network is still in the leading place to maintain the equipment and the manufacturer still has the major market share of spare parts. But this is more by accident than design. Do you know who your major aftermarket competition is? Do you know your share of overall market for spare parts on your products?

For the vast majority of manufacturers the aftermarket remains an afterthought, because the business is built around the product rather than profitable opportunities for customer service. However, if we look at profitability it becomes clear that something is wrong with the existing view. Market pressure has seen new equipment margins fall to between 1-15% whilst aftermarket margins remain a far healthier 30-60%. With the ever increasing size of the installed base, the traditional dynamic where Customer Support was a cost of doing business is reversed. Instead of simply being an incentive offered to ease the new sale, the aftermarket has become the hidden driver of corporate profitability. Innovative manufacturers have recognised this shift and adapted their business strategy to thrive.

For example; 20 years ago Rolls-Royce existed to manufacture and sell aircraft engines. Today, Sir Ralph Robbins, chairman of the company, views new engine sales within the context of their overall life cycle, describing current product shipments as "creating huge imbedded value". In 2000, aftermarket value on Rolls-Royce new engine sales stood at $14 billion over the next 25 years, far greater than the original. Like many of their peers, these companies continue to focus on cutting costs in the supply chain, but they have also recognised the competitive advantage in better supporting their customers in what Michael Hammer, author of Re-engineering the Corporation, has called the 'support chain'. This encapsulates the process and systems that come into play after the equipment sale, and manages the aftermarket relationship.

Building the support chain

The support chain is a highly complex business. The performance of the equipment drives both manufacturer profit and operator satisfaction, be it in telecommunications, aerospace, discrete manufacturing or any number of markets. The process has traditionally been time-consuming, labour intensive and costly. The sheer volume of information that underlies the support chain has meant high quantities of paper, large teams of customer support and inefficiencies that lead to equipment downtime and less profitability. The speed and dynamism of the Internet and the emergence of e-business strategies and XML technology, dramatically alters this situation. Complex technical information can be issued to the customer and spare parts ordered all at the press of a button.

Consider the following examples:

GE Aircraft Engines

The $11 billion manufacturing company with $3 billion aftermarket launched a customer web centre on 1st January 2000, moving one of the most complex industrial support chains on the web. Within its first year, the CWC carried $1 billion in revenue from spare part sales, and $50 million in additional revenue from existing customers.

Giving real-time access to over 1 million pages of content – the maintenance manuals, illustrated parts catalogues, and service bulletins that drive customer efficiency – makes GWC easier to do business with.

Pratt & Whitney

When it costs an airline $25,000 per hour for a Boeing 747 to be grounded, the productivity of maintenance staff becomes a key factor in corporate profitability. At North American Aerospace manufacturer Pratt & Whitney, innovative support chain strategies are enabling customers to foster collaboration between technical staff to share best practices and boost productivity. Such collaboration has reduced maintenance times by 10%, saving key customers literally days of lost aircraft time.

Perkins Engines

With 7 million engines in use around the world, Perkins is using the Internet to connect their global dealer network in one support chain. By improving their access to maintenance information and parts data, as well as encouraging cross- and up-selling, the company increased parts revenues by 5-10%. The Department of Trade and Industry (DTI) has recently begun using this as a case study in best practice for e-business in manufacturing.

Growing revenue

Rather than continuing to squeeze the supply chain for incremental improvements, there is a significant opportunity for manufacturing companies to apply emerging b2b tools – to grow revenue in the support chain. By leveraging their inherent advantage as manufacturer of the product, companies can profitably increase their share of their customers' lifetime value.

Many companies are not structured to see these opportunities and are uncertain how to react when they do. The company is seen in terms of the product manufactured, rather than in terms of the need met.

This is a classical marketing challenge, but also a unique opportunity. Manufacturing companies still tend to be dominated by Engineering and Sales, with Marketing still largely a tactical weapon for the support of new product sales. By taking a 'whole company view' the support chain takes the customer to the heart of the business and puts Marketing on the executive agenda.

Graham Wylie is marketing director at Enigma Europe.

7 steps to building the support chain:

- Evaluate the aftermarket for your business – is there a requirement for ongoing support?

- Map the existing processes for customer support and follow-on sales.

- Identify aftermarket competition and market share.

- Identify your unique value (support information, spares, warranty etc.).

- Leverage this value as the platform for the support chain.

- Apply appropriate technology to improve the process.

- Collaborate with key customers to measure shared cost reductions and revenue gains.

Source: *Marketing Business*, July/August 2001.

Questions

1. The Case Study refers to 'a product-centric era'. Give two examples of how competitive advantage used to be established, compared to ways in which firms are now trying to achieve it.

2. Explain two ways that companies have added value to their distribution channel through use of the Internet.

3. Explain the term 'aftermarket' as it is used in the Case Study.

SUMMARY OF KEY POINTS

In this Session, we have introduced the distribution element of the marketing mix, and covered the following key points:

- The distribution channel gets the product to the customer and adds quality and value in the process.

- The players of the 'place' mix include:

  - Wholesalers.

  - Agents.

  - Distributors.

  - Retailers.

  - E-commerce sites.

- Channel members play various roles in getting the product to the customer, and careful thought needs to be given before disintermediating.

- The criteria for selection of a channel to market include:

  - Organisational objectives.

  - Customer characteristics.

  - Competitor activity.

  - Nature of the product.

  - External environmental factors.

  - Relationships and conflicts.

Improving and developing own learning

The following projects are designed to help you develop your knowledge and skills further by carrying out some research yourself. Feedback is not provided for this type of learning because there are no 'answers' to be found, but you may wish to discuss your findings with colleagues and fellow students.

Project A

Talk to colleagues in your marketing department about different distribution channels that are used to reach target segments in your organisation.

Are all segments reached through one channel?

If not, how do they differ, and why?

Project B

Choose an organisation that only deals direct with its customers.

Use the Internet to establish how it deals with the aspect of physical distribution.

Project C

Talk to someone in your organisation who is responsible for buying equipment and consumables.

Find out about the channels that are used to get products to them.

Do the channels used to supply the company with stationery differ from those used to supply equipment?

Feedback to activities

Activity 8.1

Advantages of switching from a traditional distribution channel to a VMS.

1. Traditional distribution channels are often subject to conflict between members about the best way to get goods to the customer.

2. VMS (Vertical Marketing System) links the members of the channel together in one of three ways:

   - Corporate – where we would own the other members of the channel.

- Contract – where we have formal agreements with other channel members.

- Administered – where we are able to control the channel because of our size or power.

3. VMS offers efficiency and cost effectiveness.

4. There will be an initial cost involved, but in the long term we should be able to gain some competitive advantage through better service and improved customer satisfaction.

Activity 8.2

You will probably have found that the consumer site (Amazon) has a 'warmer' feel to it. It is friendlier, and is very easy to search for specific items; either the whole range or by product type. There are several ranges of products – books, music, videos and DVDs, and electronic goods, for example.

The PC World Business site has 150 product categories, in eight different groups – computers, peripherals, cables, etc. It can also be searched for specific items.

Both offer the opportunity to order online, and offer special deals on their Home Page. Both also carry information about their customer services policies.

Activity 8.3

To: N. Todd – Marketing Manager   Date: 22.9.02
From: A. Thornhill - Marketing Assistant

Subject: Moving to Internet only distribution

In response to your query about switching distribution to Internet only provision within three years, I would advise as follows:

- Our torches are currently sold through many different types of retailer, who are located all over the country.

- They are supplied by wholesalers, who stock mainly electrical goods.

- We are currently able to supply wholesalers in bulk, and they re-package for DIY, camping stores, garages, supermarkets, and many more.

- Although we currently have to keep our prices relatively low, to allow for the margin charged by the wholesaler and the retailer, supplying via the Internet will involve us in increased costs for both packaging and delivery.

- Retailers are able to advise customers about the best product for their need.

I recommend that further research into the costs involved in such a move before final decisions are made. Our distribution channel currently adds value to our product, which we would have to supply ourselves if we disintermediate.

Regards

Session 9

Managing marketing relationships

Introduction

This Session moves beyond the marketing mix, and looks at the many relationships involved in managing marketing effectively, and how each contributes to overall operations. It may be that certain elements of the marketing mix are managed by different individuals – for example, a Product Manager and a Communications Manager, and only good relationships between these individuals and others will ensure that all elements are integrated. The Session goes on to look at the role of relationship marketing and key account management in developing deeper relationships with customers. Internal marketing relationships, and the relationship between the organisation and society as a whole, are covered in Sessions 10 and 11.

LEARNING OUTCOMES

At the end of this Session you will be able to:

- Understand and appreciate the marketing operations process and how it can be delivered through multiple relationships.

- Explain the relationships with various members of the supply chain, and their role in meeting customer needs.

- Explain relationship marketing.

- Outline the key account management process.

Stakeholders

Traditionally, especially in the view of economists, only the owners were interested in the success of a company. More recently, it has been recognised that other 'stakeholders' need to be considered. These stakeholders, or 'multiple publics', can be defined as any group that has an actual or potential interest or impact on an organisation's ability to achieve its objectives.

There are a number of stakeholder groups that are important to an organisation and which need to be considered in the formulation and implementation of marketing plans:

Customers

As the decision makers, i.e. the people who actually buy the products, customers are considered by most marketing-oriented organisations as being the most important stakeholders. Truly marketing-led organisations will have a culture where all departments are committed to customer service. Improved understanding of customers is essential to building relationships, which means that market research is needed to uncover customer motivation and characteristics. Segmentation strategies are vital for identifying and then effectively targeting the key market segments. Personal selling is one of the key forms of promotion in business-to-business and service markets, which has led to the growing importance of relationship marketing and key account management in many industrial and some consumer markets.

Shareholders

This group includes the owners of the company, who have invested capital or who have bought shares. Their prime objectives are the long-term survival of the company and the dividends that can be acquired. Senior managers of an organisation may belong to this group, which means that they have a vested interest in balancing short-term objectives with the longer-term corporate goals.

Employees

Communication between the management, workers and staff within a company is known as internal marketing. This will be covered fully in Session 10. It normally relates to the effective collaboration between departmental functions and increased permeability of boundaries. Organisations encourage employees to treat other departments as internal customers. Internal marketing strategies include:

- Recruitment and retention of qualified, experienced employees.

- Formal and ad hoc training programmes.

- Open communication between employees and management.

- Human resources policies, such as continuous personal development.

- Shared corporate vision.

- A culture that encourages employee empowerment and involvement.

- Measurement systems for internal satisfaction.

Suppliers

This group includes all companies that supply raw materials, finished goods or services to the organisation. It is very important for organisations to build good working relationships with all members of the supply chain. Suppliers can be critical to the success of a company and can enhance the product offering to the end user.

General public

There are a number of subgroups under this heading, which include the government, regulatory bodies and financial institutions. There may also be pressure groups and other community based organisations or individuals that can influence the market.

Agents/distributors

Management and relationship building with members of the supply chain is crucial for business success. This group is particularly important for manufacturing organisations which sell their products through resellers, such as wholesalers.

Competitors

Other companies within the same industry can influence an organisation's ability to operate successfully. Many companies build strategic alliances or partnerships to grow or change the industry, or to introduce new standards. At the very least, companies should be aware of competitor activities which may affect their market position.

Activity 9.1

For your own organisation, or one that you know well, write notes identifying the key stakeholders, and how the relationship between the organisation and each group is managed.

Supply chain relationships

Business transactions take place over an extended period of time with varying degrees of interaction along the supply chain, but generally they rely on mutual interdependence. The focus within many industrial and consumer contexts has been towards partnerships with companies along the whole supply chain.

Channel co-operation is essential for all members in a supply chain. Policies must be designed to support all channel members, otherwise a weak link could destroy the chain. It is beneficial if all channels' members share common goals and agree to direct their efforts towards a common target market. It is also important for individual channel members to have precisely redefined roles and tasks that they are expected to perform.

Suppliers

Relationships with suppliers are being transformed from adversarial to co-operative. The aim is to produce a win-win situation where both parties benefit from improved relations. The drivers for these changes in attitude include: global competition, quality improvement programmes and a general effort to operate more efficiently. The ultimate goal of buyer-seller relationships is for both parties to share resources and outcomes. The need for a strong relationship with suppliers increases with the value and importance of the products being sourced, the type of product and the support services required. It is more likely that a company will seek to establish a long-term relationship with a supplier of a new order processing system than with a supplier of copier paper.

Agencies and consultancies

Some departments of an organisation may not be directly involved in sourcing products or components for manufacturing, but need to find external suppliers for other goods and services. The last decade has seen a marked trend towards out-sourcing as companies return to their core competences and become more specialised. This means that organisations are learning how to work with external agencies and consultants in many areas, from recruitment and training, to catering and cleaning. For example, marketers use outside agencies for market research, database marketing, telesales, advertising and promotion. It is important that strong relationships are built with this type of supplier, who can directly affect the company's marketing communication strategy.

Distribution channels

Most companies sell to the end consumer through a channel of distribution, which varies according to the type of product and the company's position in the supply chain. Choice of distribution channel will also depend on the cost of various channels, the amount of technical assistance needed to sell the product and the stock levels required.

In b2b markets, a producer may sell the product through several intermediaries, such as agents and distributors. By working closely with the distributors, the supplier can learn more about the target end market and develop more suitable products and services.

Other advantages of developing close relationships include achieving rapid geographical coverage without investment in a dedicated sales force. In the same way, a company can use franchises to expand the business, at a reduced cost and risk than direct investments. Once again, it will be in the franchiser's best interest to develop and manage a good relationship with the franchisee.

Salespeople

Personal selling is the main form of promotion in b2b marketing. It is also extremely important in service markets and in some consumer markets. In markets with relatively few customers, marketers can communicate directly with all existing and potential customers. Some companies may choose to visit important customers (key accounts) only. The purchase cycle of many large industrial items is lengthy and the decision making process is complex. This means that the salesperson may have to visit the buyer and other members of the DMU on several occasions to discuss product specifications and support services, thereby creating the opportunity to develop meaningful long-term relationships.

In b2b markets, products are frequently customised to buyer specifications and salespeople can provide an advisory role; for example, helping customers to design special components. Personal selling also allows follow-up visits after the sale, to ensure customer satisfaction and correct product usage. It is imperative that salespeople are sufficiently educated, trained and provided with information about their customers' markets and needs. More importantly however, it is crucial that salespeople learn how to develop partnerships with their customers, based on modern 'need satisfaction' selling techniques.

Activity 9.2

Through discussions with members of the marketing department, find out how your company handles agencies or other suppliers, and how they build long-term relationships.

Relationship marketing

In the last decade, there has been a marked shift in theory from transaction-based to relationship-based marketing. In transaction marketing, each sale is seen as carried out irrespective of any previous or potential future business. Relationship marketing takes into account the impact of each business encounter on the existing relationship, and the likely consequences for any future business.

Relationship marketing can be described as all of the activities that an organisation uses to build, maintain and enhance customer relations. Organisations are starting to use relationship marketing to attract and retain customers by providing an appropriate mix of marketing, customer service and quality. The relationship marketing concept is based on the theory that organisations can have similar relationships to those that exist between individuals.

It is now accepted that ongoing, long-lasting relationships are essential for a business market performance and survival. In many industries, the relationship between buyer and seller does not end once a single transaction has taken place. Marketing is seen as a relationship with the customer, based on a series of transactions, rather than a one-off sale. Traditional selling techniques aimed to get that first or single sale, neglecting any possibility of repeat business. Modern selling techniques are based on development of customer partnerships and relationships to ensure long-term business.

Growth in relationship marketing

Relationship marketing was originally used in b2b marketing and in services. It has now spread into consumer goods markets, especially as these have been enhanced with value added services. The growing interest in relationship marketing has emerged with the need for non-price based competition to differentiate products and services. Relationship marketing can be used to gain a sustainable competitive advantage in an increasingly complex marketplace. The following factors have contributed toward this trend:

- Deregulation.
- Globalisation.
- Maturity and sophistication of consumers.
- Lower market growth rates: important to retain existing customers.
- Explosive growth in technology.

Consumer markets

Technology such as the Internet, email and data mining software, has enabled the building of one-to-one relationships between companies and customers. There are several emerging variations on relationship marketing, such as loyalty marketing, e.g. cards or points systems. Database marketing and permission marketing are also attempts to personalise communication to customers and build relationships. For organisations with many customers, however, it is difficult to achieve personal relationships with even a small percentage of the customer base.

B2b markets

In industrial marketing, long-term relationships are very important. Buyers and sellers will often meet several times to share information and co-operate to find mutually beneficial solutions to problems. Development of specifications and price negotiations can be a lengthy process, requiring a number of encounters between the buying and selling companies. It is beneficial to both parties to develop long-term relationships in order to be aware of each other's needs and capabilities.

Service markets

Relationship marketing is critical in service marketing. Due to the inseparable and intangible nature of services, the customer's perception and satisfaction relies heavily on the attitude and appearance of the person providing the service. Frequently, the customer is purchasing the personal qualities and skills of the service provider, so the ability to develop close relationships and win customer confidence is crucial.

Cost and benefits

For the organisation initiating the relationship, there may be costs, such as those associated with the investment in technology, salespeople recruitment and training, internal marketing and new customer contact methods. In addition to the competitive advantage that the company hopes to achieve, there may be additional benefits from motivated employees and improved quality. In reward for loyalty, customers can reduce their perceived risk and increase confidence levels by using a known supplier and save time not searching for an alternative supplier.

Successful relationships

Several elements have been identified which are necessary for relationship marketing to be effective:

- Development of core service.

- Core products or services augmented with extra benefits.

- Relationship customised to individual's needs.

- Pricing that encourages loyalty.

- Marketing to employees.

- Use of two-way communication.

- Trust, warmth, commitment, intimacy, honesty and respect.

- Awareness of all stakeholders.

Key Account Management

Key Account Management (KAM) is most important for companies operating in business to business or service markets, where the customers are other organisations, or in exceptional circumstances, wealthy individuals.

Companies will identify that some of their customers may be more valuable than others and these are generally termed key customers. Other terms include: key accounts, major accounts and national accounts, and these accounts may be managed separately from the rest of the customer base. The process of managing these important customers is sometimes considered within channel management or distribution policies, especially where key accounts may be wholesalers or other distributors.

Key account management processes are the activities, mechanisms and procedures that enable effective management of a company's key customers. KAM is an evolutionary process that does not seem to be well documented in the majority of companies. It can be frustrating and complex, especially once the key accounts realise their status and potential power over the company.

Customers can be chosen as key accounts for a variety of reasons. The level of importance is often determined by their contribution to sales volume, revenue or profit. There may be some customers, such as opinion leaders or highly respected companies in the industry, who could offer valuable references. Other key accounts may be influential in other ways, for example providing access to a new network or industry sector. There may be unique technology or procedures used in a customer's operation that can be obtained through building a special relationship with the buyer.

In addition to current active customers, key accounts will usually include significant potential customers, lost or lapsed customers.

Segmentation and targeting

B2b customers will normally be segmented and targeted according to the demographic factors and by product type. Most companies understand the 80/20 rule, as it applies to their customer base, i.e. 20% of their customers contribute 80% of the revenue or profit. In general, therefore, it makes sense for companies to concentrate their attention on the top 20% of customers, without neglecting the other 80% or those customers who are not active, i.e. potential or lost customers. The 80/20 rule is also known as Pareto's rule.

In reality, of course, the 'top 20% of customers' is a moveable feast. As customers within the 80% stop buying, and others start to buy more, then the customers that get the 'Key Account' treatment need to be reviewed and adjusted.

Stages of Key Account Management

There are a number of key account development models, all of which describe the process for transforming relationships through various stages, from simple, transactional dealings into more complex, collaborative interactions.

- Pre- (or exploratory) stage: No interaction has yet taken place, but the potential key account has been identified by the seller.

- Early (or basic) stage: Several transactions may have taken place, but the supplier is still one of many used by the customer. There is limited contact between buyer and seller.

- Mid- (or co-operative) stage: There is now increasing commitment to the relationship on both sides. The seller may have achieved preferred supplier status. There are complex interactions between several people in both the buying and the selling organisation.

- Partnership (or interdependent) stage: The buyer and supplier may share sensitive information and will be working together to solve problems for mutual gain. There is likely to be collaboration at all levels of the organisation.

- Synergistic (or integrated) stage: At this stage in the relationship, borders between the companies have become blurred and the integration is evident. Many business functions are jointly managed and it would be difficult for either party to leave the relationship.

The relationship may have to be dismantled in the following circumstances:

- Change in personnel.

- Breach of trust.

- Cultural mismatch.

- Quality problems.

- Changing market position.

Successful KAM

Several factors have been identified that contribute towards effective key account management:

- Active participation and commitment of senior management.

- Focus on customer problem resolution.

- Strong product and process capabilities.

- Collaborative culture.

- Wide and deep networks of relationships with customers.

- Definition and selection of key accounts by aligning buyer needs and supplier capabilities.

- Generic and bespoke processes and strategies: limited resources mean that all customers cannot be treated individually, but customisation should be made available for key accounts.

- Interdependence in supply chains.

- Excellent information systems: key account managers should become experts in gathering, processing and distributing information through the organisation in their role as relationship facilitator.

Activity 9.3

Write a short report recommending a KAM process for your organisation, or one that you know well.

Case Study – Nothing ventured

When Cable & Wireless decided to enter the high-growth market for hosted business applications, top managers decided that even with the company's global reach, it needed partners to make the venture a success. A-Services, an application service provider, was launched last autumn with Microsoft adding software clout and Compaq computer hardware skills to C&W's own telecoms expertise.

It was a timely reminder that globalisation is making the world too big for even the mightiest corporations to conquer alone. Turn to almost any industry, and there is likely to be an unprecedented level of alliance building. "There's been an explosion of partnerships over the last five years," says Jon Van Duyne, director of the Routes to Market Association, a non-profit organisation part-owned by consultancy Via International.

Van Duyne points out that channels to market are becoming increasingly complex. "The ability to participate in rapidly segmenting markets is only possible through partnerships and alliances," he says. "You can't expand yourself everywhere. You can't buy everybody."

"If you haven't had experience with alliances, you will," predicts Professor Mitchell Koza, director of the acquisitions, merges and strategic alliances programme at Cranfield University School of Management. "We are managing in a period of disorder and that means the pace and direction of change are unpredictable. An alliance is a way of driving forward a company's strategy in a period of disorder."

Yet despite their potential for business benefit, it is certain that a high proportion of companies that enter alliances will end up disappointed with the results. The alliance upside offers benefits such as market penetration, critical mass, new skills, and broader product offerings. The downside threatens to derail business strategies, waste investment, disappoint customers and compromise brands. No partnership is risk free.

One of the greatest dangers is that many firms go into partnerships with too little thought about the strategic intent and what each can gain from the combination, argues Koza. That wasn't the case at Cable & Wireless, which did some deep strategic thinking before making its move into the competitive ASP marketplace.

"The first thing to define was the proposition," recalls Peter Fisk, a strategy specialist at PA Consulting Group, who worked on the A-Services project. "We had to work out what C&W wanted to offer and who it wanted to offer it to. Then we were able to define what extra we had to add to the existing C&W brand for potential customers to believe in the proposition."

C&W found it needed to add a mixture of competencies – key skills other firms could provide which it lacked – and to build a credible image to make its ASP product a market-killer. Partnering with Microsoft and Compaq added both expertise and market profile. And, importantly, it was also clear what each partner would gain from the alliance. C&W bought an entry ticket to a new market while Microsoft gained software licensing revenue and Compaq sold more hardware.

Prominent partners

C&W had the global profile to attract equally prominent partners. Others may find it more difficult. So how should you select an alliance partner? Van Duyne has a five-point checklist. "Firstly, there have to be complementary skill-sets and products. Secondly, it's highly desirable to have the capability of entering new markets. Thirdly, there must be a clear understanding of the commercial arrangements before the partnership is sealed. Fourthly, there should be good chemistry between the participants. And, finally, I think it is beneficial to have some shared intellectual capital – something that comes out of the partnership that neither could offer separately."

Koza believes that the ability to learn from your partner is one of the key reasons for entering an alliance. "You can learn about local geographic or product markets, about competencies and managerial skills as well as about brands and technologies," he says. "An alliance is a remarkable way of going to school on another company."

With markets fracturing under the force of new technologies, it's not difficult to see why established brands should want to use partnerships to learn how to operate in the new online world. Take established bricks and mortar names enviously eyeing the clicks and mortar world. One was Waitrose, the up-market supermarket chain owned by the John Lewis Partnership. It wanted its own slice of the burgeoning online grocery market, predicted to be worth as much as £25 billion in ten years' time.

But instead of building its own web-based grocery business, like rival Tesco, it has partnered with Ocado (formerly Last Mile Solutions), an ambitious dotcom start-up founded last year by three ex-Goldman Sachs bankers. Ocado has recruited an A-team of top management, including former food directors from Marks & Spencer, and provides the technology and fulfilment infrastructure of the new operation. Waitrose, which has so far invested £46 million for a 40% stake in Ocado, contributes its broad product portfolio and the strength of its trusted brand.

Ocado itself has partnered with BOC Distribution Services, which has skills in food distribution and logistics, to co-run its 300,000 square-foot distribution centre in Hatfield. Waitrose expects Ocado will help it penetrate markets outside its south-east heartland. And because it has taken a stake in the operation, it will also share in the capital value created as Ocado grows. This looks like a partnership destined to succeed because the interests of the parties are closely aligned and cemented through shared ownership.

But taking a stake in your partner is not essential for success. Further down the high street, Tesco has teamed up with iVillage.com, a Nasdaq-quoted company, to create a UK-based web site aimed at women. Again, the strength of the partnership is based on a clear understanding of what each company contributes and gains. Tesco is providing £12 million in cash and kind – mostly marketing promotion – as well as its expert knowledge on UK customer relationship management. iVillage provides its brand name, intellectual property, web site content and online community building expertise.

John Browett, chief executive of Tesco.com, expects the supermarket to win new business as the exclusive grocer on the iVillage.co.uk web site. It also gains placement opportunities for products on other parts of the iVillage network. "The partnership allows iVillage and Tesco to combine our respective strengths of retailing and community building," he says. Hilary Graves, co-managing director of iVillage.co.uk, believes the web site will benefit from Tesco's marketing support, including in-store promotions and mailings.

Both Waitrose and Tesco's joint ventures are in their early stages when optimism tends to be high. And it is a truth universally acknowledged that success smoothes the path of partnerships. "You tend to have fewer disagreements with your partner when the money is pouring in the window," notes Koza. But as inevitable problems arise, the strength of any partnership is tested by the way it is managed.

Van Duyne says, "open and honest communication is critical. For example, in one of our alliances, we're also dealing with our partner's competitor. But because we're very upfront about it, it's not threatening to our partner". Van Duyne recommends that venture parties have face to face communication.

Peter Gorle, managing director of international marketing consultancy Metra Martech, says it is important to "respond, not react" when a problem arises. That means listening to what your partner is telling you and understanding the subtext of any issues they may be raising. Many problems can be avoided by resolving the leadership question early in the alliance formation. "If there is a serious problem about who is going to be the leader, then the partnership usually won't work anyway," says Gorle.

Common point of view

How do you judge the success of a partnership? Much depends on its purpose in the first place. "The most important thing is to have a clear understanding of what the intent of the relationship is," says Koza. "That is obvious when you say it, but it's remarkable how often companies really don't have that internal understanding. Marketing takes one view, sales another and production something else – they haven't accumulated a common point of view. Once you understand the intent, you can design and manage the alliance process to raise the odds of success."

Just because a partnership lasts only a short time doesn't necessarily make it a failure. "The time horizon of the alliance must be understood in the context of what the intent of the relationship is," says Koza. "For example, if you partner with a company that's the best in the world at running focus groups, the fact the alliance runs a long time could be a sign of your firm's inability to internalise the learning from your partner. If it finishes quickly, it could simply be that the learning cycle is complete, you shake hands and part as friends."

PA Consulting Group's Peter Fisk sees partnerships becoming a critical component of business success in the future. "Customers want convenience and they don't want to go to many different sources for fragments of a solution. There is a wider recognition that you can do more by working together."

Partnership success at a glance

- Choose partners with complementary skills, products, markets.
- Understand the 'strategic intent' of the partnership.
- Adopt the most appropriate partnership structure.
- Resolve the leadership issue at the outset.
- Define the benefits expected from the partnership.
- Communicate the purpose and intent of the partnership internally.
- Keep communicating with your partner and anticipate problems.
- Define an exit strategy for failure at the outset.

- Monitor the benefits the partnership delivers.

- Recognise that a company may need multiple partnerships in a global business market.

Source: *Marketing Business*, September 2001.

Questions

1. What advantages are there in working in partnership to offer a customer solution?

2. What are the disadvantages of such relationships?

3. Explain relationship marketing, and how it applies to managing multiple relationships.

SUMMARY OF KEY POINTS

In this Session, we have introduced the need to manage multiple relationships in order to achieve successful marketing operations, and covered the following key points:

- The marketing manager's role involves relationships with many stakeholders of the organisation, all requiring slightly different attention.

- Developing relationships with suppliers as well as the onward supply chain helps achieve improved customer satisfaction.

- Relationship marketing recognises that retaining customers and building relationships with them is more profitable than constantly having to attract new ones.

- Key Account Management involves developing relationships with the 20% of customers who produce 80% of your profits (Pareto's rule).

Improving and developing own learning

The following projects are designed to help you develop your knowledge and skills further by carrying out some research yourself. Feedback is not provided for this type of learning because there are no 'answers' to be found, but you may wish to discuss your findings with colleagues and fellow students.

Project A

Draw a stakeholder map for your organisation, making brief notes against each group identified, about what their specific needs are.

Project B

Talk to colleagues in your marketing department about your supply chain – both suppliers and intermediaries.

How reliant is your organisation on one supplier?

What changes have been made in the past two years?

Project C

Through discussion with colleagues in several departments, explore the existing relationships for your organisation. How many of these meet the criteria for successful relationships, mentioned in the last section?

Feedback to activities

Activity 9.1

Whatever type of organisation you chose, it is likely that they have several stakeholders. There will always be customers for the products or services, who may be the buyers or the end users. Your organisation will also have a number of suppliers. Unless you are a sole trader or partnership, the company will have employees and be subject to external pressures from competitors and other influential organisations.

Activity 9.2

You may find some established relationships with agencies or other suppliers which are based on mutual trust and understanding.

Activity 9.3

The process should have included the identification of key accounts using the methods outlined above and a recommended approach to handling these customers.

Session 10

Marketing operations in an internal context

Introduction

Increasingly, organisations are realising that the behaviour of their staff towards customers reflects in their overall 'brand'. In an environment where change is constant, and much is demanded of all staff members, internal marketing plays a role in building relationships with employees, and keeping them informed of the need for change. This Session explains the role and importance of internal marketing, and techniques used in its implementation.

LEARNING OUTCOMES

At the end of this Session you will be able to:

- Demonstrate the adaptation of marketing operations principles in an internal context.

- Explain the importance of internal marketing.

- Identify internal customers.

- Explain techniques for internal marketing.

Adapting marketing operations to internal audiences

Implementing marketing activities challenges the manager to adopt an approach that draws on the knowledge and skills of the team, whilst working in co-operation and in an inclusive way. The individuals in the team may possess very different disciplinary skills or they may complement one another in their organisational skills. Whatever their make-up they need to work together to effectively implement marketing activities.

Job roles need to be designed so that each employee complements another. For example there may be one individual who is excellent at negotiating with suppliers and external agencies whereas another may be shy and prefer to organise paper-based activities. Both these roles are valid and need to be seen as part of a whole team approach to work organisation.

The main goal of the marketing department is to keep the customer satisfied and brand loyal. Customer service is paramount and the internal organisation needs to be designed to be customer facing. In the marketing department there will be two groups of customers – internal and external. Internal customers may be the sales departments and members of sales teams who act on the sales leads generated by marketing efforts. Senior management and shareholders are also internal customers; beneficiaries of profits that are generated through business growth. Marketing departments may also co-ordinate the actions of external agencies such as advertising, PR, research and sales promotion.

The marketing mix can be defined in a similar way to the external marketing mix. Promotions can be targeted at different internal groups to raise awareness of marketing activities and to motivate employees. Events such as social and sports days, Christmas dinners, quiz nights etc. can all help to generate enthusiasm. Briefings about marketing strategy and feedback from customer research can help to ensure that everyone is working to achieve the same goals. Circulating press clippings and exhibiting marketing activities can raise awareness of what's being achieved whilst newsletters can celebrate internal as well as external successes.

Training and motivation of employees is critical to achieving the marketing objectives. Keeping up to date with technology through visiting exhibitions and attending CIM local branch events to hear case histories of good marketing practice, will keep ideas fresh.

Organisations that follow the culture of continuous improvement and TQM (Total Quality Management) are creating a focus on improvement. Poorly performing products will be withdrawn from sale for redesign. Marketing provides a feedback loop from the customer to the production department that can enhance product performance. This approach to business can save money and time and improve return on investment.

Good communication is essential to motivating marketing personnel and co-ordinates their efforts. Marketing managers need to communicate at all levels of the organisation, negotiating budgets and influencing strategy at senior level and encouraging marketing employees to keep open dialogues with other departments. Information systems can support activities such as budgeting, sales analysis, performance evaluations and preparing reports.

The role of internal marketing

Internal marketing is aimed at employees to encourage commitment and motivate enthusiasm to improve performance to satisfy customer needs.

Organisations such as the Body Shop organise sports fun days so that all the employees get together and feel a camaraderie, building common ground and shared values. Anita Roddick used to invite employees to her home on a regular basis, making people feel like part of a big family. This approach demonstrated her commitment to both the company and the people, without whom her vision would have been impossible.

Virgin Airlines and the founder Sir Richard Branson had a similar philosophy, inviting employees to his home and to his holiday villa. The reservations staff organised 'events' every month to motivate the call centre staff – dressing up, giving away prizes and generally making work fun.

Organisations that wish to achieve true marketing orientation have to adopt the same values and working practices both internally and externally. Although motivating staff to treat the customer with respect may be considered a human resources function, motivation is of vital importance to marketing implementation. When the customers communicate with an organisation they expect to be treated with the same attention and warmth throughout the company, whether it's sales, production, finance or despatch personnel. That means that everyone has to adopt similar attitudes and courtesies.

The marketing mix can be used as a framework to guide internal marketing in a similar way by segmenting employees into groups with similar characteristics and using methods of communication appropriate to each type of group – e.g. senior managers, sales teams, administration etc.

The main objective of internal marketing is to improve the relationship between the organisation and its employees. When people are happy, secure, motivated and kept interested in their work through new projects and initiatives their commitment remains stable. Part of this process is effective communication, so marketing activities like new product launches should be an internal and external event. Staff can also be ambassadors in the marketplace for products and services.

Internal communication is the key aspect of internal marketing and many of the external promotional ideas can be used internally to transmit messages. Employees need to understand the importance of the brand and how to generate customer loyalty. Scotts Tissues embraced green environmental policies because of the implications of paper waste. Their internal marketing activities focused on community activities and organising local events. This achieved the objective of creating environmental awareness and promoted the company brand as caring for its local community.

The importance of internal marketing is paramount to a cohesive interdependent culture. To achieve corporate and marketing objectives employees and senior management need to communicate effectively and share similar values. The marketing philosophy in a company has to focus on the customers' needs, both internal and external.

Activity 10.1

Segment your internal employees into groups with similar characteristics so that you can decide which types of marketing activities would be appropriate for launching a new product.

Identifying internal customers

Internal customers fall into two main categories – either they **directly** request products and services from the marketing department or they are **indirectly** influenced by the results of the marketing activities.

In many 'business-to-business' organisations, sales and marketing teams work in partnership to achieve joint goals. The sales team may be targeted to achieve revenue and profits and the marketing team to produce materials and support the sales effort by organising events and presentations to customers. In organisations producing FMCG (Fast Moving Consumer Goods) marketing may be working more remotely from the sales team because their role is to sell to distributors with supporting marketing activities. Either way the sales team are direct customers of the marketing department.

The sales team need to be kept informed about marketing activities. It can be very embarrassing to visit a client who has been targeted with a mail shot or seen a special offer advert that the salesperson is not aware of. Promotions and marketing efforts need to be planned jointly to support sales. The departments need to be interdependent – not trying to control each other's efforts.

For production departments, marketing activities may not appear to make a direct impact on their work, however customer feedback about product improvements has an indirect influence on what they are producing and the quality of the products and services they provide.

In some companies the technical function or R&D is separate. Millions of pounds are wasted each year with technical innovations that are never produced because there is no market demand. Customer research is an essential role of marketing and the outcomes should inform and influence decisions made to produce and modify new products.

Finance is not just the role of the accounts department. Budgets are allocated to each department and whether those budgets are achieved directly influences the cash flow and profit of the company. Marketing budgets need to be managed so that any deviations from the budget and cash flow are communicated immediately. Major expenditure, for example on an exhibition stand or large print runs, could upset the company cash flow and cause stress and financial problems if working capital is not sufficient to cover large invoice values.

Human resources and personnel functions are a supplier to marketing, recruiting new staff, training, and contracts of employment. Both recruitment and training are key functions to the development of the marketing team and an ongoing relationship can enhance the type of training provided. It may be that there is an internal marketing budget for training that is negotiated between HR (Human Resources) and the marketing manger, or it may be up to the individual to obtain funds for marketing training. Some larger companies run in-house training using external providers and marketing needs to update HR with current and future requirements based on objectives and challenges in new skills.

Within the marketing department itself there are customers and suppliers of information and skill. For example the manager requires the staff to accomplish various projects that combine to achieve overall objectives. Equally staff need information and shared knowledge about marketing plans so that they can provide the marketing activities appropriately. Customer and supplier relationships are characterised by mutual exchange and relationship management, in a similar way to external customer relations.

Activity 10.2

Identify a range of internal customers.

Compile a table that highlights the needs of each sub-group.

Evaluate how effective you are at meeting those needs.

A second table can be developed for internal suppliers so that you can assess how effective your department is at meeting their expectations.

Internal marketing techniques

Internal marketing is approached in the same way as planning to communicate with external customers and suppliers. A plan with a budget needs to be developed with specific, measurable objectives and a budget. The following framework may assist the planning approach:

Internal environment

Assessing the current situation is important to establish the scope of communications that need to be planned. What perception does the organisation have of the marketing department at the moment? Do you need to change the image of how you work and what is being achieved? What awareness exists about the products and services being offered? Maybe an internal survey would help establish the current position.

Positioning

Depending on the results of your internal customer survey, deciding on your positioning is important before embarking on an internal marketing programme. What messages need to be transmitted? What relationships do you have with other departments and do you need to involve them in your activities? Are you taking the role of 'informer' or are you trying to influence a changed attitude to marketing?

Objectives

What do you want to achieve? Are you creating awareness or do you need to provide more in-depth knowledge so that employees take on the role of product ambassadors? The quantifiable objectives can be related to a further survey checking on people's changed attitudes to marketing as result of the internal campaign.

Segmentation

The process of dividing staff into sub-groups such as departments or by lifestyle characteristics. For example, the administrative staff may be more motivated by a social activity rather than a more formal activity for senior managers.

Product

Which products and services will be promoted internally and how? Will you need to demonstrate something highly technical or can you get staff to experience the product? For example in the travel business, staff are sent on exploratory trips so that they can more effectively sell the country and hotels. It's also possible to use customers to explain to the staff the quality and performance of products – factory visits could be made if complex machinery is installed at customer sites. The 'product' in this sense may also be the change that is being communicated, or the new corporate plan.

Place

How will you organise the marketing activities – will they happen in-house or will you have to pay to hire external facilities? What kind of venues will be suitable and in keeping with the image you are trying to transmit?

Promotion

The promotion of your events and activities are important. Creating hype and desire are just as important internally and a range of media can be used, such as:

- Notice boards.
- Exhibition panels.
- Promotional materials.
- Intranet.
- Email.
- Presentations.

Price

What are the 'costs' of internal marketing activities – the time and other resources used to communicate with your internal target audience.

Action plan

The timeframed action plan with key milestones and responsibilities is important for implementation and adds the practical dimension to the internal marketing plan.

The marketing plan itself can be a valuable document for sharing with certain departments and individuals the necessity for the marketing activities and the objectives you are trying to achieve.

Case Study – A winning strategy

Clients and sales prospects are not the only targets for some companies' marketing effort. Growing numbers invest in marketing to their own staff too, as David Sumner Smith explains.

Profit sharing, bonuses, home working, flexitime and paternity leave are all becoming commonplace in the work environment. With unemployment at its lowest level since 1975 and skills shortages now widespread, it is essential that businesses make themselves perceived as good places to work. As well as helping to attract and keep good staff, it also brings benefits to the company brand.

According to the Chartered Institute of Personnel and Development (CIPD), flexible working arrangements and other 'family-friendly' policies are particularly good tools for retaining skilled staff. Businesses also benefit from operational flexibility through increased cover in the case of job sharing or staff being allowed to work from home. Absenteeism is lower and staff are more productive and highly motivated. "People's employment decisions are influenced by a number of factors," says Maureen O'Donnell, Human Resources Manager of business Internet provider UUNet. "The opportunity to work in an interesting environment, pay, culture and – increasingly – quality of life."

According to Andrew Oswald, Professor of Economics at the University of Warwick, for many people this 'package' of factors does not add up, and only 36% of British workers are happy in their jobs. This dissatisfaction is costing money, with staff turnover being a growing problem. The CIPD calculates the average cost of labour turnover per employee to be £3,546. This cost – which includes the replacement and indirect costs such as loss in customer satisfaction – is highest for professional employees at £5,206, but still a substantial £1,127 for unskilled manual workers

Marketing to the job market

In order to minimise these costs by attracting and retaining good staff, businesses need to market themselves to the market. Effective marketing of this not only strengthens the company brand on the jobs market: it also adds valuable, positive qualities to the company brand in personal communications between staff and customers. "When people enjoy their work, it is clear from their body language and the tone of their voice," Ross Urquhart, managing director of brand experience consultancy RPM. "They give off positive messages about their employer and will go the extra mile for clients too. The company brand enjoys a very boost as a result."

The tactics adopted by leading firms achieving this goal range from practicality to panache. Many focus on parenthood issues. American Express, for example, offers an on-site nursery, while drug manufacturer Pfizer has playcare facilities for 70 children and two full-time childcare co-ordinators to help staff find carers for their offspring.

Other companies focus on different aspects of family life. Intel provides staff with free home computers, while holiday cottages are provided to staff by Agilent Technologies and Maersk shipping at subsidised rates or entirely free of charge. Asda even offers unpaid leave to staff needing to look after grandchildren.

Concierge services

For most businesses, the marketing effort is focused on the workplace. Growing numbers of companies offer staff facilities such as workplace gyms and health-centres, free food and drink, hairdressers and dry cleaning. Amongst the most comprehensive packages is the concierge service provided by consultants Accenture. It employs five full-time staff to handle personal tasks such as collecting cars from garages, shopping for gifts and waiting at home for workmen or deliveries.

In some eyes such facilities are wasteful, irrelevant or simply frivolous. But growing numbers of firms are investing resources in marketing themselves to their staff. The concept is easy to understand. By making the company more unusual, exciting and a better place to work, a company improves staff morale, increases the commitment of its personnel and attracts a higher calibre of human resources.

While it is difficult to quantify, attracting and keeping high quality staff with a positive attitude to their employer also brings a 'halo effect'. Communications with clients and prospects are likely to be more enthusiastic and committed, with staff imparting subtle, positive messages that enhance the brand value of their employer.

'Duvet days'

Amongst the most eager practitioners are a number of companies in the marketing industry. Within the PR world, for example, August.One Communications has received favourable reactions from staff and media alike to its 'duvet days'. The concept permits staff to treat themselves to a day in bed, twice a year, without the need to take sick leave. Managing director Tariq Khwaja says, "This is an important recognition on our part that people are human beings and not machines. We work in a high pressure industry and to get the best from staff, we need to make sure that working conditions are at their most conducive."

August.One uses other innovative measures such as a massage day every month, where a visiting masseur goes round the consultancy. The company also pays for a day of pampering London's fashionable Sanctuary health and beauty club for staff who have performed beyond the call of duty and there is a 'morale budget' that staff can use for lunches or to relax in an off-site environment.

"People spend most of their time at work, so it has got to be fun and fulfilling – even if it is hard work," says Ross Urquhart. "A number of clients have remarked how positive our staff are about their work despite the extreme effort they sometimes need to put in. By making our personnel demonstrate positive sentiments about our company, we are adding valuable qualities to the RPM brand. I have no doubt the investment would be worthwhile on that count alone."

Career breaks

RPM has recently introduced a monthly 'experience fund' which allows staff the chance to win funding for their personal dream experience, whatever and wherever that might be. First experiences include trips to Lapland's Ice Hotel, a Tokyo fish market and a company-wide flotation tank experience. RPM also provides paid career breaks for longer-serving staff.

Somewhat smaller, but equally innovative, is the London-based PR agency Eulogy. With 15 people, it has nevertheless managed to achieve the title of the fastest-growing PR agency in the UK over the last 5 years. Working as it does in consumer, dotcom and professional services, PR means any attempt to make the workplace a different, more enjoyable environment must appeal to the various styles of account handler within the agency, according to joint managing director of Eulogy, Adrian Brady.

"The key thing about the work environment is marrying flexibility with pragmatism. Some time ago we carried out an anonymous survey with the team at Eulogy to identify what would best motivate them. We had our own ideas, but felt it was critical that those enjoying the benefits should play a key part in their establishment."

Fun, fulfilling and fair

Amongst the programmes that Eulogy now runs is First Friday. On the first Friday of every month the agency closes early to encourage people to get away for the weekend. All the staff go for a regular night out, and at Christmas the entire staff had a two-day trip to New York City.

As well as an extra day of holiday for each year of service there is also the 'Day on Eulogy' where anyone can nominate a member of the team for an extra day off as reward for a particular achievement or positive contribution. Brady concludes, "We have a policy of not working late and never working at weekends. Hopefully our additional perks ensure that this culture of enjoying work within the working week is genuinely reflected, in our actions."

"If we can create an atmosphere of genuine enjoyment at the office, there is no doubt that this translates to happy clients and excellent journalist relations," says Brady. It has also been effective in selling the agency to high-calibre PR professionals, he believes. "In a people business such as this, our staff are our ambassadors. By ensuring they are giving off positive messages about the company, they are helping us to build the Eulogy brand in the PR marketplace."

St Lukes Communications has gone one step further. It is an employee-owned company describing itself as the world's first ethical, stake holding advertising agency. It defines itself as a stakeholder organisation and was founded on the belief that work should be fun, fulfilling and fair.

New employees are entitled to become shareholders after a probationary period and the number of shares held by an employee is related to their length of service, with shares re-allocated at the end of every year. There are no job descriptions within St Lukes, and everyone is encouraged to work outside their remit. Starting and finishing times are left up to the individual employee. Employees work in project teams that are very much self-managed.

St Lukes also runs a 'make yourself more interesting' campaign which helps finance employees to take courses that are unrelated to work. Every five years, employees are entitled to a four-week sabbatical that they can take for whatever purpose they wish.

Dignity and respect

Young marketing and PR agencies are not the only businesses to embrace the principle of marketing themselves to staff by making work more fun. Bacardi-Martini UK Limited, for example, is a large, well-known company and 139 years old. Thanks to leadership from 38-year-old managing director Stella David, the company has developed a wide range of employee-friendly benefits and practices, including generous family-friendly policies, dry cleaning, a gym, an Internet cafe and special birthday gift – with a card from the managing director. All employees are encouraged to take part in management forums, nearly one in five are regularly allowed to work from home, and last year all its staff were given a 33% company performance-related bonus on top of their personal bonuses and their annual salaries.

Jonathan Austin, managing director of Great Place to Work UK, agrees that the best employers boost their brand in both the employment and commercial markets. "The organisations we have identified in the Sunday Times 'Best 50 Companies to Work For' have unearthed a simple, yet valuable secret and they are flourishing as a result," he says. "It is not just about posh perks, it is about something more fundamental: treating others' dignity and respect, and putting people first."

At a glance

- Only 36% of British workers are happy in their jobs.

- The best employers boost their brands in both the commercial and employment markets.

- 'Duvet days' mean that staff can treat themselves to a day in bed without having to take sick leave.

- Many companies focus on improving family life as a way of attracting and retaining quality staff.

- Other perks provided include concierge services, 'pampering days', birthday gifts and morale boosting days out.

Source: *Marketing Business*, May 2001.

Questions

1. List three reasons why internal marketing is important, highlighted by the article.

2. Identify 10 examples of actions companies take to 'market themselves to their staff'.

3. Outline the stages of the marketing plan as it applies to an internal market.

SUMMARY OF KEY POINTS

In this Session, we have introduced the role that internal marketing plays in managing change in organisations and improving customer satisfaction, and covered the following key points:

- Organisations have recognised the need to have good relationships with employees in order to provide excellent customer service.

- Internal marketing plays an important role in maintaining open communication between management and staff.

- It can also help inform and reassure during periods of change.

- Internal customers can be segmented in a similar way to external customers, to aid effective communication.

- Marketing planning techniques can be adapted to the internal market.

Improving and developing own learning

The following projects are designed to help you develop your knowledge and skills further by carrying out some research yourself. Feedback is not provided for this type of learning because there are no 'answers' to be found, but you may wish to discuss your findings with colleagues and fellow students.

Project A

Talk to colleagues in your marketing department about any pro-active internal marketing planning that is undertaken. Find out if a formal internal marketing plan exists.

Project B

List all the methods used by management in your organisation to communicate with internal staff. How effective is each in achieving its purpose?

Project C

How are your organisation's corporate plan and objectives communicated to staff? How often does this take place?

Feedback to activities

Activity 10.1

Segmenting is the process of dividing groups into sub-groups with similar characteristics. For example, senior managers may prefer to mix within their own group, concentrating on business needs so they may want to have a more formal meeting where new products are presented with supporting research and a complete marketing plan giving samples of packaging and associated proposed advertising.

Sales teams usually respond well to lots of hype, so they may be invited to a major product launch with their customers that is high profile, such as a day at the races or a motor sports event.

The administrative staff may like to have a social event; perhaps a briefing then a meal out with dancing.

Segmenting the internal staff into sub-groups means that you can appeal to them at the level of their wants and needs, the same way you would approach buying behaviour for the external customer groups.

Activity 10.2

Customer	Needs and Expectations	Effectiveness
Marketing Manager.	Marketing activities completed on time. Budget variances kept within agreed variables.	The advertising campaign was a month late for the spring issue of Vogue but we kept to budget.

Supplier	Needs and Expectations	Effectiveness
Human Resources.	A programme of training courses that meet the long-term needs of the marketing department such as: ■ Working with innovation. ■ Financial cash flows and budgets. ■ Negotiations skills.	This year's programme included topics such as time management which were not helpful for our particular needs.

Activity 10.3

The presentation needs to follow a logical sequence, each section linking thoughts towards a coherent, cohesive approach to internal marketing.

Slide 1

Introduction –	Internal marketing is used to help communicate change, or new objectives and plans within the organisation.
Internal Environment –	Internal survey may reveal staff opinion and level of morale.
Positioning –	Consider message, and purpose – to inform or influence?

Slide 2

Objectives –	Set clear and measurable objectives. Consider what you want people to do, feel, perceive at the end of the campaign.
Segmentation –	Divide staff into groups to help shape the message and media used – this may reveal supporters, opposers and neutrals.

Slide 3

Product –	This may be the new corporate plan, or the reason for changes that are taking place.
Price –	This may be the 'opportunity cost' of holding a Conference, as well as the physical cost of the event. If the Conference is held in working hours, what sales may be lost?
Place –	How and where will the message be 'distributed'?
Promotion –	What promotional tools and techniques will be used? What is the message to be communicated?

Slide 4

Action Plan –	Who is to be involved? Will the CEO deliver the key message to give it credibility? When must each step of the campaign be complete? Are there information packs to be prepared for example?
Control Measures –	Refer back to the objectives set. How will you know you have succeeded?

Session 11

Marketing operations and ethics and social responsibility

Introduction

This Session looks at the fact that marketing has recently had to respond to a move towards satisfying the needs of society as a whole. It looks at social responsibility and ethics in marketing, and the way in which an organisation's image can be enhanced when it adopts an ethical stance. It also looks at the background to consumerism and environmentalism, and their role in driving social responsibility.

LEARNING OUTCOMES

At the end of this Session you will be able to:

- Demonstrate the adaptation of marketing operations principles in the context of relationships with the wider public and society.

- Explain the importance of marketing ethics.

- Explain the impact of social responsibility.

- Outline the background to consumerism and environmentalism.

- Identify strategies for fulfilling a firm's social responsibilities.

Societal and cause-related marketing

In Session 9, we introduced the many stakeholder groups with which organisations need to develop relationships. These include customers, suppliers, employees and competitors, who may directly shape the business environment. There are other groups of stakeholders who may indirectly affect the industry, such as the governmental bodies that regulate the business and legal environment, financial institutions, consumer and community groups. There are highly influential groups, such as lobbyists or pressure groups who can fundamentally change the business horizon. Special interest groups, such as industry associations, can be massively powerful in changing business practices and regulations. Advanced technology and increasing globalisation have contributed to the creation of specialist communities, such as web-based Internet communities, that can communicate and share information easily.

In recent years there has been a growth of interest in societal marketing, which is focused on satisfying the needs of society as a whole. Other issues related to societal marketing are cause-related marketing, marketing ethics and social responsibility.

Cause related marketing

This type of marketing can be defined as the linking of a company, or brand, to a relevant social issue or cause, to the mutual benefit of both parties. It is important that the company and the cause share a similar territory, so that the customer can identify why the particular cause is applicable to the brand. A company may develop a strategic alliance with a charity or voluntary organisation committed to the specific issue concerned. This partnership approach offers advantages to both parties. The charity itself will have specialist expertise in the topical issues related to their particular cause and to what motivates people to respond to their appeals. Teams of volunteers may already be established, and they can help to disseminate the campaign. Charities are often powerful brands in their own right and the company can benefit from this 'halo effect'. For the charity, there is the expectation of increased funds, raised profile and the possibility of attracting other supporting companies or benefactors. An example of a successful partnership is Ambre Solaire skin products and cancer charity Marie Curie.

A company may design a campaign to directly address the cause itself, with no involvement from another organisation or institution. This may offer the benefit of ownership and control of the campaign, but the company will not have the support of the charity's human resources and knowledge of the target market.

Tesco, one of the largest food retailers in the UK, has relaunched its 'Computers for schools' campaign, and is an excellent example of a successful direct approach.

Many companies have philanthropic departments who look for worthwhile causes to support. For example, hundreds of companies donated funds to the charities that were established after the September 11th terrorist attack in the US.

Other companies prefer to support educational programmes, for example some of the medical device companies in the Johnson & Johnson group either own, or fund, training institutes for surgeons, doctors and nurses.

Affinity cards have become increasingly popular as a way for charities and non-profit organisations to increase their incomes. This type of cause related marketing appeals to individuals who find it a more convenient way to make smaller regular donations to a favourite cause.

Organisations must carefully monitor changes in market forces and stakeholder attitudes, in order to prepare clear and effective responses. Marketers have to provide members of society with products, services and activities that they want and to eliminate the activities that are not acceptable.

Stakeholders have the ability to influence markets either directly or indirectly and can be regarded as threats or useful to an organisation. Therefore, stakeholders are extremely important and relationships need to be actively managed and considered throughout the whole organisation.

Activity 11.1

Using the Internet and search engines, look for examples of cause related marketing, other than the ones mentioned above.

Marketing ethics

Marketing ethics are moral principles that define right and wrong behaviour in marketing. The most fundamental ethical matters have been formalised through the legal and regulatory system to meet the standards of society. Most organisations will operate within these laws and regulations, but marketing ethics are more complex.

Ethical decision making

There are a number of factors that influence an individual's ethical decision making process:

- Individual factors: individuals use their own judgement of what is right and wrong to make decisions in their personal and professional life. Individuals may use different moral philosophies according to the circumstances.

- Organisational relationships: individuals will also make ethical decisions based on their environment. An organisation's culture may offer guidelines for behaviours and how to resolve problems. Friends, family and colleagues may also influence an individual's decision making process.

- Opportunity: if an individual acts unethically and it goes unnoticed or even rewarded, then that individual is likely to behave in the same way in the future. It is important that organisations have professional codes of conduct and policies on ethics that encourage acceptable behaviour.

Codes of ethics

These ethical guidelines describe what type of behaviour the organisation expects of its members or employees. Formalised rules and standards such as these minimise the opportunities for unethical behaviour, by prescribing or limiting certain activities. Top management should provide leadership in implementation of the guidelines.

Look at http://www.connectedinmarketing.com/cim/abo/html/memCod.cfm and read the Chartered Institute of Marketing's Code of Professional Standards, Ethics and Disciplinary Procedures.

Ethical issues related to the marketing mix

Product

Marketers occasionally neglect to inform the public about risks or other essential information related to a product, e.g. changes to a product's ingredients. With pressure from regulatory bodies and consumer groups, most organisations have improved packaging and labelling to offer more detailed product information, often emphasising product safety. Examples of this can be seen in the food industry, especially in relation to GM foods and nutritional analysis, e.g. fat content. Certain products may be regarded as unethical, e.g. tobacco, pornography, high interest rate loans. Targeting certain vulnerable markets may be regarded as unethical, e.g. children, elderly or underprivileged sectors.

Pricing

Ethical issues in pricing include predatory prices, price fixing and failure to disclose the full price of a product purchase, i.e. hidden costs. Legislation is in place to deal with some of these issues – look at http://www.oft.gov.uk/Business/Legal+Powers/Competition+Act+1998.htm for information on this UK legislation.

Distribution

There may be unethical relationships or conflict between producers and other members of the supply chain, such as suppliers and intermediaries. Producers may use unethical methods to persuade distributors to handle certain products or agree to unreasonable terms.

Promotion

There are many examples of unethical behaviour in marketing communication, which may destroy the trust that consumers have in an organisation, including:

- False and misleading advertising.

- Manipulative or deceptive sales promotion or publicity efforts.

Advertising abuse includes:

- Exaggerated claims, which cannot be substantiated, e.g. a herbal remedy claming to cure cancer.

- Concealed facts, such as a fruit flavoured product that contains no real fruit.

- Being unfair to a competitor, such as publishing comparisons based on limited information or testing.

- Breach in acceptable levels of decency: use of children or sex in advertising.

In personal selling, ethical issues may cause problems for organisations if sales methods used are perceived to be unacceptable. In most industries, sales personnel are well educated, well trained and professional. They use modern selling techniques to uncover and then satisfy customer needs with appropriate solutions. However, there are sales organisations, for example, double-glazing, which sometimes use questionable practices, such as aggression, manipulation and pressure selling.

Market research

Marketing research to gather and analyse customer information is essential to effective marketing planning and implementation of strategies. It is essential that ethical guidelines be established for marketing research and that these are followed by all members of an organisation or agency. Areas of concern have traditionally been:

- Researcher's honesty and competency.

- Manipulation of research techniques or of respondents, e.g. leading questions.

- Data manipulation: the clients or the public may not be informed about flaws or biases in data.

- Invasion of privacy: door-to-door surveys or unsolicited mail.

- Failure to disclose the purpose or sponsorship of a study, e.g. pretending it is on behalf of an industry rather than a single company.

One of the main problems that has affected the image of marketing research is the practice known as 'sugging', which is selling under the guise of research.

Activity 11.2

Write notes about your organisation's Code of Ethics, if one exists. If not, recommend a basic Code, based on the above information.

Social responsibility

Social responsibility in marketing relates to an organisation's obligation to maximise its positive impact and minimise its negative impact on society. Where ethics relates to individual decisions, social responsibility concerns the impact of an organisation's decisions on society.

The four dimensions of social responsibility are:

- Economic: be profitable, i.e. make money.

- Legal: obey the law and play by the rules.

- Ethical: i.e. avoid harm and do what is right, just and fair.

- Philanthropic: be a good corporate citizen, i.e. contribute resources to the community and improve the quality of life.

Most organisations have been concerned with the first two dimensions, in order to survive. Many are now actively seeking to take action on the other two factors.

Society becomes concerned about marketing activities when the actions produce negative or questionable results. There are many recent examples of companies behaving unethically, where consumers have reacted with concern or even anger. Society expects marketers to enhance the standard of living and protect the general quality of life. Society's concerns provide threats and opportunities for marketers.

The marketer must determine what relationships, obligations and duties exist between the organisation and society. Successful marketers monitor social trends and changes, in order to develop and enforce suitable policies. The challenge for organisations is to discover what society as a whole wants. This is difficult as society is made up of diverse groups, often with conflicting goals. There are costs associated with social responsibility and marketers need to assess how much the members of society are willing to pay for what they want. For example, consumers may demand cheaper fuel, but still want a reduction in car emissions.

Growth of corporate social responsibility

The increased visibility of corporate social responsibility has encouraged companies to account for their actions in a wide range of areas, including employee relations, environmental policies and practices, and community involvement. Increasingly, a broad range of stakeholder groups is seeking specific information from companies on their social and environmental performance. Government regulators, financial analysts, employees, non-profit organisations, trade unions, community organisations, and the news media are among the groups pressing companies to divulge greater amounts of information on decision making, performance and targets. In addition, many customers – both consumers and business-to-business customers – are factoring social and environmental performance into purchase decisions. One result is that many companies now conduct regular assessments or audits of their social performance and report their findings to stakeholders and the public at large.

Government regulators at all levels are calling on companies to increase the quantity and quality of information they disclose to the public about their practices and performance. Particularly in the area of the environment, companies are facing new and growing amounts of regulation and legislation aimed at increasing their accountability to society.

The Internet has provided companies and those seeking greater corporate accountability an unprecedented ability to share and exchange information – both accurate and inaccurate – on a large scale. A number of companies now use the Internet to report proactively on their social and environmental activities. At the same time, a variety of organisations have established Internet sites that provide detailed information about companies' environmental performance, philanthropy, and other social impacts.

> **Activity 11.3**
>
> Search the Internet for examples of companies that have made public statements about their social responsibility programmes.

Consumerism and environmentalism

Social responsibility issues include: community relations, diversity, green marketing and the responses to the consumer movement.

Community relations

Marketers are becoming aware of their role in helping to overcome social problems, such as health and safety, education, welfare and equal rights. Organisations are more prepared to support communities through the contribution of resources such as money, time and products. The recipients of these donations may be local charities, the arts, recreations and disadvantaged groups. These programmes have a positive impact on local communities, but also help organisations to create goodwill and a positive image with customers and other stakeholders.

Diversity

Stakeholders are seeking a greater awareness and acknowledgement of demographics and lifestyle issues. Examples of these issues include equal opportunities, integration and an appreciation of differences. Organisations are being forced to consider the utilisation of an increasingly diverse work force, including women and ethnic minorities. Successful companies have realised the benefits of countering racism, sexism, and more recently ageism, through the introduction of company policies.

Environmentalism or 'green marketing'

The concern for the environment has been around since the 1960s, and has increased significantly in the last decade. There is a growing social awareness that the planet's natural resources are scarce. Green marketing refers to the specific development, pricing, promotion and distribution of products that do not harm the environment. Examples of green issues include conservation, air pollution, water pollution and land pollution.

The green movement has gained momentum and is committed to increasing public awareness of the environment and instigating changes in production, marketing and consumption. To date, increased awareness has led to significant changes in packaging and production methods, from design to disposal.

Green issues are not simply costs and threats to the organisation but may offer opportunities for cost reduction and revenue enhancement through interaction and co-operation with customers and other organisations. Environmental awareness can offer competitive advantage and opportunities for companies to work with stakeholders, to gain their approval and support. Involvement of environmental groups in the new product development process may be beneficial, when customers and suppliers may not have the appropriate knowledge. For example, McDonald's received assistance from the Environmental Defence Fund in changing its packaging.

The rising importance and role of green issues must not be underestimated. Examples of the effect of environmentalism include the following:

- Changes in labelling to support environmental claims, e.g. energy consumption on white goods.

- Development of recycled paper products and goods with recyclable packaging.

- Introduction of recycling banks for bottles, clothes and newspapers.

- Increased concern about waste disposal.

- Awareness of dangers of green house gases and biodegradability of certain materials, e.g. plastics used in disposable nappies (diapers).

- 'Cleaner' cars and fuel that produce fewer emissions.

Consumerism

After the environmental lobby and the green movement, the latest pressure group that has directly impacted on organisations is the consumer movement. Consumers now expect the right to be informed, the right to be heard, the right to be protected and the right to quality of life.

The consumer movement is a diverse collection of individuals, groups and organisations that demand the protection of the rights of consumers and campaign on issues such as environmental protection, product performance and information disclosure. Interest groups and individuals can use various actions to promote the cause of consumers, such as lobbying government officials and agencies.

Pressure groups use letter writing campaigns and often place articles or advertisements in national, local or trade press. Consumer groups will encourage the boycotting of companies or their products if they are deemed to be irresponsible or unethical.

Consumer activism has led to legislation related to safety features in cars, and produced many of the consumer protection laws in the UK and throughout the developed world. For example, in the UK there has been a rising interest in consumer issues, as evidenced by publications such as *Which?* magazine and television programmes such as *Watchdog* and *Rogue Traders*.

Marketers should embrace this increase in consumerism, as it can only lead to better marketing and higher standards. By improving information, organisations should be able to develop better relationships with all stakeholders. Dialogue between companies and stakeholders can provide valuable insight into their communities and society as a whole. This will help marketers to understand how their companies are perceived by community groups and other stakeholders, and will alert them to future issues and concerns that may affect their operations.

Strategies for social responsibility

Social responsibility may seem to be a theoretical ideal, but is becoming more important to the success of a company. In enlightened companies, social responsibility is a crucial factor in major marketing strategy decisions. Evidence shows that organisations ignore social responsibility at their peril. If marketers pursue socially unacceptable activities, they are likely to lose the trust of their customers and possibly face the intervention of regulatory bodies. Either way, this can mean a reduction in potential or actual revenue and an increase in cost.

There are four basic strategies for handling social responsibility issues:

Reaction strategy

An organisation using this type of passive strategy will allow a situation or potential problem to go unresolved until the public learns about it. The problem may only be known to limited parts of the organisation, such as the senior managers, or the public may discover it first. The organisation denies responsibility, but attempts to resolve the problems, and deal with the consequences, whilst continuing to do business.

Defence strategy

Organisations will sometimes try to minimise or avoid their social obligations linked to a problem or situation. Usual defence tactics include legal manoeuvring and involving trade unions that endorse the company's way of operating and support the industry. Organisations may use lobbying to avoid government action or regulation.

Accommodation strategy

This is a reactive strategy where the organisation takes full responsibility for its actions. A company may adopt an accommodation strategy where pressure groups are encouraging a particular activity or if there is a threat of government intervention.

An example may be a company that decides to review its production facilities in response to workers' claims that there may be health and safety issues.

Proactive strategy

This is the most positive strategy that a company can adopt as it takes full responsibility for its actions and responds to accusations made against it without outside pressure or government intervention. This strategy requires that a company proactively manage all its activities related to a particular cause or issue. An example would be a corporation undertaking a diversity audit to ensure that equal opportunities are encouraged.

Leadership companies are developing a wide range of management systems to measure, apply and report their efforts to integrate corporate social responsibility into all aspects of their operations. These systems are designed to build a culture that supports and rewards social responsibility at all levels. Systems range from long-term planning to everyday decision making, including processes for designing products and services and practices used to hire, retain, and promote employees.

Companies using more proactive strategies can hope to achieve:

- Reduced costs: The enhanced communication that is often part of corporate social responsibility efforts can help build trust between companies and stakeholders, which can reduce costly conflict and improve decision making.

- Increased attractiveness to investors: some shareholders will screen companies for social and environmental attributes and may only invest in "socially responsible" funds.

- Improved organisational effectiveness: The process of self-assessment and evaluation that is part of a social responsibility programme can have a beneficial impact on company operations. For example, social and environmental auditing and reporting give companies the opportunity to assemble more comprehensive information on operations. This information can help co-ordinate and maximise efficiencies across departments, facilities, and business units.

- Decreased risk of adverse publicity: Socially responsible companies may be better prepared to address the concerns of customers or other stakeholders. Organisations may communicate more effectively with stakeholders about their interests and concerns and address those concerns in business implementation processes. In this way, companies may be able to avoid the bad publicity associated with negative actions such as boycotts organised by consumer groups.

Examples of social responsibility:

- Nike partnered with a non-governmental organisation to help design and implement the company's factory monitoring and community involvement programmes worldwide. The partnership helped Nike gain an awareness of local and global community issues and provided technical expertise in factory monitoring.

- British Telecom (BT) publishes various social and environmental reports and has a large social section on its web site.

Case Study – Café Direct

This Case Study was introduced in Session 4, and questions were posed about suitable promotional activities to communicate the fact that an organisation is taking an ethical stance. It is reintroduced here to highlight issues of ethics and social responsibility.

Café Direct holds approximately three per cent of the UK fresh ground and freeze-dried coffee markets despite very little marketing spend. The company began trading in 1991 as a non-profit joint venture involving the following ethical trading organisations: Equal Exchange, Oxfam Trading, Traidcraft and Twin Trade.

Cutting out the middlemen is key to the organisation's success. The company buys coffee beans directly from small co-operatives in Latin and Central America and Africa. Café Direct guarantees an agreed trade price for the coffee beans which means they have occasionally paid suppliers more than twice the normal market rate. If the international coffee price rises above the agreed trade price, they pay the international price plus a ten per cent 'social premium' which the co-operatives distribute as they see fit. Café Direct also provide an upfront subsidy of up to sixty per cent of the value of one contract. It also provides regular updates on world coffee prices. This is important because the fourteen co-operatives who supply the company only sell a quarter to one half of their beans to Café Direct.

What does all this ethical trading mean for the consumer? The recommended retail price for a 227 gram jar of roast or ground Café Direct is £2.09. A jar of the leading brand Kenco costs £1.99. Café Direct's 100 gram freeze-dried product retails at £2.39; Nestle Gold Blend sells for £2.19. The UK supermarkets have maintained their profit margins and have passed on the cost of ethical business practices to the consumer, a number of whom are clearly willing to pay a slight premium if they believe the company behind the brand is operating ethically.

The issue of ethical trading has been driven by publicity about poor working conditions in factories and plantations in some developing countries. A recent documentary focused on the relationship between a major supermarket chain, and one of its larger suppliers of peas in Zimbabwe where it revealed that out of the retail price of a 99 pence pack of peas, the pickers got less than 1p. Supermarkets have been prompted to initiate audits of their supply and production lines and make public statements about their commitment to ethical trading. For example Tesco recently set up a team of ethical advisors to help monitor the goods it sells in its stores and develop an ethical trading policy. Other major chains, such as the Co-operative, have signed up to participate in a project with the Fair Trade Foundation to investigate the mechanics of implementing independent auditing procedures to meet international ethical trading standards. These include agreements to negotiate with independent worker organisations and to honour or better any locally agreed minimum wage.

As the profile of ethical trading increases, the retailers' position that consumers will have to pay a premium may become untenable – especially if one of the supermarket chains takes a more definite ethical stance to distinguish itself from the other companies.

Questions

1. Define and explain the strategic approach taken by Café Direct, the Co-operative and Tesco to the social responsibility issues raised by ethical trading.

2. Outline the marketing operations issues that should be included in the development of a code of ethical trading.

3. How does the Case Study describe what ethical trading means to the consumer?

SUMMARY OF KEY POINTS

In this Session, we have introduced ethics and social responsibility, and covered the following key points:

- Marketing ethics are moral principles that define right and wrong behaviour in marketing.

- Social responsibility refers to an organisation's obligation to minimise its negative impact and maximise its positive impact on society as a whole.

- The consumerist and environmentalist movements have been responsible for driving organisations towards pro-active strategies in these areas.

- There are four main strategies for social responsibility – reactive, defensive, accommodating and pro-active.

- Organisations taking a pro-active stance can enjoy an improved image.

Improving and developing own learning

The following projects are designed to help you develop your knowledge and skills further by carrying out some research yourself. Feedback is not provided for this type of learning because there are no 'answers' to be found, but you may wish to discuss your findings with colleagues and fellow students.

Project A

Identify any actions your marketing department has taken to respond to consumer groups in your country. How has this impacted on:

i) Customer perception of the organisation?

ii) Profits?

Project B

Through discussion with your colleagues, find out what impact any environmentalist issues have had on your organisation. What changes have been made? How are these actions reflected in your Annual Report & Accounts?

Project C

Talk to colleagues in your marketing department to establish what strategy is in place to deal with social responsibility. Look at your organisation's web site and its Annual Report & Accounts to look for evidence of this.

Feedback to activities

Activity 11.1

You may have found a number of companies linked with the children's charity NSPCC or various cancer charities.

Activity 11.2

Your response to this Activity will vary depending on which organisation you select. It is likely that whoever you work for, you found a number of areas where improvements could be made to the marketing activities.

Activity 11.3

Examples of this type of activity are becoming increasingly easy to find on corporate web sites, and you may have identified several examples. For example, www.heinekencorp.com and their investment in 'water', and www.sainsburys.com and go to 'Our Company', Ethical Trading.

Session 12

Marketing operations in a business-to-business context

Introduction

This Session is the first of four that look at marketing operations in specific contexts. This Session considers the business-to-business, or industrial marketing context, which is made up of organisations that purchase specific types of products, either for re-sale, to use in the manufacture of other products or in their day-to-day operations. In particular, it looks at the ways in which the context impacts on the marketing mix.

LEARNING OUTCOMES

At the end of this Session you will be able to:

- Demonstrate the adaptation of marketing operations principles in a business-to-business context.

- Identify characteristics of business to business and industrial markets.

- Explain business buyer behaviour and the role of the DMU.

- Identify factors impacting on the organisational buying decision.

- Identify and explain key differences in marketing mixes used in a business-to-business context.

Marketing Operations in Context – Business to business (b2b)

Business-to-business describes a situation where one business is selling its goods or services to another organisation that will use the goods or services itself, or combine them with their own product or service and pass them on up the supply chain. Types of business-to-business market are:

Producer markets

This category is made up of individuals or companies that purchase goods to use in their own production facilities or to use in their daily functions. Organisations in this group purchase raw materials, components, semi-finished and finished goods. These markets include a broad range of industries from manufacturing to business and personal services. For example, a production plant such as a canning factory sources aluminium for the cans.

Reseller markets

This group consists of intermediaries, such as wholesalers and retailers, who buy finished goods and sell them to make a profit. Most consumer goods are sold through reseller markets, except those that are sold directly from producers to the public, e.g. specialist or made-to-order furniture. Intermediaries may alter the packaging of the products handled, for example, breaking down a bulk order into smaller units, but do not change the basic physical characteristics of the product itself.

Wholesalers purchase products from manufacturers and generally sell on to retailers, other wholesalers or producers. They can often carry a large variety of stock, which makes the buyer's role much easier as they can find most items they require, from different suppliers, in one place. Retailers purchase products and re-sell them to final consumers. Retailers include supermarkets, department stores and grocery stores, which may stock thousands of product lines and brands. The decision making process usually depends on the size of the store.

Government markets

National and local government make up this group of buyers. These markets purchase a variety of products and services to support their internal operations and provide the general public with education, healthcare, utilities, defence, etc. Types and quantities of products bought by this group depend on the social demands made by various government agencies, and on the country or region. Decision making processes can be complex and slow, due to the huge value of the contracts that government markets can award.

Institutional markets

This group of buyers includes schools, universities, churches, charities and other non-profit organisations. Institutions, like governments, can spend vast amounts of money in support of their various members. For example, a private hospital must source medical equipment as well as the furniture and furnishings.

Information needs and segmentation

Industrial marketers have easy access to a large amount of customer information through government and industry publications. Like marketers in other sectors, b2b marketers can use marketing research to identify potential customers, find out where they are, and estimate their purchase potential.

Industry type

Most information about industrial customers is based on the Standard Industrial Classifications (SIC) system. This categorises all industrial, commercial, financial and service organisations by various economic characteristics. The kind of information available about industrial markets includes: value of shipments, number of establishments, number of employees, export and import data, industry growth rate and major producing regions. The SIC system allows b2b marketers to divide industrial organisations into market segments based mainly on the type of product manufactured or handled. Once the target segments have been identified, the marketers can identify and locate potential customers using the Internet or business directories such as Kompass. Look at http://www.insitepro.com/sic_b.htm for a list of SIC codes.

In industrial marketing, it may be more beneficial to segment markets by benefit sought, rather than by customer characteristics. If a b2b marketer can gain a good insight into his customer's needs and understand the end use of the product, he is more likely to discover opportunities. For example a precious metal supplier could segment his market into those customers needing purity, and those customers requiring strength.

Purchase potential

To estimate the purchase potential of b2b customers, the marketer has to find a relationship between the quantity purchased and a variable available from the SIC data, such as value of shipments or revenue. If the marketer knows that on average, the products he supplies are a known percentage of the buying organisation's costs, then he can calculate an average potential.

The above types of business-to-business markets are also used when segmenting and targeting. Bases for segmenting business-to-business markets include:

Company demographics – for example, how long has it been established, where is it based, how many employees does it have, what is the turnover in monetary terms.

Purchasing approach – for example, is buying done centrally or is it decentralised, what are the buying criteria, what are the buying policies.

Situational factors – for example, size or frequency of order, urgency of purchase.

Operating variables – for example, the way the products or services are used.

Personal characteristics – individual characteristics of the buyers within firms still have an impact on purchase behaviour. However formal the buying structure, individuals' personalities will still affect the way relationships are built, etc.

Activity 12.1

With reference to the SIC system, draw up a table or spreadsheet which defines the key industries to which your organisation supplies. If your organisation does not operate in b2b markets, use the example of a paper production plant.

Characteristics of business-to-business and industrial markets

Characteristics

Fundamental differences exist between b2b markets and consumer markets. The first of these relates to the quantities of products that are bought by b2b buyers. Suppliers often prefer to sell in large volumes as they make more profit than by selling to smaller buyers. Generally b2b purchases are negotiated less frequently than consumer goods. This may be because of expensive capital items, such as machinery which is used for a number of years without needing replacement. Other products may be used frequently, e.g. small components, but the contract for the supply of the components may be a long-term agreement, only seldom re-negotiated.

Negotiations may take much longer than for consumer markets. Purchasing is often made by a committee or buying group. Orders can be large and complex, and there may be several people involved in the decision making process.

Business buyers are generally better informed about the products they purchase than the average consumer buyer. This is not surprising, as their jobs often depend on it!

They will often require detailed information about the product's functional features and technical specifications. In addition to objective criteria for the selection of various products, the organisational buyer may have less rational, more subjective motives for choosing a supplier. It is important that industrial marketers recognise these psychological needs that may relate to their personal goals.

Concerns and needs of the business buyer

B2b buyers will consider a number of factors when they make purchasing decisions. These are usually related to the following:

- **Quality:** B2b buyers need to ensure a certain quality level in the products that are supplied to their customers. Therefore they usually buy products on the basis of explicit product characteristics, namely specifications. This means that the buyer has a checklist for the products that are being considered and can reject any that do not meet all the criteria in the specifications. On the other hand, a b2b buyer is unlikely to purchase a product that is over-specified, as this will normally increase costs. Suppliers to b2b markets need to ensure that their products are designed to match carefully customer specifications.

- **Service:** Suppliers to b2b markets can achieve competitive advantage by offering value added services, even when the product specifications are the same as all the other competitors. Examples of the most commonly expected service include: market information, inventory maintenance, on time delivery, warranties, repair services, replacement parts and credit facilities.

- **Price:** The actual price of the product is important to the buyer as it has a dramatic effect on operating costs and the total cost of goods sold, which in turn influence the selling price and profit margin. The purchase of major pieces of equipment is considered by the b2b buyer as capital investment. Often, the buyer will need to calculate depreciation and total cost of the item over a fixed period of time. Marketers can influence the buying process through non-price competition by emphasising the intangible features and benefits of the product, such as service quality.

Types of b2b purchasing

Straight re-buy: this is a repeat purchase of an existing product or service that has given satisfactory performance in the past. No new information is needed for this type of buying situation. The existing supplier is usually difficult to displace as they have gained the trust of the buyer and it is easy for the buyer to maintain the status quo.

Modified re-buy: The buyer may be dissatisfied with the existing product or supplier and in this case the buying decision has to be reconsidered. In many markets, this means that the incumbent supplier loses the business to a competitor, usually as a result of incompetence or neglect.

New task buying: In this situation, there is no previous history. The buyer is looking for a product or service that he has not sourced before and therefore all potential suppliers have the same chance of winning the business.

Activity 12.2

From discussions with your colleagues in the purchasing department, find out what they look for in a supplier and define their most important concerns under the categories of quality, service, and price. Does your organisation have a 'preferred supplier' list?

Business buyer behaviour and the role of the DMU

B2b buying behaviour relates to the purchase behaviours of individuals or groups in the producer, reseller, government and institutional markets described previously.

In industrial marketing, decisions are frequently taken by groups rather than by individuals. Sometimes the official buyer does not have the authority to make the final decision. This approach allows individuals with relevant expertise to be included in the process, where possible. The group of people who are involved in the decision making process in business-to-business markets is often known as the Buying Centre or Decision Making Unit (DMU).

A DMU may comprise of the following individuals or sub-groups:

- **Users:** These are the people in the organisation who will actually use the product or service being purchased, e.g. the machine operators or supervisors. They often initiate the purchase and write the product specifications. They are also involved in the product evaluation post-purchase.

- **Influencers:** These individuals are usually involved in developing the product specifications and evaluating alternative products. Influencers such as technical personnel are often involved into buying situations involving new or innovative technology.

- **Buyers:** This individual or group has the formal authority to write purchase orders. They are usually the ones who locate and meet with the suppliers and negotiate the terms of purchase.

- **Deciders:** Sometimes known as Approvers, these are the people in the organisation who actually make the decision to buy or who formally authorise the decision. For routine purchases, deciders and buyers may be the same individuals. For more complex buying situations, for high value items or for new task purchases, a decider may represent a more senior level of management compared to the buyer.

- **Gatekeepers:** These people have the power to stop the sellers reaching other members of the decision making unit. They may be secretaries or technical personnel and can interrupt the flow of information to, from and between DMU members.

The size and characteristics of an organisation's DMU are influenced by the number of employees, its market position, types of product being purchased and the company culture.

Stages of the decision process

Recognise the problem

One or more members of the DMU, or other individuals inside and outside the company may identify a particular problem or need. For example, a secretary may realise that a new photocopier is required.

Develop product specifications to solve problem

The individuals involved assess the scale of the problem and try to determine a solution. During this stage, users and influencers such as technical personnel can provide information and advice.

Search for products and suppliers

Members of the DMU may search the Internet, company records and trade directories. They may contact suppliers, visit trade shows, and examine catalogues and trade publications. This stage can last from a few hours to several months. In some cases, the solution may need to be specially designed and built to suit the specific problem or need. The result should be a shortlist of suppliers and product options.

Evaluate products and suppliers relative to specifications

The buyer attempts to match products with their specifications. Suppliers are evaluated according to criteria such as quality image, price and support services.

Select and order most appropriate products

Based on the results of previous stages, the buyer chooses the best product for the job. Several suppliers or products may be selected, especially to reduce the risk of supply disruption, e.g. shortages or bankruptcy. Many organisations today prefer single sourcing and choose to build long-term relationships with a single supplier.

At this stage, specific details regarding terms, credit methods and technical support are also agreed.

Evaluate products and supplier performance

In this final stage, the product's performance is assessed against the specifications. Even though the product may meet the agreed specifications, the problem may not be completely resolved, which means that the specifications have to be revised. The performance of the supplier is also evaluated, based on some of the quality and service criteria mentioned earlier. If there are deficiencies in the service levels, the buyer may seek corrective action or switch supplier. The results of performance evaluations become feedback for the other stages in the decision making process and influence future purchasing decisions.

The full b2b buying decision process described above is almost always used for new task purchases. The process may be simplified, with fewer stages, for straight re-buying or modified re-buying.

Activity 12.3

Through discussions with your purchasing department, identify the DMU in your organisation or one that you know well.

Factors impacting on organisational buying decisions

Business-to-business buying decisions can be influenced by four key factors:

Environmental factors

These are the uncontrollable external forces that face all industries, and normally fall under the STEP headings:

- Social, demographic and cultural issues, e.g. changing consumer lifestyles.

- Technological, e.g. innovation.

- Economic and legal, e.g. competitive actions.

- Political and regulatory, e.g. changes in local or national regulations.

Changes in one or more of these environmental forces can dramatically affect buying decisions, especially when whole industries are affected, e.g. the convergence of some of the companies in technology sectors.

Organisational factors

The buyer's various objectives, e.g. a limited timeframe for negotiations, will have an influence on the outcome and process of making decisions. Purchasing policies, such as the standard procedures that are normally followed for large items of expenditure, may impact on the decision. Other influences include the company resources, for example the budget and need for credit facilities from the supplier. Finally, one of the greatest influences on the decision making process is the size and structure of the DMU. The more individuals are involved, the more complex the decision making process is likely to be.

Interpersonal factors

Relationships amongst the members of the DMU will significantly influence the buying decisions. Some members of the DMU will hold greater power or authority in the organisation or they may have better skills in communicating or persuading others. There may be open conflict between individuals, or there may be hidden agendas, which can be even more of a challenge for the b2b marketer attempting to sell into the DMU.

Individual factors

These are the personal characteristics of the individuals on the DMU, such as age, education, personality and motivation level. Buyer attitudes and behaviours are frequently influenced by values and beliefs, which are closely related to their personal characteristics. The marketer will need to be aware of the individual negotiating styles and how to manage these within the DMU.

The way that an individual in the DMU behaves is also related to his or her position in the organisation and income level. It will be considerably different for a marketer to deal with an inexperienced junior manager compared to a seasoned purchasing director.

How much influence all these factors will have on a buying decision depends on the buying situation, the type of product being purchased, and whether the purchase is a straight re-buy, a modified re-buy or a new task purchase.

Activity 12.4

For the DMU that you described in an earlier activity, write a short report that summarises these factors and what they mean for the organisation.

Key marketing mix differences for business-to-business markets

Product and service

In industrial or b2b markets, especially when all suppliers can meet similar specifications, it is important to establish a differential advantage. Although b2b buyers appreciate a wide product range and innovative products, it is more likely that they buy from suppliers who provide the best added value services. B2b marketers tend to place a greater emphasis on services such as on-time delivery, quality control, custom design, availability of parts and technical advice. There is usually less emphasis on packaging, other than having a purely functional role, i.e. suitable for transportation, storage and communication of essential information – e.g. dosage information for pharmaceuticals.

Price

Price levels in industrial markets tend to be fairly stable in comparison to consumer markets. As always, there are exceptions to this, such as oil, and computer chips, for example. B2b buyers are becoming aware that good quality and reliability are only achieved at high prices. Marketers are also using their competitive advantage in added value services such as training, flexibility and payment terms, to achieve premium pricing.

There are three common ways to determine the price of an industrial product:

- **Administered price:** the supplier may publish list prices for all buyers, or from which certain discounts can be applied, dependent on the buyer.

- **Bid prices:** sealed bids are quotations submitted to the potential buyer, which are not seen by other companies pitching for the same project. Normally the lowest priced contract wins the business. Open bids are made public.

- **Negotiated pricing:** even when list prices and discount structures exist, the buyer and seller may still prefer to negotiate the final price. This may be beneficial to both parties, as specifications can be altered, the product can be customised and extra services can be agreed.

Place

Distribution channels tend to be shorter for b2b than for consumer markets. There are four main options for distribution:

Direct: this is the most common channel, in over 50% of b2b transactions, where the producer sells the products directly to the company that will use them. This is especially appropriate in cases where the product is highly technical, complex and expensive, e.g. Rolls-Royce sells engines directly to aircraft manufacturers.

Distributor: this method is used by producers who want an intermediary who can hold stock of the product and provide credit terms to the purchasing company. Distributors can be specialists in the buyers' industry and stock a wide range of products for that industry. They may specialise in a certain type of product, in which case they may hold other products in the same category. In the former case, there may be a disadvantage that the distributor does not have sufficient technical knowledge to sell the product effectively. In the latter case, the distributor may have a conflict of interest between competitive brands.

Agent: The third method of distribution in b2b is through an agent. These people are normally independent and sell complementary products. They do not hold stock and have no control over pricing or negotiations. They are usually rewarded for their sales efforts via commission.

Agent and distributor: The final method for b2b is for the producer to sell the product through an agent, to a distributor. In this way, the producer can avoid hiring a sales force, yet achieve good geographical coverage in a short time, with minimal investment.

B2b suppliers often need to invest heavily in logistics due to high product cost or special physical characteristics, e.g. raw materials that require special handling, storage and transport. Cost of channels, amount of technical assistance needed and inventory levels required will also influence the choice of distribution channel.

Promotion

Personal selling is the main form of promotion in b2b marketing. The conditions that lend themselves to personal selling are as follows:

- Relatively few customers: marketers can communicate with all existing and potential customers.

- Complex or technical selling: products require face-to-face explanation and demonstration.

- Purchases are high in value: it is cost effective to have a field sales force.

In b2b markets, products are frequently customised to buyer specifications and salespeople can provide an advisory role, for example, helping customers to design special components. Personal selling also allows follow-up visits after the sale, to ensure customer satisfaction and correct product usage. It is imperative that salespeople are sufficiently educated, trained and provided with information about their customers' markets and needs. Telemarketing can support field sales, usually in appointment setting or in handling incoming enquiries. Sales promotion is normally limited to trade shows and exhibitions. Industrial marketers usually have limited budgets, based on historical expenditure.

Advertising

B2b marketers generally use printed trade publications, the financial press, direct mail, catalogues and web sites to communicate with their target customers. Industrial advertising is often designed to create the initial awareness and to generate leads for the sales force. Advertisements often need to convey more technical and factual information than advertisements for consumer goods. They also have to work over a longer period of time, with the extended purchase cycles found in b2b marketing.

Activity 12.5

To see how b2b industries target their customers, look at the following web sites and follow some of the links to see how organisations within these industries use the Internet for marketing communication messages.

www.steel.org.uk
www.britglass.co.uk

Case Study – Hitting new targets

No matter how creative, promotional marketing is often the element of the mix that gets lost in the background or overshadowed by expensive advertising or high-profile PR campaigns. Marketing activity in the business-to-business (b2b) environment often tends to go even more unnoticed, even though its ability to change behaviour and build awareness can play a vital role in generating new business and sales leads.

The tendency for companies to focus on their end-users, i.e. consumers, can result in limited resources and energy invested in incentivising and promoting to the various third parties that feature along the route to market. John Sylvester, director of motivation at performance and motivation company P&MM, believes this oversight is often at odds with the energy that companies pour into building their brand image.

"What we're talking about companies investing in, is the point of contact at which their carefully crafted brands hit the consumer. There are huge marketing budgets spent on creating those brand and corporate images and reputations, which are then taken to market, predominantly through people at some point or other. There is a very strong case for a higher level of investment in the development of those individuals so that they can represent the brand and maximise the investment that's been made in building up the brand and the equity that goes with it."

An obvious example of b2b campaigns that focus on third parties with the ultimate intention of improving brand communications with consumers, can be found in promotional marketing targeted at car dealerships. P&MM has worked closely with Skoda over the last few years to help rebuild and reposition the brand amongst its end consumers. "The dealership network has changed and grown substantially over the last few years," observes Sylvester. "We have had to adapt and develop the motivation proposition from Skoda to meet the changing needs of the brand. The old profile was very much a back street garage-type profile, but Skoda is now working with major dealer groups and is a highly respected brand."

Mark Huntley, director at Tarantula, believes that marketing in the b2b marketplace remains relatively immature, because sales functions still take the lead role in establishing and maintaining relationships with customers. Huntley believes this might change soon. "Technology and margin pressures in most forms of commerce are bringing about radical reviews of the role of what is often singularly the most expensive communication conduit, the sales force. B2b companies are looking to develop complex channels of marketing communications to help prospect, develop trial and repeat purchase, where formerly a salesperson would have spearheaded these roles."

Boring campaigns

If b2b campaigns are to catch up with consumer-targeted campaigns in terms of quality and effectiveness, there is a need for more attention to be paid to creativity. The fact that the targeted audience is positioned within a business environment does not justify the use of boring campaigns.

Spencer McHugh, planning director at direct marketing agency MBO, has found that this is often the case in b2b promotions, particularly when it comes to direct mailing campaigns. "In direct mail, creativity is often one of the most overlooked aspects of the medium. Even for business mailings, you can't get away with a dull mailing – it needs to stand out and make the reader take notice."

Frankie Holloway, partner at communications agency Mustard, says the creativity that accompanies b2c campaigns, will produce similar results in the b2b world.

"Companies and agencies could be smarter by using the knowledge gained from consumer-facing activity and overlaying this into the b2b environment. For example, cut-through is crucial and this is where creative inspiration comes into play together with an in-depth knowledge of understanding how to incentivise your target audience to act."

However, companies may be missing a trick if they simply apply the same b2c marketing techniques in the business environment. Sylvester says: "There is an opportunity to be more sophisticated in the b2b market than you can with sales promotion techniques. This is because in channel marketing, you are essentially really wanting to change a more complex set of behavioural patterns than at consumer level."

Targeting decision makers

Targeting b2b campaigns effectively is more complex than when planning b2c campaigns, given the number of key people likely to be involved in making a purchasing decision. McHugh notes: "The key to any b2b marketing campaign is properly understanding the decision making process. The chief differential is the role of the influencer verses the decision maker – the individual who controls the budgets or signs the cheques who needs to be won over."

MBO recently worked on a campaign for GNER that focused on trying to encourage business people to travel first class. "Here is a good example of who to approach," says McHugh. "It's not the travellers themselves but rather the accounts department who have to authorise the expense."

Omaid Hiwaizi, executive creative director of Hubbard Hiwaizi McCann, agrees that targeting is all-important in b2b campaigns, although as there are a number of different roles within the decision making process, companies usually have the opportunity to do more intricate, smarter marketing than in b2c campaigns. "The cost is higher per contact and it is much more important to get to the correct decision making individual." For this reason, notes Hiwaizi, it is vital to pre-qualify leads.

Broader objectives

Achieving varied objectives is another key difference between b2c and b2b campaigns. "This is an area of development in our industry," says Sylvester. "Objectives are getting broader and more sophisticated. Increased sales is just one objective. More and more we are working with campaigns where there are a whole lot of objectives, including loyalty, relationship building, service quality development and knowledge skills development."

For example, explains Sylvester, instead of rewarding increased sales, a b2b campaign might reward staff for successfully completing a product knowledge questionnaire. Staff are then rewarded for gaining the knowledge that will help them sell more, rather than just being encouraged to sell.

"Making a difference"

How do promotional campaigns within a b2b environment differ from those in a b2c environment? Ian Humphries, marketing manager of Dixons Group Business Services, suggests marketers take note of the following key differences:

- **Offers.** These have to have a business benefit, as usually the buyer is not the owner. Taking up a self-reward offer is often not allowed in modern business culture. A way of getting around this could be by offering a discount alternative to any added value and always contacting the recipient to ensure that they are happy to receive it.

- **Cut-through.** The business buyer has less time and is more likely to reject any unsolicited mail. Creatively this makes it a much more demanding market.

- **Service follow-up.** The business decision maker demands detailed product knowledge in any follow-up calls which often means it is impractical to use a telemarketing agency. Mailings often have to be phased to allow account managers the time to follow up any leads generated.

- **Cost.** Because of the similar target markets in general, it is usually necessary to measure the lifetime value of a customer when calculating the ROI on any programme, not just one-off order values. Unit costs also tend to be far higher than in b2c marketing.

Questions

1. The Case Study highlights that it is important to understand the DMU in the business-to-business marketplace. Explain how the DMU might be made up, and give examples of ways in which the marketing mix might accommodate this.

2. Write two examples of marketing objectives for the business-to-business market, which focus on areas other than increased sales.

3. Explain why the Case Study says it is important for b2b campaigns not to be boring.

SUMMARY OF KEY POINTS

In this Session, we have introduced the way that business-to-business marketing needs a changed marketing mix, and covered the following key points:

- The business-to-business (b2b) marketing mix has similarities to the business-to-consumer (b2c) mix, but its nature means that adaptations are necessary.

- The b2b marketplace is made up of producers, resellers, government markets and institutional markets.

- B2b markets can be segmented by company demographics, their purchasing approach, their operating variables, situational factors, and the personal characteristics of the buyers.

- Purchases can be categorised as new-task, straight re-buy and modified re-buy.

- Business buying is often done through a Decision Making Unit (DMU) made up of a user, an influencer, a buyer, a decider and a gatekeeper.

- Business buying decisions are influenced by environmental factors, organisational factors, interpersonal factors, and individual factors.

Improving and developing own learning

The following projects are designed to help you develop your knowledge and skills further by carrying out some research yourself. Feedback is not provided for this type of learning because there are no 'answers' to be found, but you may wish to discuss your findings with colleagues and fellow students.

Your approach to these projects will differ, depending on whether you work in a business-to-business environment or not. If you do, then look at your own company – if not, try and talk to one of your suppliers about the way they approach their marketing.

Project A

Find out and make notes about the way in which your company segments its market.

Project B

Talk to one of your organisation's salespeople about their experiences of selling to companies, and how they have found DMUs to be made up.

Project C

Talk to colleagues in your marketing department about the way in which the marketing mix is adapted to accommodate the characteristics of your target markets.

Feedback to activities

Activity 12.1

Using the example of paper, the customers are likely to be in the producers market, for example printing companies buying rolls of paper for use in book production. Resellers could be buying finished blocks of paper to sell on to wholesalers or retailers such as stationers. Government or institutions may be buying finished paper products such as paper towels, in bulk, directly from the paper manufacturer.

Activity 12.2

It is likely that their criteria covers some, if not all, of the factors mentioned here.

Activity 12.3

If you work in a large organisation, it is likely that the DMU for high value purchases, such as capital equipment, is made up of several individuals, possibly spanning several different departments.

Activity 12.4

It may have been difficult to complete this activity unless you know the individuals in the DMU very well. Nevertheless, it demonstrates the challenges that face the b2b marketer in designing marketing programmes for b2b customers.

Activity 12.5

You may have picked out many examples. These include:

Glass Pages – a directory of members.
Steel – a moving banner of colour photos showing various steel structures.
News – about both industries.
Statistics.
Information.
Opportunity to register with the site for more and updated information.

Session 13

Marketing operations in a service context

Introduction

This Session continues our exploration of marketing operations in specific contexts, by looking at services. A service is any activity or benefit that one party can offer to another that is essentially intangible and does not result in the ownership of anything. Service marketing can incorporate not-for-profit sectors such as education, healthcare and government. Most commercial services are found in profit-making areas such as entertainment, tourism, finance, personal services and professional services.

LEARNING OUTCOMES

At the end of this Session you will be able to:

- Demonstrate the adaptation of marketing operations principles in a service context.

- Identify the characteristics of services.

- Explain the elements of the extended marketing mix.

- Explain the importance of service quality.

Marketing operations in a service context

There are a wide variety of service industries and products, which can be grouped into two categories: consumer services, performed for an individual or private buyer, e.g. hairdressing, and business services, purchased for use by an organisation, e.g. management consultancy.

The service sector has been one of the fastest growing parts of many developed and emerging economies. In the UK and in Europe, as in the United States, service industries contribute to around two thirds of the economy.

The driving force for the growth in the service sector is increasing economic prosperity and stability. Consumers are buying in more services, e.g. eating in restaurants rather than cooking meals at home. Consumers also have more leisure time, and their desire for fitness and recreation has lead to a boom in the leisure industry. For companies, the increased use of technology and the need for flexibility and specialisation has meant that more businesses services are contracted out, e.g. recruitment. As it has grown, it has also become increasingly competitive, and marketing therefore has an important role to play.

The importance of the marketing mix

All of the 4 Ps of the marketing mix are applicable to services marketing, with some modification. The aim of marketing is to satisfy customers, by offering a product or service with an advantage over the competitors. For services, creating and sustaining this differential advantage is a challenge, due to the characteristics of services.

Product

Most conventional marketing tools related to product can be used for services, such as the product life cycle and New Product Development process. It is more difficult, however, to conduct market research or test new concepts, as it is not easy to explain an intangible service unless the consumer can actually try it out. However, some large organisations in the service industry do spend large budgets on researching customer needs, customer satisfaction, etc. Few barriers to entry mean that competitors can copy successful innovations or initiatives. One of the key advantages of a service is the possibility of customisation that can be used to create an effective product feature or unique selling proposition.

Service companies may consider the development of complementary services or diversification into new markets in order to equate supply and demand.

Additional services such as warranties and after-sales guarantees can also be regarded as important service elements, often in support of a physical product.

Price

The basic methods of price determination and alternative strategies, such as skimming and penetration, can be used with services. The key to success in services marketing is the careful matching of supply and demand; therefore a more flexible approach to pricing and margins is appropriate.

To avoid the possibility of over-supply or excess capacity, companies can offer special prices or discounts to even out demand, e.g. last minute air fares and bargain break holidays. The intangible nature of services tends to increase the use of price as an indication of quality. For example, a customer may choose the most expensive holiday that the travel agent offers, to guarantee a certain standard.

Place

The inseparability of service marketing often means that direct selling is the only possible method of distribution. The scale of a service operation may be limited unless a service provider can reduce the need for him or her to be physically present, e.g. by using franchise systems and agents. For example, a management consultant may belong to a large network of consultants who work on different projects at different times.

Promotion

Marketing communication and branding is more important for services than for physical products and the supplier has to create a strong company and brand image. The supplier has to emphasise the benefits rather than the features of the service through selling and promotional activities. Service providers will often look for ways in which to increase the tangibility of their products, e.g. through demonstrations, exhibitions, promotional literature or web sites.

Some service providers are prohibited from advertising directly to consumers, e.g. the Health Service.

Activity 13.1

Using the Internet and other forms of electronic or printed media, find at least three examples of services (for example, a Hotel, a Health Club and a Bank) that are being promoted and consider how the companies are using the first 4Ps of the extended marketing mix with these services.

The characteristics of services

There are several key differences between services and physical products. They can be summarised into the five categories below.

Intangibility

Most physical products, especially consumer goods, can be seen, touched and possibly even sampled before purchase. Most services are based on a concept or idea that cannot be observed or experienced before use. Purchase decisions for services have to be based on previous knowledge, word of mouth recommendations and often on the physical manifestation, i.e. the place or person providing the service. For example, a consumer looking for a new hairdresser may ask around, look for advertisements and visit the salon to see the premises and meet the stylist personally, before deciding to go ahead with the transaction. This lack of tangibility presents a number of problems for both the consumer and the supplier of services.

Inseparability

Another key feature of service marketing is that the service provider and the service provision are closely linked with the customer and the service consumption. For the service to take place, the provider and the customer usually need to meet at some time, and in the same place. Examples may be going out for a dinner in a restaurant or the use of a library. With personal services such as a massage, the consumer actually has to be present! With professional services such as accountancy, the outcome of the service depends on the co-operation of both parties, supplier and customer, to achieve the end result, e.g. a completed tax return. This need for 'togetherness' has implications for the channels of distribution and the scale of the service operation. Centralised mass production of services is therefore not possible.

Perishability

One of the key features of services is that they cannot be stored. Physical products can be kept in stock indefinitely and sold at different times after manufacture, dependent on the type of product. A durable consumer good such as a washing machine could be kept up for several months, even years, whereas a fast moving consumer good such as a packet of crisps will have a shelf life of a few weeks.

Services have to be consumed immediately, at the time of production and cannot be used at a later date. This is due to the inseparability feature, which means that the service has to be consumed at the point of provision and not afterwards. For example, an airline has a number of seats on a particular flight. If not all the seats are sold, then the airline loses the revenue that could have been made on those seats. The availability of the seats cannot be kept and used later. The matching of supply and demand becomes very important in service marketing.

Heterogeneity

Otherwise known as variability, this feature is a result of the human factor involved in the provision of services. With many services the customer relies in the skill and expertise of the supplier, who may be an individual or a group of individuals. It can be very difficult for both the supplier and the consumer to ensure a consistent quality of service, especially during repeated interactions. Standardisation and quality control are very difficult to achieve and measure. An example of this challenge is for a utility company to guarantee a minimum level of service when call centres employ hundreds of people and a customer could speak to a different person each time they make contact.

Non-ownership

The final distinguishing feature of a service is that the customer does not gain ownership of the product at the end of the transaction. The customer pays the price of the service in order to obtain access to the service or have temporary use. An example would be using a taxi service.

Activity 13.2

Write a short report or draw up a table, comparing the implications of each of the features, under the headings of perishability, intangibility, heterogeneity, inseparability and non-ownership, for the following examples:

- Shoe shine.

- Rail travel.

The elements of the extended marketing mix

In addition to the conventional 4 Ps of the marketing mix, there are 3 further Ps that need to be considered in services marketing.

People

Due to the inseparable and intangible nature of services, a key factor in the customer's perception and satisfaction with the service is the person actually providing the service at the point of contact. Often the extent to which the customer is happy with the service relies heavily on the attitude, skills and appearance of the person providing the service. Very often, especially in personal services, the consumer will use a service precisely because of the person that he or she deals with. Examples of this type of customer loyalty can be found in services where we use the word 'my', such as 'my dentist' and 'my hairdresser'. The importance of the people factor in services should not be underestimated. Companies must allow adequate time and resources for employee recruitment and training.

Often the customer is purchasing the personal qualities and skills of the service provider so the ability to develop close relationships and win customer confidence is crucial.

Physical evidence

As most services are intangible, it is necessary to provide some physical manifestation of the service to help the customer choose. Physical factors should be designed to create a positive image of the service provider and influence the customer perception of the service. For example, a quality restaurant will pay great attention to the ambience, décor and table setting. The menus should be easy and pleasant to read and the food should be cooked and presented in an attractive way.

Service marketers can use design and graphics to portray the service in an attractive way. Promotional materials, especially including photographs of the service provider or place where the service is provided, can be important in helping the customers decide which service to use.

One of the characteristics of services, lack of ownership, can be turned to an advantage by stressing benefits this gives, e.g. out-sourcing office cleaners means that the customer does not have to employ permanent staff or use their own equipment.

Companies can build strategic partnerships and alliances with other service companies and make use of shared facilities, such as offices or exhibition stands, in order to portray a company image or demonstrate services.

Process

The final factor of the services marketing mix is the delivery system. There are several elements that are included in the process factor, which relates to the way in which services are provided. As we have mentioned previously, it is important to build some level of consistency and quality into the service provision. This can only be achieved if there are systems and procedures in place for dealing with all customer contact. Organisations can use processes to ensure consistency in many areas, including order processing and dealing with customer enquiries or complaints. For example, McDonald's have employees' manuals that outline all of the procedures that the staff in their fast food outlets must use, from cleaning of the restaurant and kitchen areas, to preparation and serving of the meals. Wherever possible, all systems, procedures and ingredients in the service package should be standardised, to avoid any variability.

Services cannot usually be protected by patents, so it is important for companies to protect trade secrets and tacit knowledge that give them a competitive edge. Use of registered trademarks is one method companies can use.

Service companies also need excellent logistics systems to balance the fluctuations of supply and demand. Many companies will achieve this through well-managed booking and reservation systems. Other types of service organisations rely on good administration and project management skills.

Activity 13.3

Through discussion with your colleagues, think of the some examples of where well-known service providers use the above 3 elements of the marketing mix.

The importance of service quality

Services are very difficult to evaluate, because of the characteristics described previously. Service quality is defined as a customer's perception of how well a service meets or exceeds their expectations. It is the primary role of a services marketer to close any gaps between customer perception and reality. Marketers must examine their service quality from a customer's point of view. Therefore service organisations need to determine what customers expect and then develop products that meet or exceed those expectations. For example, a restaurant may offer wonderful food in a great atmosphere, but the customer may be more concerned with the waiting time or the cleanliness of the washroom facilities.

Customer evaluation

The greatest obstacle to the evaluation of services is the intangible nature. Customers have to trust the provider of the service and believe that they will deliver on their service promise. Customers can use five criteria to judge service quality:

Tangibles

These are the factors that are known as physical evidence:

- Appearance of physical facilities.
- Appearance of service personnel, e.g. attractive uniforms.
- Tools or equipment to provide the service.

Reliability

The most important in determining customer evaluations of quality, related to the consistency and dependability of the service:

- Delivering as promised, e.g. train runs on time.
- Accuracy of paperwork, e.g. accurate electricity bill.

Responsiveness

Willingness of employees to provide the service:

- Returning customer calls.
- Providing prompt service.
- Handling urgent requests, e.g. emergency appointments.

Assurance

Knowledge and competence of employees and their ability to instil confidence:

- Knowledge and skills, e.g. qualifications and training record of employees.
- Company name and reputation.
- Personal characteristics of employees, e.g. good problem solvers.

Empathy

- Listening to customer needs.
- Caring about customer interests.
- Providing personalised attention.

Service companies should be aware that the majority of these criteria relate to employee performance, making the 'people' factor critical to service success.

Delivering exceptional service quality

In order to provide consistent high quality service, organisations must manage the four factors that make up service quality:

Understanding customer expectations

- Marketing research: surveys and focus groups can be used to discover customer needs and expectations. Feedback forms are often used in hotels and restaurants to get customer ideas about service levels.

- Open internal communication: employees can be an excellent source of information, especially those that interact regularly with customers.

Service quality specifications

- Service goals: to ensure that the standards are achieved, the company must establish acceptable target levels, against which the actual levels can be measured. These goals must relate to the customer expectations.

- Management commitment to service quality: It is essential that all employees and managers within a company be committed to providing a quality customer service.

Employee performance

- Training: Employees in service companies need to be carefully recruited and trained to perform their customer contact roles effectively. Customer service employees are the vital link to the customer and their performance is critical to customer perception of service quality. In order to understand their roles, companies can provide them with information on the customers, service specifications and on the organisation itself.

- Evaluation and compensation systems: Manual service employees are paid on the basis of output or other type of quantified measurement. It may be more beneficial for service organisations to evaluate and reward their staff according to customer-oriented factors, such as friendliness, effort and customer satisfaction.

Managing service expectations

- Advertising: service companies should aim to deliver what they promise in all forms of marketing communication. They must set realistic expectations about their services that avoid any disappointment on the part of the customer.

- Good internal communications: Ideally, all departments within a service organisation must be involved in customer service. For example, it is crucial that the marketing department of a bank informs the operations team of any special promotion or new product that they have launched, e.g. new mortgage.

It is becoming increasingly recognised that all products have a service component and that this service element has a substantial influence on customer choice. Therefore many of the concepts of service marketing and in particular service quality are being applied to all areas of marketing, including business-to-business products and consumer goods.

Case Study – Amplify reputation

Laurie Young is the first global head of marketing for the corporate finance and recovery division of professional services firm PricewaterhouseCoopers (PwC). Laurie has given a lot of thought to how the evolutionary curve of marketing operates in different industries at different times.

It starts in the early days of an industry, when it's young and innovative and can usually sell everything it can make. So there's little need to embrace the discipline of marketing. The focus is on selling and promotional activities like brochures and events.

But the industry starts moving up the evolutionary curve as it begins to approach market maturity. At that stage, companies in that sector have to begin to embrace marketing that is professional and targeted if they want to stay the course. It's not an option but a necessity, he believes.

The routes of this evolution lie back in the late 1950s/early 1960s, when the grocery business with companies like Mars, Unilever and Procter and Gamble approached market maturity: "Marketing came of age as they began to build marketing into their businesses." It's also why a lot of early teaching and theory about marketing is FMCG-orientated, he believes.

In the 1970s it was the turn of the car industry, which began the process of understanding customer requirements and building that into products aimed at target segments. Again, according to Young, it was driven by necessity.

He sees it happening now in the computing and telecoms sectors, both industries he worked in prior to his arrival at PwC just over a year and a half ago. "And they are struggling to find a value proposition," he believes. "I predict that the survivors will be those who build marketing into the very guts of their businesses. There are skilled individuals and examples of excellent campaigns in those industries but marketing hasn't been embedded into the organisations."

And the professional services sector could be the next candidate in the coming years. "The symptoms that point to professional services being at the beginnings of market maturity include changes in market conditions and regulations, changes in the structure of the industry with more activities like mergers and acquisitions, and clients becoming more sophisticated," he says.

Becoming more marketing oriented will not be a case of a straightforward transferring of the principles that define consumer goods marketing to professional services, however. Young, who has overseen the Canon of Knowledge in services marketing for CIM, is a firm advocate of the need to look at services marketing through a somewhat different lens.

Defining professional services

And he defines professional services as any professional service where professional skills have been used as a barrier to entry, whether headhunting, law, architecture, accountancy or consultancy. Till now, professional services has been about what he describes as asymmetric information, where the professional knows more than the client. But as clients become more familiar with the process, their purchase criteria change as they move from being naive to informed buyers.

That's forcing a debate about the nature of professional services, which Young is keen to be part of. So, in 1999, having just sold his own marketing services consultancy, the head hunters who approached him to become the first head of global marketing in PwC's corporate finance and recovery division were knocking on an open door.

What impressed him and continues to do so, he says, is the breadth and depth of the firm, not only in terms of the skills it can offer but its geographic spread. It's the world's largest professional services organisation, formed from a merger of Price Waterhouse and Coopers & Lybrand in 1998. It has revenues of around $20 billion, roughly 9,000 partners of 150,000 staff and a presence in 150 countries.

Room for improvement

Young's division oversees activities like international reorganisations, mergers and acquisitions, bankruptcies and turnarounds.

During the recruitment process what persuaded him that this would be the right move was the recognition by all the partners that the division's marketing needed to be improved.

Unlike auditing, for example, which is regular and what Young describes as 'annuity' business, services like consultancy and corporate finance operate project by project. And corporate finance, because it encompasses a wide range of services, has to confront a huge range of competitors such as merchant banks, the other 'big five' firms, boutiques offering recovery services, strategy firms, and so on.

So in an organisation like PwC the key drivers are the quality of the people and the standard of the work they do for clients. These factors combine to contribute to the firm's reputation and attract client referral, which in turn builds up the brand as a whole. It's a complex process based on the intermingling of the firm and the individual partners.

Because Young believes in getting to grips with where a business is now, not where it thinks or hopes it might be, his first step was to collect objective data about the firm's position in the market. "What is the reputation of PwC in the corporate finance/recovery market, and what about the lead individuals in those markets? So if you first measure that, and then use marketing techniques to amplify that reputation, what happens is that you create demand pull. If products are about push, professional services are about creating demand pull."

Marketing in this environment works at three levels. First there is contact marketing, which is everything done face to face with clients, from proposals to corporate hospitality. At the next level is what he calls capability marketing, which is the industrial expertise the firm offers through articles, books, thought leadership pieces – whatever contributes to leading edge knowledge. The third level is company marketing, where the brand and reputation comes into play.

Having spent the first year defining how the services should be marketed, he then set up about half a dozen trial programmes to see if a highly targeted marketing initiative would increase demand pull. "These are straightforward marketing techniques," he declares. "There is nothing mysterious about them. You look at the target market the group lives in and decide how we can enhance the natural momentum of the business to create more revenue at less cost."

The results of those trials have been encouraging, with increased revenues from more effective targeting combining with substantially reduced costs from the more streamlined relationships with marketing suppliers. Backing this up is a new tracking survey of all PwC's corporate finance partners across Europe. It's based on interviews with clients once a deal has been completed, and benchmarked against competitors. Young sees it as a virtuous circle, since having such precise data is becoming directional in terms of helping individuals understand their markets better, and thus understanding where to direct their efforts more precisely.

Role of brand

The role of the brand is critical in a market like this because in the world of professional services, the brand usually means the corporate brand: "With products, branding is a proven technique. In services it's different. Every service has a process through which a client moves. And that can be disconcerting because the supplier tends to be in control of the process because you can't make a brand out of a service as you can with a product."

"What happens is that emotionally users look behind the service offered to the company behind it. So for professional services firms it's the corporate brand that matters." Since the merger, in fact, PwC has developed a number of initiatives to bolster the brand, including carrying out an annual firm-wide brand tracking survey based on interviews with people around the world to measure attributes like loyalty, awareness and familiarity.

Despite the importance of branding, too few in professional services have really grasped the role it plays. Young argues, "Most professional services workers –whether law, architecture, or whatever, who work for a firm with a well-known brand, get so used to clients coming to them for work that they build up a sort of arrogance. And so some begin to discount the value of the brand – until they leave." And then they find life isn't as comfortable without the backing of a powerful brand. What they have failed to appreciate is the symbiotic relationship between the individual professional and the corporate brand.

No central marketing department

Young has purposely not created a large central marketing department, something that would sit awkwardly in a culture that is flexible, diverse and entrepreneurial and where persuasion rather than imposition works best. Instead, he has been encouraging the emergence of a professional marketing cadre who help their local practices in the way they go to market. "My priority has been to enable the organisation to let these people deliver their work. And we've tried to do that by taking a structured approach to the development of marketing as a competence," he says.

A chartered marketer himself, Young would like to see more senior marketers in the higher echelons of companies influencing the way their companies go to market, rather than seeing marketing in terms of the next campaign. At a senior level, he argues, it should be about organisational learning and competence. Marketing is still a fairly young profession. But it's time for it to grow up a bit, he muses: "We need to toughen up as a profession and show how marketing activity contributes to shareholder value."

Source: Amplify Reputation, *Marketing Business*, February 2002.

Questions

1. The Case Study refers to 'the quality of the people and the standard of the work they do'. Explain the 'people' and 'process' elements of the extended marketing mix for professional service firms.

2. Explain the characteristics of services that necessitate an extension to the traditional marketing mix.

3. Explain the terms 'contact marketing', 'capability marketing' and 'company marketing', as they relate to services marketing.

SUMMARY OF KEY POINTS

In this Session, we have introduced the marketing of services and how the mix might be extended to take account of differences between products and services, and covered the following key points:

- Services differ from products because they are intangible, inseparable, perishable, heterogeneous and cannot be owned.

- Although the traditional 4 Ps are still important for services, the mix has been extended with a further 3 Ps – people, process and physical evidence.

- Customers measure their satisfaction with services against criteria such as their quality, and reliability, and the responsiveness and empathy of the staff delivering the service.

- The four factors that make up service quality are:

  - An understanding of customer expectations.

  - Service quality specifications.

  - Employee performance.

  - The management of service expectations.

Improving and developing own learning

The following projects are designed to help you develop your knowledge and skills further by carrying out some research yourself. Feedback is not provided for this type of learning because there are no 'answers' to be found, but you may wish to discuss your findings with colleagues and fellow students.

Project A

Next time you visit the theatre or the cinema, look for evidence of the 'people', 'process', and 'physical evidence' elements of the marketing mix and make notes about them.

Project B

Write a short report outlining a your recommendations for delivering exceptional service quality within your own organisation.

Project C

Talk to colleagues in your marketing department about the importance of customer service in your own organisation.

How is it handled?

Are complaints welcomed?

Are regular surveys carried out?

Feedback to activities

Activity 13.1

Depending on the media that you searched, it is likely that you will have found examples of personal services such as banking, restaurant or home services such as plumbing. You may also have found professional services such as office cleaning, accountancy, or virtual secretaries.

Activity 13.2

Your observations may have included the following:

Shoeshine

- Perishability: if the supplier can't find enough customers, then his income for the day will suffer.

- Intangibility: the only way to demonstrate the service is to show a picture of a pair of clean shoes.

- Inseparability: Customer and supplier have to be in the same place at the same time.

- Non-ownership: this is a lasting service – the customer gets to keep his clean shoes.

- Heterogeneity: consistency of service depends on the individual supplier.

Rail travel

- Perishability: if seats are not sold, then the rail service loses revenue.

- Intangibility: difficult to describe a rail journey, except in the benefit of getting from a to b.

- Inseparability: customer and supplier do not necessarily have to be in same place at same time, e.g. someone can purchase a ticket in advance for another person to travel. However the traveller needs to connect with the train.

- Non-ownership: there is no lasting impression after the journey, apart from being in a different place.

- Heterogeneity: service should be fairly consistent.

Activity 13.3

Some examples:

Singapore Airlines – known for their excellent cabin crew (people).

Hard Rock Café – known for the ambience of their restaurants (physical evidence).

Accenture – known for their systems (process).

Session 14

Marketing operations in a not-for-profit context

Introduction

This Session looks at the way not-for-profit marketing differs from that practised in commercial markets. These differences include the overall objectives that are in place for the organisation, the different target audiences that exist, and ways in which these factors then influence the marketing mix.

LEARNING OUTCOMES

At the end of this Session you will be able to:

- Demonstrate the adaptation of marketing operations principles in a not-for-profit context.

- Explain how organisational objectives differ from commercial markets.

- Identify the target audiences.

- Outline the key marketing mix differences.

- Identify ways in which to measure marketing performance.

Marketing operations in a not-for-profit context

The Chartered Institute of Marketing defines marketing as 'the management process of identifying, satisfying and anticipating customer needs profitably'. This implies that marketing is only appropriate for organisations that have profit as one of their objectives, and whilst that may have been the case several decades ago, it is clearly not the case now.

Charities and the public sector now pro-actively use marketing, even though their objectives, their messages, and their audiences may be very different to those of commercial organisations.

Even the Police in the UK used marketing to try to improve recruitment through a TV campaign, raising awareness of the more difficult aspects of the job, and the need for recruits to have special qualities.

Road Safety campaigns and Health Awareness campaigns are also implemented, passing on important messages to the general public. For example, the dangers of driving under the influence of alcohol or driving while tired are shown through hard-hitting TV advertisements.

The British government recently launched a campaign, 'UKOK', targeted at potential visitors to the UK, with a very positive message aiming to change attitudes about Britain as a tourist venue. One of the government's objectives is to ensure that the economy is growing. The tourism industry provides a valuable contribution to the economy, and it is therefore in the government's interest to invest in a campaign to try to aid its recovery.

Many of the organisations involved in tourism are small businesses, and they are finding their own ways of promoting their services to a wider audience through use of the Internet. The government is taking responsibility for putting right some of the damage that it contributed to by 'closing the countryside' during an outbreak of foot and mouth disease, by promoting 'the country' as a venue.

Activity 14.1

Try to find three different examples of not-for-profit marketing in your own country.

What types of organisation are you able to identify?

What elements of marketing were you initially alerted by?

Differences in objectives

Marketing is beginning widely accepted and practised by:

- **The government and political parties**
  Who look to influence the opinion of the general public on many political issues, and encourage individuals to vote for them.

- **Schools and universities**
  Who look to build relationships with parents or attract students from home and overseas markets.

- **The health sector**
  To change public perception, and to influence the purchasers of health services to buy from them.

- **The leisure services of local councils**
  Who look to improve the quality of life of members of their local community by changing attitudes to fitness.

- **Social services**
  Who need to promote their services.

- **The church**
  Who need to stop a move away from religion and worship.

- **Charities**
  Who look to attract funds for good causes, or create awareness with the general public.

- **Voluntary organisations**
  Who look to raise awareness and attract new members.

From the above list it is apparent that the objectives of these organisations are different to those of commercial organisations, although schools, universities, the Church and voluntary organisations could be said to be looking to grow market share.

Barnardo's (a worldwide children's charity) states its overall objective to be 'to help the most vulnerable children and young people transform their lives and fulfil their potential'.

The British Heart Foundation states its overall objective to be 'to play a leading role in the fight against heart disease so that it is no longer a major cause of disability and premature death.'

A local council states its purpose to be 'to secure quality services, delivered fairly, courteously and responsively by well-informed employees who take pride in what they do', and goes on to say that they aim to 'define our customers and understand their requirements', showing a customer focused intention.

The overall organisational objectives may be stated very differently to commercial organisations, but once these are broken down to the level of marketing communications objectives, for example, then they are similar. Not-for-profit organisations still need to:

Differentiate themselves from other organisations providing the same services, or with the same goals.

Remind the public of their existence, and their purpose, keeping their organisation in the mind of the target audience.

Inform the public or potential users, members or donors of the good work they are doing.

Persuade new members to join, donors to give money, the public to behave more responsibly, etc.

Activity 14.2

Look at www.nhs.uk and www.cancerresearchuk.org to establish their overall objectives or purpose.

Not-for-profit target audiences

Just as there are several different types of not-for-profit organisation now using marketing, there are also different categories of target audience from those of commercial organisations. Let's consider each type of not-for-profit organisation in turn.

Charities

The different stakeholder groups that charities have to satisfy are many and varied. Since charities have started to use sophisticated marketing techniques, they have had to balance the need to satisfy their Charitable Boards of Trustees that investment in marketing will increase awareness, and, in turn, increase the volume of donations.

Their target audiences for marketing messages are:

Donors – corporate and individual – in the same way as commercial organisations, charities can profile their donors and segment their market.

Charitable Board of Trustees – who oversee the decisions made by the organisation.

Volunteers – who may help with collections of funds, or work in High Street retail outlets that sell goods to raise funds.

Employed staff – who need to be kept informed of activities in the same way as the staff of commercial organisations.

The Government – for issues related to the charity. For example, some countries will grant tax relief against regular charitable donations.

Beneficiaries and their families – who may need persuading to take up the help on offer.

Voluntary groups

The Church, the YMCA and the Girl Guides are examples of voluntary organisations that have been existence for a considerable number of years, and which are losing members. Their target audiences include **donors**, to raise the funds necessary to improve the image and services offered. Research is needed to find out how services can be improved to attract members today, and then potential members need to be targeted to tell them about the changes.

Health, education and social services

Target audiences include the **Government**, to secure funding and **potential users** of their services. They also include the **general public** to raise awareness and help recruit appropriately **qualified staff**, as well as younger people into the profession.

Government and local authorities

Target audiences are the **general public**, to encourage votes, as well as users of the services offered and policies introduced, to persuade them that they are the right actions for the good of all.

How the marketing mix differs

We have seen that not-for-profit organisations need to set marketing objectives and carry out research. They also need to monitor their external environment, and competitor activity, as they will be competing with other charities for available funds.

Let's now look at each element of the marketing mix:

Product – the package of services offered. In the case of some charities, there may be physical products offered through retail outlets. The charity will need to ensure that these 'fit' the image they are putting across. For example, fair trade products, or child-safe toys.

Price – in the main, this will be the amount of money that is generated for the service that is given. It is not a 'price' in the traditional sense, as it is not generally 'charged' to anyone. It is the total of donations in the case of a charity, or the amount of funds won from the government in the case of health, education or social services.

Promotion – the main issues here are those of image, and awareness. Many promotional tools are used, including TV advertising in recent years.

Place – charity shops that raise funds and awareness are a consideration.

People – this is an important element of the mix in the not-for-profit environment. Much activity is carried out on a face-to-face basis, and the attitude of and approach used by the 'people', be they staff or volunteers, is important.

Process – for charities and other not-for-profit organisations, the 'process' is that of donating money, accessing services, or accessing information.

Physical evidence – again, it is important that this element ties in with the 'image' that the organisation wants to be associated with. It would be inappropriate to be seen to be investing too many funds into buildings, for example, when the main aim of the organisation is to raise funds for another purpose. However, it is important that something can be 'seen' as being achieved through donations, or payments made for local government services for example. Many organisations' web sites show how funds are being invested or used, and marketing promotions can again play a part in communicating this information to those concerned.

Activity 14.3

Your local school has decided to run an 'after hours' club for children.

Develop an extended marketing mix for this voluntary organisation, considering the two main target audiences – parents, and children.

Evaluating marketing effectiveness

Not-for-profit organisations state their overall purposes in terms that are not particularly measurable. However, this need not be the case with marketing and marketing communications objectives.

SMART objectives are always the first stage in being able to measure the effectiveness of your activities, and progress to your plans. It is in the need to be seen to be using money wisely that not-for-profit organisations differ from commercial organisations. Although marketing departments in companies are accountable for their actions, and may well be questioned if objectives are not achieved, charities in particular are only just winning the argument that high marketing spend can be justified by the amount of funds that are raised as a result. They have to be very careful to set achievable objectives, and to ensure that they can be justified.

Generally, measurements can be made in very similar ways to those in companies, although what is measured is volume of funds raised, rather than volume of sales attracted.

Objectives set in terms of raising awareness, for example, may be measured through pre- and post-testing, and objectives set in terms of customer satisfaction can be measured through regular postal questionnaires.

Case Study – Democracy online

Think hard. Have you recently ticked any questionnaire boxes allowing your email address to be distributed? If so, you could soon be the lucky recipient of some political email. Yes, despite a well-deserved reputation as techno-dinosaurs, British politicians have finally caught on to the potential of the Internet as a marketing tool. Until recently barely 16% of all MPs had their own web site – and that figure excludes Tony Blair and most of the Cabinet. But since the American presidential elections, when stories about Internet campaigning began to waft across the Atlantic, all the main parties here have redoubled their efforts to exploit the potential of the web.

Earlier this year the grandly titled Webmasters for George Bush and Hilary Clinton's Internet sites shared their wisdom with a British political audience, passing on the message about the power of fund-raising and canvassing online. Their British cousins listened in awe to stories about the millions of dollars raised through Mr Bush's personal web site, then scuttled off to re-examine how to use their own piece of cyberspace. But is the Internet likely to bring in substantial amounts of money for politicians here? Out of over $3 billion raised during the US campaigns last year, only $50 million – that's just over 1. 5% – was raised online.

Dr Phil Harris, of Manchester Metropolitan University, is chairman of the Academy of Marketing and an expert in political campaigning. He is sceptical about the web's likely impact as a fund-raising tool. In the United States people have the ability to make instant donations for a wide variety of causes. If you want to raise money you can even download your own fund-raising kit from the net. "A higher level of Internet use, plus a greater culture of donating via the web, means US parties are better placed to take advantage of it. "The starting pistol is about to go off here, and I suspect there will be a bigger effort to appeal for money through e-donations, but up till now voters are more used to phoning a donation hotline or posting a cheque."

Web campaigning

All the parties will have to include the cost of Internet campaigning within their overall election budget, and individual MPs – soon to become prospective parliamentary candidates – must take care not to overstep their own budget. Depending on the size of their constituency, this is likely to be less than £10,000. Calculating the amount spent on web campaigning could prove tricky. "The whole issue of how much you can spend on your web site, especially if it was developed before the campaign began, is a grey area" says Dr Phil Harris. "I suspect e-expenditure will amount to between 5-40% of the total bill."

Not surprisingly, the teams at Tory Central Office and Labour's Millbank Tower are reluctant to reveal the secrets of their Internet strategy. Rumours abound about a six-figure sum spent by the Conservatives to develop and rebrand their site, Conservatives.com. A Central Office spokesman would only say that the party was aware of the need to market itself through the web. A small in-house team is backed up by a twelve-strong effort from an Internet consultancy, Uovo, which has written the software. Anyone visiting it during the past few months will have been treated to a web-version of the banner advertising used for billboards. The site is a content-rich mix of policy information and photos of the shadow Cabinet. Labour has also used its web site to repeat its billboard campaigns. With its internal audience in mind, the site has also been used to offer candidates a 'Web in a Box' service. This do-it-yourself kit, branded with Labour colours, is an off-the-shelf product offering users regular policy and news updates at a start-up cost of just over £200.

Selective targeting

Like the Tories, Labour's Internet team are also coy about the effort which has been ploughed into their campaign. What is clear is that all the parties have been working hard to build up a database of emails which they can use to canvass voters. Mark Pack, in charge of the Liberal Democrat Internet campaign, says the party is particularly keen to use cyberspace as a communication and fund-raising tool. "As the smallest of the parties we think it can be very effective for us. It's a great medium for addressing niche areas, like the environment for instance." He says the party has used the web for direct marketing. "It's something we have been experimenting with. The important thing is to target the way you email people. There is a wide range of quality in the email lists on the market, so it's important to be selective." Neither of the other two main parties will say how they have built up their database of addresses, though Labour claims it has no intention of buying lists. Like his counterparts, Mark Pack believes politicians are a long way from understanding how to campaign most effectively through the Internet. "In five years' time we will know what works and what doesn't, but at the moment no one knows."

Dreams of using the Internet to fill campaign coffers may be unrealistic, but all the parties believe it offers them and their candidates a chance to talk to key voters and develop loyalty at a local level. Shadow Home Secretary Ann Widdecombe, soon to become the Tory candidate for Maidstone and the Weald, is streets ahead of her colleagues when it comes to selling her own brand online. Her WiddyWeb – now famous among journalists and political groupies alike – had more than 6,000 hits in one week after the last Tory party conference. This despite, or perhaps because of, its lack of emphasis on policy. True, surfers can opt to view the official press releases, but most will be drawn to the pictures of Ms Widdecombe's two cats, Caruthers and Pugwash, or the series of constituency snapshots showing her out and about among the fetes and awards ceremonies of her local patch. Colleagues, she admits, may scoff at the 'Ann out and about' section, which features everything from prize pigs to school prize givings, but she is undeterred. "I wanted it to be a way of relating to my constituents right from the start, especially youngsters. There is a genuine interest in the personalities of public figures, as well as an interest in what drives people." There are even plans for a 'Widd-eo'. A web cast from the WiddyWeb could leave more technologically-challenged colleagues gasping. "I'm not a techno-wonk, but I really believe this is the communication tool of the future," argues Ms Widdecombe. "I would say to other MPs, don't run away from modem technology or you will be like a maiden aunt who hasn't learned to drive."

Internet election

The Labour backbencher, Derek Wyatt, who helped to put together Labour's 'Web in a Box' system, agrees that the Internet is important for individual MPs as well as parties. He suspects, though, that politicians need to be wary of expecting too much. "Web sites need to be updated and maintained, and many politicians don't have the time. I get less than 30 hits a day from my site, but as many as 80 emails a day. The important thing is for people to realise they can use email to contact me." Despite the use of the Internet in the US elections, Mr Wyatt says it didn't have a huge effect on the proportion of people who went out to vote. "You couldn't call the recent US election an 'Internet election', not in any substantial sense."

Nevertheless, candidates in the forthcoming British campaign are being advised to make the most of the medium. Ann Widdecombe will use her local party site to email constituents during the election period. She's already included the new blue and yellow Tory branding into her own web site, but is adamant that uniformity shouldn't go too far. "A template is fine, but I am against control." The idea of using the web to project a personal as well as a party political image is, she argues, a logical thing to do. "The web site is a communication channel I am in control of, unlike a TV appearance. I am not interested in image for its own sake, but nor am I against using it as a tool for putting across what I stand for."

The majority of MPs who have ventured into cyberspace have been more willing to allow their own personal brands to be obscured by their party image. Those who take Ann Widdecombe's view stand out from the crowd. Labour's Paid Flynn offers visitors to his site a mix of information and "gossip from the Commons terrace", while the Liberal Democrat Evan Davy is one of several MPs offering links to other local sites – thus providing an interactive service to constituents. The shadow Chancellor, Michael Portillo, has taken the idea of personal image further than most, with a front-page photo-portrait against a dark, some might say Machiavellian, background. Interactive it is not. E-literate voters are politely requested to use the old snail mail system or phone Mr Portillo's office if they want their MP to take up a burning issue on their behalf.

Build loyalty

Few experts believe the Internet will be used to its full potential in this general election campaign. A recent investigation by the Hansard Society, the educational charity which promotes parliamentary democracy, concluded that we could be looking two elections ahead before we really see its effect on the electorate. But in marginal seats the Internet may prove a vital tool in the battle to get the voters to the polling booths and to build voter loyalty in the long term. It is also an easy way of providing instant information to local and national media.

Online chat sessions

According to Ann Widdecombe, its significance is yet to be felt. "I suspect that, by the time the election after this arrives, my main means of talking to constituents will be via email and the web. There's no reason why I can't hold online chat sessions. When I started out, the public meeting was the mainstay of campaigning, but the public meeting is dead." And, as the electorate becomes increasingly cynical about the brand values of the political parties, the power of the personal brand can be exploited via the web without damaging the party image. "A web presence reinforces the image for the candidate and for the party," says Dr Phil Harris. "The web is a way of attracting young voters, and the more interactive a site, the better it will be. The use of the Internet by MPs has been patchy up to now. It remains to be seen how many successful candidates arrive at Westminster without a friendly party anorak to create or update their web page. After almost three weeks of e-canvassing and campaigning, British political cyberspace could look very different."

Source: Democracy Online – *Marketing Business*, April 2001.

Questions

1. Identify from the Case Study the main objectives of politicians in setting up web sites.

2. List the target audiences that you can identify from the Case Study material.

3. A politician from a party in your country has approached you to advise them on the benefits of having a web presence. Write notes for your meeting with them.

SUMMARY OF KEY POINTS

In this Session, we have introduced not-for-profit marketing and how it differs from commercial marketing, and covered the following key points:

- Not-for-profit organisations, including charities in particular, are increasingly using the tools of marketing to meet their objectives.

- Not-for-profit organisations include charities, voluntary organisations, health, education and social services, as well as the government and local councils.

- Whilst the overall objectives of these organisations may differ from those of commercial organisations, marketing objectives may be similar.

- Not-for-profit organisations have many audiences to communicate with. These often include donors, and the recipients of services.

- The elements of the marketing mix may need adapting to service the specific needs of this type of organisation.

- It is just as important, if not more so, for marketers to evaluate the effectiveness of their activities.

Improving and developing own learning

The following projects are designed to help you develop your knowledge and skills further by carrying out some research yourself. Feedback is not provided for this type of learning because there are no 'answers' to be found, but you may wish to discuss your findings with colleagues and fellow students.

Project A

Gather four pieces of marketing communications material from not-for-profit organisations in your own country.

Look at the overall objectives and purpose that are stated.

How do they differ from the objectives of commercial organisations?

Project B

Identify an example of a charity or voluntary organisation that has secured sponsorship from a commercial organisation.

Make a list of the benefits that each party may attract from the relationship.

> **Project C**
>
> Look at the marketing activity of your college or university.
>
> How were you attracted to study there?
>
> Talk to other students and see how they made their decisions.

Feedback to activities

Activity 14.1

Answers to this activity will vary depending on the organisations you identified. Were they government linked, charities, voluntary organisations, health/social services, or educational establishments? What form of communication did you see?

Activity 14.2

The NHS states its purpose as – 'to provide healthcare for all citizens, based on need, not the ability to pay.'

The Cancer Research Society states its purpose as – 'to cure cancer patients faster, cut numbers of people getting cancer, bring better treatments to cancer patients, train more doctors, nurses and scientists for research, and to maximise resources available for cancer research.'

Both of these objectives are very ambitious and not SMART in the way in which they are worded. However, they both clearly demonstrate the difference between the objectives of commercial organisations and those of not-for-profit organisations.

Activity 14.3

Product

The 'product' or service in the mix is the club itself, and the attractions it offers.

Price

If it is to be run as a voluntary operation, then it may be free, or may charge a small attendance fee that will be supplemented by the organisation.

Place

This is the location of the club. It may be run on school premises, or in a local hall.

Promotion

This is the way in which the club will be promoted to potential members, and their parents. It may combine announcements in school, letters home to parents, posters on school notice boards, etc.

People

It may be run by teachers who volunteer their time, or parents, or other volunteers to act as youth workers. It will depend on the objectives of the club as to what qualifications may be needed. For example, if it is to encourage children to take part in sports, then volunteers may need to be qualified as coaches, or if it is to improve IT skills, then other qualifications may be appropriate. The club will have to be careful that it only uses suitable volunteers, because of the vulnerable nature of the potential members.

Process

How will children apply to join? Will there be a waiting list?

Physical evidence

This applies to the environment in which the club is run, and the ambience and atmosphere that is created.

Session 15

Marketing operations in an international context

Introduction

Successful organisations use segmentation to target the market sectors offering the best potential, often using a different marketing mix for each segment. International marketing can be regarded as a similar approach, where further segmentation by region or nation is used. Companies operating in international markets have various levels of international involvement and they will usually devise different methods of doing business in these markets.

LEARNING OUTCOMES

At the end of this Session you will be able to:

- Demonstrate the adaptation of marketing operations principles in an international context.

- Describe how an organisation can obtain marketing information to meet its needs.

- Identify the differences in the marketing environment, and how these should be managed.

- Outline how an organisation may choose between the various structures available for marketing in an international context.

- Explain how the marketing mix may need to be adapted for international markets.

Marketing operations in an international context

Definitions of the different types of international marketing include:

- Global marketing (sometimes called transnational marketing): truly global organisations operate around the world, with fully integrated manufacturing, sales and marketing bases in different countries.

- Multinational marketing: multinational organisations adapt some of their marketing activities for each country.

- International marketing: international companies are actively involved in the marketing activities and sometimes production in foreign markets.

- Export marketing: export companies manufacture their products in the home market, and then sell them into foreign markets.

- Domestic marketing: domestic organisations limit their marketing activities to the home market.

There has been an increasing trend towards globalisation in recent decades, as a result of some significant driving forces:

- International monetary framework: rapid development of the international financial markets. For example, the introduction of the Euro has enabled foreign trade and the even closer alignment of European Union members.

- World trading systems: development of the World Trade Organisation and the regional trading blocs, e.g. EU, ASEAN, NAFTA.

- Increase in global peace: despite recent terrorism and continued violence in the Middle East, there is greater global understanding.

- Domestic economic growth: developed markets have become even more receptive to imports.

- Communications and transportation technology: enables business to be conducted globally.

Global marketing

True globalisation (with standardised products and marketing activities) seems to be achievable in very few industries, usually those that demonstrate the following characteristics:

- Technology based.
- Innovative products.
- Homogenous customer tastes.

Some industries are more suited to globalisation, e.g. aircraft construction, where there are large advantages to using global business systems and a low need for local product adaptation. Other industries are more suited to local operations, e.g. breweries, where there are not many advantages from operating global systems and there is a huge need to adapt to local tastes. For most international marketing, there is a need for balance between standardisation and adaptation.

Comparative advantage

Conventional economic theory explains all international trade. One country has an absolute advantage over another in terms of producing a specific product because the factors of production (wage costs, materials costs, capital costs, etc.) are more favourable. The main advantage of international marketing is the ability to locate certain activities, such as production, in those countries with the most favourable cost or quality factors, e.g. producing computer components in Taiwan. However, in reality, deficiencies in management accounting, especially dealing with transfer pricing and the allocation of overheads, can distort the cost structures so that comparative advantage is not clearly defined.

Economies of scale

Concentrating the total demand of a number of countries on a limited number of plants, with shared logistics and global marketing communication, should lead to economies of scale and give international companies a cost advantage.

Desire for growth and profit

To survive, companies must meet their business objectives, whether that is measured in return on capital invested to shareholders, market share or profitability.

Most of these objectives require growth. Organisations may have to look outside their domestic markets to find the required growth, for example if the home market is stagnating or shrinking, or if the industry is experiencing difficulty or massive change. It may be more favourable to develop business opportunities internationally, in newly emerging markets.

Interestingly, one of the major requirements for international success would seem to be established success in a strong domestic marketplace.

However, many companies underestimate the difficulties that they may face in dealing with customers and other foreign organisations such as local agents and regulatory bodies.

Activity 15.1

Through discussion with your colleagues, find out what kind of international involvement your organisation has, and how this has developed.

Marketing information needs for international marketing

Market research

In order to compile a shortlist of countries that would appear to offer potential for market entry, a company must gather all the available information about those markets. Although in many ways this is no different to researching new domestic markets, there is the inherent danger of making too many assumptions, based on domestic experience. It is important to involve marketing personnel who have experience of international markets, in writing the research brief, conducting the research and interpreting the results.

Secondary research

The first step in analysing a foreign market should be collecting basic market information from secondary sources. Foreign market information can be gathered from data published in reports and surveys. Some of these reports may be freely available but most need to be purchased from the organisation that commissioned the research. Suppliers of data include: banks, libraries, governments and trade bodies such as the Department of Trade & Industry. Commercial suppliers include: market research agencies, publishing companies, consulting firms and database providers.

Types of information

General information about the market such as economic indicators (GDP, inflation, interest rates) can be gathered through chambers of commerce and foreign trade organisations. More detailed information about specific industries can be collected via local trade associations or regional development agencies. Previous export marketing research such as country market sector surveys and global market surveys can be obtained from many sources, especially some of the regional or global trade organisations, for example the EU and WTO, or from publishers e.g. Euromonitor, Economic Intelligence Unit (EIU).

Primary research

In addition to the environmental analysis which can be undertaken using social, technological, economic, political and cultural information (see next section), companies may also need to obtain more specific data related to their target market potential. There are several choices to be made for conducting this type of research. Using in-house resources is not recommended, as they are unlikely to have the necessary experience. It is preferable to employ specialist agencies with local knowledge of customers and the culture. One option is to use a local agency in each country, but this approach requires a significant amount of time to visit the market, brief the agency and supervise activities. A much simpler method is to use a multinational agency that has links in the local markets. This relies on the quality of the local subcontractors used by the agency. A good compromise is to use a domestic agency that can co-ordinate several foreign agencies.

It is highly likely that primary research will be necessary to establish issues concerning market access, such as local standards, patents, trademarks and import regulations. Product potential can be gauged through research into local customer needs and desires, attitudes towards foreign goods and competitor products.

Even more thorough research is needed to write the export marketing plan for a foreign market. The company should estimate sales potential by forecasting the sales volume based on buyer behaviour and price expectations. All cost elements will need to be considered, including internal distribution and promotional expenditure. Forecasts and budgets should take into account other effects on profitability such as competitor activity and exchange rates.

Marketers must be aware that collecting information on foreign markets can be difficult and data is often scarce. All sources must be carefully checked, to ensure the reliability, validity and comparability of data.

Techniques of data collection may have to be adapted to suit different countries. There may be serious obstacles towards research in certain countries, for example, differing attitudes towards privacy or freedom of speech. It may be more difficult to interview people in countries which have strong privacy laws or less freedom of speech. Language issues can also complicate research projects. In some of the former Yugoslavian countries, the languages are similar but it would cause great offence if a questionnaire in Serbian were used in Croatia. In countries like Brazil or Italy, the postal system may not be as reliable as in other countries for delivering research questionnaires.

The cost of researching foreign markets can be considerably higher than research into a domestic market. This may be a result of the large number of markets that need investigation, as well as the complexity of the research projects. Marketers may need to spend more time and money to handle unfamiliar cultural practices and overcome language barriers.

> **Activity 15.2**
>
> For any industry type, search for information on exporting or setting up business in France.
>
> You can use any published sources or look at the following Internet web sites:
>
> www.ft.com
> www.economist.com
> www.insee.fr
> www.eiu.com

The differences in the marketing environment in an international context

There are fundamental differences between countries and even regions within countries. The identification and analysis of these differences between markets is critical in deciding which markets should be entered and in developing effective marketing strategies for these markets. Organisations can use an adaptation of the STEP model to analyse the external environments of the markets being considered for entry.

Social and demographic

Marketing activities have a social orientation and need to consider the institutions of family, religion, education, health and recreation.

- Size of population: There may not be enough people living in the country to support a marketing operation. It is important to analyse the socio-economic distribution and any class systems.

- Natural resources: there may be massive differences in climate and unpredictable weather conditions that affect the markets.

- Literacy rates, educational and skills levels: it is important to consider the local population, in terms of consumers, i.e. audiences for marketing communication, and as potential employees for local operations.

- Family roles: these can affect the choice of target audience for marketing communication.

- Sport and leisure: these vary widely across national boundaries and may affect marketing activities such as sponsorship.

Technological

Some of the marketing technology used in the industrialised regions of the world may be totally inappropriate for some less developed countries. For example, using the Internet to promote products is not an option in countries where computer ownership is low or non-existent.

- Accessibility and distance: It is now relatively easy to travel and transport products between many countries, but there are still some remote countries that are not on the existing trade routes.

- Infrastructure and communication networks, including transport systems, i.e. adequate roads, railways and airports will affect logistics and distribution.

- Media: The marketer will need to establish how well the local market can support the Internet, email and other modern methods of marketing communication.

Economic

Desk research can be used to assess the overall level of development by using indicators such as:

- Economic growth, GDP and GNP.
- Stability and control of currency, exchange rate and inflation.
- Balance of payments.
- Per capita income and distribution across the market.
- Disposable income and expenditure patterns.

Research may also have provided an insight into the perceived role of foreign trade in the local economy. Companies may also want to find out about the various business infrastructures in place, for example, local agents and distributors.

Political and legal

It is important to examine the current system of government and the following:

- Political stability and continuity.
- Ideological orientation.
- Government involvement in business and in communications.
- Attitude towards foreign trade.
- Bureaucracy.

There may be regulatory issues that will affect the attractiveness of the country, such as restrictions on imports, e.g. tariffs and quotas. Some countries may impose legal bans on certain products, usually to protect domestic supply. Restrictions may be placed on foreign ownership of local companies. In some fragile economies, currency restrictions have been set up to prevent the 'export of currency' which means that profits cannot be extracted from the country. There may be favourable terms for entering the market, if the exporting country and the importing country are both members of a trading bloc, e.g. European Union.

Culture and language

The additional, and possibly the most crucial, element that needs to be considered in assessing a market is its prevailing culture. Values and beliefs underpin a culture and these are difficult to reveal and often impossible to change. Culture influences customer preferences, assumptions and ultimately, behaviours. Different cultures assign different meanings to objects, sounds, symbols and colours. This has a massive implication for all elements of the marketing mix, from product development to promotional activity. It is also important for the marketer to take account of the differing social norms, i.e. the unwritten rules that govern the interaction of individuals in a society. For many companies, knowing the correct business etiquette in any particular culture can make or break a deal.

The language barrier can prove to be the most difficult to overcome for many organisations, especially from the English speaking nations. It may be possible to find a local agent or interpreter, but a company needs to understand the local language to become integrated into a market.

Activity 15.3

Using the STEP + Culture format, write a short report on the country that you researched in the previous section.

Structures for international marketing

Methods of market entry

There are a number of ways in which an organisation can enter a new international market, from relatively simple exporting to the most complex Foreign Direct Investment (FDI). Different methods are available to a company wanting to enter a market, which give different amounts of control, risk and involvement in the marketing operation.

Export methods

The company can choose to operate through a third party, in which case the agent assumes most of the risk. The exporting company only need invest a small amount of time and money to 'test the water' and a low level of commitment means that the decision to enter an international market can be easily reversed. However, the exporting company may lose a large element of control over the pricing, promotion and distribution of the product and has to accept a lower profit margin.

Contractual methods (licensing or franchising)

A company wishing to enter an international market can offer all their intangible assets, such as patents, know-how and trademarks, to another company in that market who can manufacture the product locally, in return for a license or franchise fee. This method allows rapid market entry, with low investment and better potential returns than exporting. However it still means that the licensor relinquishes some control to the licensee and could risk losing some of their competitive advantage.

Trading companies

These organisations provide links between buyers and sellers in different countries. They are responsible for getting products from one market to another. They may also help organisations to assess the possibility of directly investing in a foreign market by providing research information and practical help such as legal assistance and foreign exchange.

Direct investment methods

Joint ventures

Two or more organisations can pool their assets or knowledge to create a new company, with shared joint ownership and control. A company that wants to enter a foreign market may instigate a JV by working with one or more local partners. Benefits include the sharing of risk, access to local knowledge, business contacts and existing distribution channels. Disadvantages may be the possibility of power struggles, hidden agendas and conflict of interest.

Wholly owned subsidiaries

The establishment of subsidiaries in the local markets is often known as Foreign Direct Investment (FDI). It gives the organisation the greatest level of control over all marketing and operational activity and can offer the highest potential rewards.

However it also requires a high level of initial investment and carries the greatest risk. It can also be slow to set up and may meet resistance from the local regulators. Acquisition of a local company may be preferable to allow quicker access to the market, and to reap the benefits of existing business relationships. This in turn may lead to problems in clashes of culture and incompatibility between the various elements of the marketing mix (including the people!) in the newly merged company.

Strategic alliances and partnerships

Alliances have become quite popular in recent years, as companies have seen the advantages of sharing the cost and the experience of dealing in foreign markets.

Partnerships can be based on technology – where companies work together to transform entire markets or to create industry standards. Smaller companies may work together for global competitiveness, to defend against industry giants. Organisations may share common distribution channels, manufacturing and R&D facilities. The key benefit of alliances is that they enable firms to respond quickly to technological change. However, the companies involved need to ensure that the rules of the alliance are clearly established and that the alliance gives all parties involved equal benefits. There are many examples of alliances, some spanning the globe, e.g. British Airways and Qantas Airlines.

Criteria for selection of an appropriate market entry method include cost, risk, control, and profit potential. Generally, as cost and risk increase, so does the potential for profit, and the amount of control the organisation has over the venture. Exporting is the simplest and cheapest option, followed by joint ventures and finally, direct investment.

Activity 15.4

Through discussion with your colleagues, find out which structure is being used for your own organisation or one that you know is involved in international marketing.

Adapting the marketing mix for international markets

As mentioned earlier, organisations can use a variety of marketing strategies in different market segments. In reality, companies will try to standardise their marketing as much as possible, but may need to adapt elements of the marketing mix to suit the target segment. Marketing internationally introduces a further complexity to this process, as you may be targeting:

- The same segment in both the home market and the international market.
- Different segments in the home and the international market.
- The same segments as the home market in some countries, and different segments in other countries.

Companies can choose from five basic strategies:

- Offer the same product with the same marketing messages to all segments and countries.
- Offer the same product with different marketing communication.
- Offer a modified product with the same market communication.
- Offer a modified product with different marketing communication.
- Offer something completely new, created specifically for each market.

Product and promotion

Modification to the product could be based on technical specification, where the products need to be adapted to the local market, e.g. electrical goods need the correct plug and voltage. It is likely that the branding remains unchanged across different markets to ensure consistent product positioning and economies of scale in promotion. For example, the name of the chocolate bar Marathon in the UK was eventually replaced by the global brand Snickers.

Some companies offer exactly the same product worldwide and these are usually well-known and well-differentiated brands such as Swatch watches. The product range may be adjusted to suit local tastes, e.g. different Swatch designs dependent on the local market. The vast majority of companies make some modifications to their products to sell internationally, e.g. Heinz tomato ketchup is made with a slightly different formulation in Spain compared to the UK product, to account for local tastes. Packaging may be different – not only the label, but the size and shape of the container, e.g. cooking oil in Italy is sold in much larger containers than in the UK. Colours mean different things in different countries and this will always have an implication for packaging and promotional materials.

Even if an organisation can standardise a product across national boundaries, it is unlikely that the marketing communication can be the same. If promotion can be standardised, the company can realise large cost savings, improve the efficiency of marketing communication and send consistent messages to all markets. Not all types of media are available in every country, which may limit advertising to local press or radio in emerging economies, without access to television or the Internet.

Price and place

Some global organisations might choose to maintain similar prices across the world, although these are subject to fluctuations in currency exchange rates. Others will attempt to set prices according to what the market will bear, leading to different prices in each country. The risk of this policy is that customers in higher priced countries will obtain products from cheaper priced countries. Worse still, distributors may do the same, and then sell on the products to make a higher margin. This parallel importing can create a grey market and undermine the marketing operation in the higher-priced country. To avoid this situation, companies may prefer to sell slightly modified products in each country, with individual order codes, even though this may add to the cost.

Distribution

From the analysis of the marketing environment, the differences in distribution channels will have been identified. Not all markets have the same sophistication of channels. For example, out of town hypermarkets or retail villages may only be found in developed countries, where the majority of the population have cars. In emerging markets, access to consumers may only be possible through certain types of outlet such as markets and smaller shops.

Other logistical decisions such raw materials sourcing and manufacturing locations will also form part of the international marketing strategy. Some global organisations may decide to move certain activities further down the supply chain, closer to the point of final consumption. For example, computer manufacturers may ship their components across the world and carry out the final assembly in the local markets.

There are practical problems related to the large distances that need to be travelled by products, especially if special conditions are required, e.g. shipping ice cream. There are also issues to be resolved linked to storage, warehousing and customs procedures. In many countries, established relationships exist within the distribution network. It may be exceedingly difficult for a company to break into a market where the competitors have tied up all the distribution channels.

Activity 15.5

Using the Internet or other media, find example of products that have differentiated strategies and which parts of the marketing mix differ across countries.

Case Study – Ford and Honda's international organisation

Rising costs and the worldwide spread of shared tastes in car styling have prompted the automobile industry's giants to exploit global economies of scale. However, rivals such as Ford and Honda have approached the task very differently.

Ford was one of the world's first multinationals. Its first foreign production unit was set up in Canada in 1904 – just a year after the creation of the USA parent. For years Ford operated on a regional basis. Individual countries or areas had a large degree of autonomy from the USA headquarters. That meant products differed considerably, depending on local executives' views of regional requirements. In Europe the company built different cars in the UK and Germany until the late 1960s.

Honda, in comparison, is a much younger company which has grown rapidly from its beginnings as a manufacturer of motorcycles in the 1950s. In contrast to Ford, Honda was run very firmly from Japan. Until well into the 1980s its vehicles were designed, engineered and built domestically for sale around the world. Significantly however, Honda tended to be more flexible than Ford in developing new products. Rather than having a structure based on independent functional departments, such as bodywork or engines, all Japan's car makers preferred multidisciplinary teams. This allowed development work to take place simultaneously, rather than being passed between departments, which speeded up time to market for new product launches.

In the 1990s both companies started to review their organisations to take advantage of the perceived strengths of other forms of organisational structures.

In 1993 the Ford 2000 restructuring programme replaced the old functional departments with multi-disciplinary product teams. The teams were based on five vehicle centres, responsible for different types of vehicles. Small and medium-sized cars, for example, are handled by a European team split between the UK and Germany. The development teams comprise of staff from a range of backgrounds, with each taking charge of one area of the process, whether technical, financial or marketing based.

Honda, by contrast, has decentralised in recent years. While its cars have much the same names around the world, they are becoming less, rather than more, standardised. In fact 'glocalisation' – a global strategy with local management – is the most appropriate term. Eventually the group expects its structure will comprise four regions – Japan, the USA, Europe and Asia Pacific – which will become increasingly self-sufficient. As a result, the latest generation Accord family car, initially launched in Japan, and recently in the USA and Europe, differs in all the regions.

Both Ford and Honda argue that their new international structures represent a correct response to the demands of the global market. Much of what they have done is similar, but intriguingly, they have chosen to adopt the same strategies at different times.

Source: *Marketing Operations* Examination Paper, June 1999.

Questions

1. As a Marketing Consultant in the automobile industry provide a report which reviews the advantages and disadvantages of the international structure of Ford (i.e. centralisation versus decentralisation).

2. Continue the above report, reviewing the advantages and disadvantages of the international structure of Honda (i.e. centralisation versus decentralisation).

3. Finally, conclude the report by highlighting the marketing mix implications of Ford and Honda's contrasting international marketing strategy (i.e. globalised versus customised).

SUMMARY OF KEY POINTS

In this Session, we have introduced marketing in an international context and the key differences that are involved, and covered the following key points:

- There are four main options for organisations looking to operate on an international basis:
  - Global marketing.
  - Multinational marketing.
  - International marketing.
  - Export marketing.

- Driving forces towards globalisation include the international monetary framework, world trading systems, global peace, domestic economic growth (in developed countries), and developments in information and communications technology.

- Differences in marketing internationally demand that research is carried out thoroughly. PEST + C(ulture) is a useful framework for identification of external factors that are relevant.

- Methods of market entry include:
  - Export.
  - Contractual – licensing and franchising.
  - Trading companies.
  - Direct investment.
  - Strategic alliances and partnerships.

Improving and developing own learning

The following projects are designed to help you develop your knowledge and skills further by carrying out some research yourself. Feedback is not provided for this type of learning because there are no 'answers' to be found, but you may wish to discuss your findings with colleagues and fellow students.

Project A

Talk to colleagues in your marketing department and find out which, if any, countries your company deals with abroad. Make notes about which products are targeted at which markets.

Project B

For each of your products and markets identified above, make a note of the market entry method used.

Project C

Unless your organisation operates globally, identify two other countries that your organisation might extend their market by entering. What criteria did you use to select these countries? What method of market entry would you recommend for each?

Feedback to activities

Activity 15.1

Your organisation may have an export department or be part of a multinational corporation, or they may not have any international involvement at all.

Activity 15.2

There is a large amount of free general information, but it is usually necessary to subscribe to a supplier to obtain detailed primary research, or to find surveys or reports related to specific industries.

Activity 15.3

You may have needed to make some assumptions about the country, given limited information.

Activity 15.4

You may have found that the organisation you examined has used more than one method of market entry. Sometimes a company will commence their international involvement by exporting, then use contractual agreements before finally investing directly in international markets.

Activity 15.5

There are many examples of products with different elements of the marketing mix used in different countries: cars, cleaning products, food. It is much harder to find truly global brands, with non-differentiated strategies, but the best examples are Coca-Cola and McDonald's.

Glossary

Glossary

Above-the-line – advertising for which a payment is made and for which a commission is paid to the advertising agency.

Account management – the process by which an agency or supplier manages the needs of a client.

ACORN – A Classification of Residential Neighbourhoods: a database which divides up the entire population of the UK in terms of housing in which they live.

Added value – the increase in worth of a product or service as a result of a particular activity – in the context of marketing this might be packaging or branding.

Advertising – promotion of a product, service or message by an identified sponsor using paid for media.

AIDA – Attention, Interest, Desire, Action: a model describing the process that advertising or promotion is intended to initiate in the mind of a prospective customer.

Ansoff matrix – model relating marketing strategy to general strategic direction. It maps product/market strategies.

BCG matrix – model for product portfolio analysis.

Below-the-line – non-media advertising or promotion when no commission has been paid to the advertising agency.

Brand – the set of physical attributes of a product or service, together with the beliefs and expectations surrounding it.

Business plan – a strategic document showing cash flow, forecasts and direction of a company.

Business strategy – the means by which a business works towards achieving its stated aims.

Business-to-business (b2b) – relating to the sale of a product for any use other than personal consumption.

Business-to-consumer (b2c) – relating to the sale of a product for personal consumption.

Buying behaviour – the process that buyers go through when deciding whether or not to purchase goods or services.

Channels – the methods used by a company to communicate and interact with its customers.

Comparative advertising – advertising which compares a company's product with that of competing brands.

Competitive advantage – the product, proposition or benefit that puts a company ahead of its competitors.

Confusion marketing – controversial strategy of deliberately confusing the customer.

Consumer – individual who buys and uses a product or service.

Consumer behaviour – the buying habits and patterns of consumers in the acquisition and usage of products and services.

Copyright – the law that protects the originator's material from unauthorised use, usually (in the UK) for seventy years after the originator's death.

Corporate identity – the character a company seeks to establish for itself in the mind of the public.

Corporate reputation – a complex mix of characteristics such as ethos, identity and image that go to make up a company's public personality.

Culture – a shared set of values, beliefs and traditions that influence prevailing behaviour within a country or organisation.

Customer – a person or company who purchases goods or services.

Customer loyalty – feelings or attitudes that incline a customer to return to a company, shop or outlet to purchase there again.

Customer Relationship Management (CRM) – the coherent management of contacts and interactions with customers.

Customer satisfaction – the provision of goods or services which fulfil the customer's expectations in terms of quality and service, in relation to price paid.

DAGMAR (Defining Advertising Goals for Measured Advertising Response) – a model for planning advertising in such a way that its success can be quantitatively monitored.

Data processing – the obtaining, recording and holding of information which can then be retrieved, used, disseminated or erased.

Data Protection Act – a law which makes organisations responsible for protecting the privacy of personal data.

Database marketing – whereby customer information stored in an electronic database is utilised for targeting marketing activities.

Decision Making Unit (DMU) – the team of people in an organisation or family group who make the final buying decision.

Demographic data – information describing and segmenting a population in terms of age, sex, income and so on which can be used to target marketing campaigns.

Differentiation – ensuring that products and services have a unique element to allow them to stand out from the rest.

Direct mail – delivery of an advertising or promotional message to customers or potential customers by mail.

Direct marketing – all activities that make it possible to offer goods or services or to transmit other messages to a segment of the population by post, telephone, email or other direct means.

Direct Response Advertising – advertising incorporating a contact method such as a phone number or enquiry form with the intention of encouraging the recipient to respond directly to the advertiser.

Distribution (Place) – the process of getting the goods from the manufacturer or supplier to the user.

Diversification – an increase in the variety of goods and services produced by an organisation.

E-commerce – business conducted electronically.

E-marketing – marketing conducted electronically.

Electronic Point of Sale (EPOS) – a system whereby electronic tills are used to process customer transactions in a retail outlet.

Ethical marketing – marketing that takes account of the moral aspects of decisions.

Export marketing – the marketing of goods or services to overseas customers.

Field marketing – extending an organisation's marketing in the field through merchandising, product launches, training of retail staff, etc.

FMCG – Fast Moving Consumer Goods such as packaged food and toiletries.

Focus Groups – a tool for marketing research where small groups of participants take part in guided discussions on the topic being researched.

Forecasting – calculation of future events and performance.

Franchising – the selling of a licence by the owner (franchisor) to a third party (franchisee) permitting the sale of a product or service for a specified period.

Geo-demographics – a method of analysis combining geographic and demographic variables.

Grey market (silver market) – term used to define a population over a certain age (usually 65).

Industrial marketing (or business to business marketing) – the marketing of industrial products.

Innovation – development of new products, services or ways of working.

Internal customers – employees within an organisation viewed as 'consumers' of a product or service provided by another part of the organisation.

Internal marketing – the process of eliciting support for a company and its activities among its own employees in order to encourage them to promote its goals.

International marketing – the conduct and co-ordination of marketing activities in more than one country.

Key account management – account management as applied to a company's most valuable customers.

Logo – a graphic usually consisting of a symbol and/or group of letters that identifies a company or brand.

Macro environment – the external factors which affect companies' planning and performance, and are beyond its control. (SLEPT).

Market development – the process of growing sales by offering existing products (or new versions of them) to new customer groups.

Market penetration – the attempt to grow ones business by obtaining a larger market share in an existing market.

Market research – the gathering and analysis of data relating to markets to inform decision making.

Marketing research – the gathering and analysis of data relating to marketing to inform decision making (includes product research, place research, pricing research, etc.).

Market segmentation – the division of the marketplace into distinct sub-groups or segments, each characterised by particular tastes and requiring a specific marketing mix.

Market share – a company's sales of a given product or set of products to a given set of customers expressed as a percentage of total sales of all such products to such customers.

Marketing audit – scrutiny of an organisation's existing marketing system to ascertain its strengths and weaknesses.

Marketing communications (Promotion) – all methods used by a firm to communicate with its customers and stakeholders.

Marketing information – any information used or required to support marketing decisions.

Marketing mix – the combination of marketing inputs that affect customer motivation and behaviour (7 Ps – Product, Price, Promotion, Place, People, Process and Physical Evidence).

Marketing orientation – a business strategy whereby customers' needs and wants determine corporate direction.

Marketing planning – the selection and scheduling of activities to support the company's chosen marketing strategy or goals.

Marketing strategy – the broad methods chosen to achieve marketing objectives.

Micro environment – the immediate context of a company's operations, including such elements as suppliers, customers and competitors.

Mission statement – a company's summary of business philosophy, purpose and direction.

Model – simplified representation of a process, designed to aid in understanding.

New Product Development (NPD) – the creation of new products from evaluation of proposals through to launch.

Niche marketing – the marketing of a product to a small and well-defined segment of the marketplace.

Objectives – a company's defined and measurable aims or goals for a given period.

Packaging – material used to protect and promote goods.

Personal selling – one-to-one communication between seller and prospective purchaser.

PIMS (Profit Impact of Marketing Strategies) – A US database supplying data such as environment, strategy, competition and internal data.

Porter's Five Forces – an analytic model developed by Michael E. Porter which analyses the competitive environment and industry structure.

Positioning – the creation of an image for a product or service in the minds of customers, both specifically to that item and in relation to competitive offerings.

Product Life Cycle (PLC) – a model describing the progress of a product from the inception of the idea via the main people of sales, to its decline.

Promotional mix – the components of an individual campaign which are likely to include advertising, personal selling, public relations, direct marketing, packaging and sales promotion.

Public Relations (PR) – the planned and sustained communication to promote mutual understanding between an organisation and its stakeholders.

Pull promotion – addresses the customer directly with a view to getting them to demand the product and hence 'pull' it down through the distribution chain.

Push promotion – relies on the next link in the distribution chain, e.g. wholesaler, to 'push' out products to the customer.

Qualitative research – information that cannot be measured or expressed in numeric terms. It is useful to the marketer as it often explores people's feelings and opinions.

Quantitative research – information that can be measured in numeric terms and analysed statistically.

Reference group – a group with which the customer identifies in some way and whose opinions and experiences influence the customer's behaviour.

Relationship marketing – the strategy of establishing a relationship with a customer which continues well beyond the first purchase.

Return on Investment (ROI) – the value that an organisation derives from investing in a project.

Sales promotion – a range of techniques used to increase sales in the short term.

Skimming – setting the original price high in the early stages of the product life cycle to get as much profit as possible before prices are driven down by increasing competition.

SLEPT – a framework for viewing the macro environment – Socio-cultural, Legal, Economic, Political and Technical factors.

SMART – a mnemonic referring to the need for objectives to be Specific, Measurable, Achievable, Relevant and Timebound.

Sponsorship – specialised form of promotion where a company will help fund an event or support a business venture in return for publicity.

Stakeholder – an individual or group that affects or is affected by the organisation and its operations.

Supplier – an organisation or individual that supplies goods or services to a company.

Targeting – the use of market segmentation to select and address a key group of potential purchasers.

Unique Selling Proposition (USP) – that benefit that a product or service can deliver to customers that is not offered by any competitor.

Vision – the long term aims and aspirations of the company for itself.

Word-of-mouth – the spreading of information through human interaction alone.

Appendix 1

Feedback to Case Studies

Session 1

1. **From the article, identify three examples of ways in which strategic and tactical marketing are differentiated.**

    Strategic –   Formed at top level.
    Long term.
    Market-led and customer focused.

    Tactical –   Implemented in the context of strategy.
    Functional.
    Includes research, NPD, pricing, promotion, etc.

2. **List three stakeholder groups that companies are expected to satisfy, and make brief notes about the prime focus of each.**

    Shareholders –   Expect to see increases in earnings per share.

    Employees –   Expect good communication, job satisfaction, pay.

    Suppliers –   Expect regular orders, payments on time, good relationship.

3. **What activities can be found in the article that constitute 'marketing'?**

    Activities suggest tactical measures:
    Marketing research.
    Product development.
    Pricing.
    Distribution.
    Advertising, promotion, selling.

Session 2

1. **Identify the main challenges in the political and legal environment that are likely to affect the BBC.**
    - Government activity – impacts on licence fees, speedy conversion to digital services, changes in policy on advertising/commercial focus.
    - Currently relying on government approval of plans for digital channels.
    - Currently controlled, and unable to raise revenue via advertising.

2. **Identify the main challenges in the social environment that are likely to affect the BBC.**

    ■ Customers' viewing habits demanding greater choice, and better quality of picture and sound.

    ■ More demand for interactive services – e.g. home shopping.

    ■ 'Global' viewers may need more choice of language broadcasts.

3. **Identify the main challenges in the technological environment that are likely to affect the BBC.**

    Developments in technology (digital TV) are presenting new opportunities, and also increasing the threat of competition.

Session 3

1. **Outline the stages in an operational marketing plan.**

    Situational analysis.
    Objectives.
    Strategy.
    Action plan – marketing mix.
    Control mechanisms.

2. **Write two SMART objectives for Diamondback, as mentioned in the Case Study.**

    To increase market share of the Diamondback within the BMX racing bike market by 10% by the end of 2003.

    To increase brand recall of the Diamondback to 60% within its target market of 16-30 year olds in the UK by the end of 2003.

3. **Outline a marketing mix for one of the products identified, and a specific target audience.**

    Product –   A high performance BMX racer, meeting customer needs.

    Price –   Slight premium for quality product.

    Place –   Combination of mail order, Internet, specialist retail outlets.

    Promotion – Combination of e-marketing, advertising, PR, sponsorship of events – to both consumers and the trade.

Session 4

1. **What is Café Direct's USP?**

   Its ethical stance in trading.

2. **Recommend an outline promotional campaign for a supermarket that has decided to take a similar stance to Tesco and the Co-operative in adopting ethical trading to differentiate itself from its competitors.**

   Outline promotional campaign:

   Advertising –   Both message and media are important here. Only those who fit the ethical stance should be used.

   Public relations –   To gain favourable coverage in the media. Also internally to get staff 'on side'.

   Sales promotions – Carefully designed POS material. Appropriate sales promotions e.g. 'Buy 2, and a small donation will be made to... on your behalf.'

   Direct mailings –   To known segments with ethical and ecological views.

   Personal selling –   Staff in store to promote the message to customers.

3. **Write 150-200 words of copy for a press release introducing the supermarket's new ethical stance on trading.**

   "The first supermarket in the UK to adopt a full commitment to ethical trading and 'Fairtrade' companies throughout the world. Buying from us, you can be assured that we are:

   ■ Dealing with our suppliers in an open and honest way.

   ■ Ensuring that suppliers treat their employees in a fair way – especially in terms of employment policies, working hours and conditions, and pay.

   ■ Paying fair prices for all goods, and not overcharging our customers.

   ■ Constantly considering ecological issues as we plan to get our goods to you.

   We live in a fast changing global environment, and your views are important to us. We will actively seek your views on the policies we adopt on an ongoing basis. Contact us on: …

Session 5

1. **You are looking to launch the Diamondback mountain bike. Set some media objectives for the launch.**

   ■ To increase sales of the Diamondback within the UK by 40% within two years of launch.

   ■ To communicate the brand essence in all activities to both Trade and Consumer, so that 40% of the target market perceive it as invigorating and daring.

   ■ To achieve 60% brand recall of Diamondback within the target market of 16-30 year old males in the UK by the end of 2003.

2. **Identify the promotional tools you will use within the launch campaign. Justify your answer.**

   Product will be launched to the consumer target market and the trade.

Tools for consumer marketing:	Tools for trade marketing:
PR – in specialist cycling press and suitable men's glossies.	**PR** – in specialist trade press.
Sponsorship – of BMX events.	**Sponsorship** – trade may benefit from same event.
Internet and opt-in email – news of biking events, and unique sales promotion offers through specialist bike retailers.	**Internet and opt-in email** – can be used. To develop relationships with trade.
Advertising – in glossy mags and specialist cycling press as above. TV is very expensive but may be used seasonally or when an event is being televised.	**Advertising** – in trade press.
	Personal selling – to selective stockists.

All tools used should have objectives linked to their use and evaluation methods used following the campaign.

3. **Explain why you have chosen not to select other promotional tools.**

   All tools used across the push and pull strategy. However, different objectives would be set for consumers and trade. Personal selling is only used to the trade as it would not be cost effective with consumers. Salespeople in retail outlets would be given POS and promotional literature, as well as communication about main benefits offered by the Diamondback.

Session 6

1. **Confusion marketing involves the use of any marketing tool. How does the article state that pricing is used in confusion marketing?**

   Pricing strategies are designed to make comparisons impossible.

2. **The article describes the way that confusion marketing can be used to achieve a premium price. Explain the term 'premium price' and how this type of pricing is usually achieved.**

   Premium pricing is the term usually applied when the highest quality products or services are sold for the highest possible price.

3. **'Marketing is a source of customer value in its own right'. Briefly explain two ways that this might be the case.**

   1. Consumer research is undertaken at a cost. It should therefore be carefully designed, and the results used to ensure changing customer needs are met.

   2. Investments in web sites should be made so that they add value to the customer offering. E.g. Personalised fitness plans for Leisure Club members, recipes for supermarket customers.

Session 7

1. **List three ways in which books differ from straightforward products for marketing purposes, according to the article.**

   1. There is little research you can undertake.

   2. You can't forecast income before the book is written.

   3. You can't write a book to set criteria.

2. **Identify one way that the product was adapted to attract more customers.**

The book was re-jacketed for an adult audience.

3. **How does the article describe the development of a 'brand personality'?**

It describes the jacket-design as being key to this process. It has a distinctive artistic style that is instantly recognisable.

Session 8

1. **The Case Study refers to 'a product-centric era'. Give two examples of how competitive advantage used to be established, compared to ways in which firms are now trying to achieve it.**

   - Used to be achieved through quality and cost.

   - Now achieved through improved 'support chain' relationships, and by adding value through information provided on the web site.

2. **Explain two ways that companies have added value to their distribution channel through use of the Internet.**

   GE Aircraft Engines –   Customer web centre selling spare parts.
                             Provision of 1 million pages of content.

3. **Explain the term 'aftermarket' as it is used in the Case Study.**

The term refers to the relationship built with the customer after the initial sale has been completed.

Session 9

1. **What advantages are there in working in partnership to offer a customer solution?**

Advantages include:

Added expertise and skills.
Market penetration.
Critical mass.
Broader product offerings.

2. **What are the disadvantages of such relationships?**

   Disadvantages include:

   Business strategies can become confused.
   Investment can be wasted.
   Customers can become disappointed.
   Brands can be compromised.

3. **Explain relationship marketing, and how it applies to managing multiple relationships.**

   Relationship marketing recognises that customers are important, even after their first transaction, as it is cheaper to sell to an existing customer than to attract a new one. It includes all activities the organisation needs to carry out to build the relationship, and so includes building relationships with suppliers and other departments in the organisation. It is closely linked with internal marketing, keeping all parts of the organisation working to satisfy the needs of the customer.

Session 10

1. **List three reasons why internal marketing is important, highlighted by the article.**

   1. Happy staff mean happy customers.
   2. Skilled staff are difficult to retain, and internal marketing can help.
   3. Improved staff relations adds positive values to the company brand.

2. **Identify 10 examples of actions companies take to 'market themselves to their staff'.**

   1. Profit sharing.
   2. Home working.
   3. Flexitime.
   4. Paternity leave.
   5. Onsite nurseries.
   6. Duvet days.
   7. Holiday cottages.
   8. Unpaid leave to look after grandchildren.
   9. Workplace gyms.
   10. Free food and drink.

3. **Outline the stages of the marketing plan as it applies to an internal market.**

Assessing the current situation – staff satisfaction surveys.

Segmentation and positioning.

Objectives.

Marketing mix – the message may be the product, the price is the cost of undertaking the activity (including lost working hours), place – may be involved if an event is being organised, and promotion includes Intranets, newsletters, noticeboards, email, presentations, etc.

Control mechanisms to evaluate success.

Session 11

1. **Define and explain the strategic approach taken by Café Direct, the Co-operative and Tesco to the social responsibility issues raised by ethical trading.**

Café Direct – pro-active strategy.

Co-operative – accommodating strategy.

Tesco – reactive strategy (only just setting up their team of advisers).

2. **Outline the marketing operations issues that should be included in the development of a code of ethical trading.**

Product – recalls, packaging and labelling, product safety, not targeting vulnerable customers.

Price – fair pricing, confusion pricing, no price fixing.

Place – no unethical relationships or policies, attention to ecological matters.

Promotion – no false or misleading claims – should be legal, decent, honest and truthful.

Research – no invasion of privacy, no data manipulation, no 'sugging'.

3. **How does the Case Study describe what ethical trading means to the consumer?**

They are prepared to pay a slightly higher price, partly as a result of the 'feel-good' factor they get as a result of knowing they are supporting ethical practices.

Session 12

1. **The Case Study highlights that it is important to understand the DMU in the business-to-business marketplace. Explain how the DMU might be made up, and give examples of ways in which the marketing mix might accommodate this.**

B2b DMU –	User.
	Influencer.
	Buyer.
	Gatekeeper.
	Decider.
Product –	Need to develop products that are easy to use (user), and add-value to package (buyer and decider).
Price –	Need to negotiate (buyer).
Promotion –	Personal selling to communicate personal message to get past gatekeeper, produce specifications (influencer and decider), communicate ease of use (user).
Place –	Need to negotiate delivery terms, and add value by installing and training if appropriate.

2. **Write two examples of marketing objectives for the business-to-business market, which focus on areas other than increased sales.**

To retain 80% of profitable customers during 2003.

To improve perception of service quality from 65% excellence for reliability to 85% for reliability buy the end of 2003.

3. **Explain why the Case Study says it is important for b2b campaigns not to be boring.**

Need to incentivise buyers to act and creativity in promotional activity may achieve 'cut-through' and both attract attention and differentiate from the competition.

Session 13

1. **The Case Study refers to 'the quality of the people and the standard of the work they do'. Explain the 'people' and 'process' elements of the extended marketing mix for professional service firms.**

   People – referred to in the Case Study as 'contact marketing'. Everything that is done face to face with clients – proposals, Reception, consultations, and corporate hospitality.

2. **Explain the characteristics of services that necessitate an extension to the traditional marketing mix.**

Intangibility	–	Unlike products, they cannot be touched or held.
Heterogeneity	–	Service is difficult to standardise because of the 'human' element of delivery.
Perishability	–	Services cannot be stored. Once a consultation appointment time has passed, the 'slot' cannot be re-used and becomes a missed opportunity.
Inseparability	–	The customer is involved in the delivery of the service. They have to be present at the consultation meeting.

3. **Explain the terms 'contact marketing', 'capability marketing' and 'company marketing', as they relate to services marketing.**

   'Contact marketing' refers to the 'people' element of the mix.
   'Capability marketing' refers to the 'process' element of the mix.
   'Company marketing' refers to the 'physical evidence' element of the mix.

Session 14

1. **Identify from the Case Study the main objectives of politicians in setting up web sites.**

   Mainly fund-raising and canvassing/campaigning.

2. **List the target audiences that you can identify from the Case Study material.**

    MPs, existing supporters, prospective voters, journalists, constituents.

3. **A politician from a party in your country has approached you to advise them on the benefits of having a web presence. Write notes for your meeting with them.**

    Benefits of web presence for political parties include:

    - Opportunity to build the 'brand'.

    - New way to become accessible to constituents.

    - Ability to build relationships and develop loyalty at a local level.

    - Email can be used as a form of direct communication.

    - Some opportunity for fund-raising.

    - Helps promote the image of the party.

    - Provision of information to local and national press.

Session 15

1. **As a Marketing Consultant in the automobile industry provide a report which reviews the advantages and disadvantages of the international structure of Ford (i.e. centralisation versus decentralisation).**

    Report

To:	**Marketing Director**	**September 2002**
From:	**Marketing Consultant**	

    Subject: Centralisation vs Decentralisation

    ---

    1. Introduction
        A centralised organisation is one in which senior management delegate little authority to lower levels of the company or to local markets. Decentralised organisations do the opposite, and allow more flexibility for adaptation to local market needs.

    2. Ford has a centralised structure. It has five vehicle centres with multi-disciplinary product teams.

Advantages:

- Consistent and standardised global marketing strategy.

- Economies of scale – less duplication of effort.

- Less confusion amongst marketing staff.

- Gives a higher level of control to senior management.

Disadvantages:

- Over-dependence on senior management.

- Lack of adaptation to local market needs.

- Managers and staff at a local level may become demotivated.

- Slower responses to local competitor activity.

- Slower responses to local customer needs.

2. **Continue the above report, reviewing the advantages and disadvantages of the international structure of Honda (i.e. centralisation versus decentralisation).**

   3.   Honda has a decentralised structure:

Advantages:

- More customised marketing strategies.

- More opportunity for local managers to make decisions.

- Greater responsiveness to customer needs.

- Encourages local innovation and better responsiveness to local opportunities.

Disadvantages:

- Less standardisation and economies of scale.

- Less control by senior management, so greater degree of risk.

- Inconsistent strategy to global customers.

3. **Finally, conclude the report by highlighting the marketing mix implications of Ford and Honda's contrasting international marketing strategy (i.e. globalised versus customised).**

4. Conclusion

Both strategies offer major advantages – globalisation brings economies of scale, and customisation lets the organisation get closer to customer needs. Whichever organisational strategy is selected, the marketing mix will be affected. Examples of these implications are shown below:

Ford – globalisation

Product – each of the five products has the same features and design.

Price – same price in each market, with the exception of local taxes, duties, etc.

Place – distribution through authorised dealers.

Promotion – standard promotional campaigns, with only language changed.

Honda – customisation

Product – different features in different markets. E.g. air conditioning may be standard in the USA, but not in Europe.

Price – reflects local demand, and environmental forces.

Place – adaptation of channel to local market.

Promotion – varied messages and campaigns to suit cultural differences.

Appendix 2

Syllabus

Marketing operations

Aims and objectives

- To build on the knowledge of marketing which you will already have gained.

- To encourage you to test and apply modern marketing theory to the understanding and solution of practical marketing problems and situations.

- To provide you with a sound understanding of the process of marketing planning (analysis, strategy and implementation) and underpinning knowledge for the Postgraduate Diploma subject Planning and Control.

- To provide you with a sound understanding of the marketing mix tools that contribute towards the effective implementation of marketing strategy.

- To be able to evaluate the relative effectiveness and costs of elements of the promotional mix providing underpinning operational knowledge for the Integrated Marketing Communications module at Postgraduate Diploma level.

- To encourage you to explore the multiple relationships which need to be formed and maintained to enable successful and ongoing marketing exchange.

- To examine the need to adapt marketing operations in a variety of contexts; business-to-business, services, not-for-profit and international.

Learning outcomes

By the end of this module, you should be able to:

- Conduct a basic marketing audit considering internal and external factors.

- Understand the process of marketing planning at an operational level.

- Develop marketing objectives and plans at an operational level.

- Understand the need to integrate marketing mix tools to achieve effective implementation of plans.

- Select an appropriate integrated mix (4P's or 7P's) for a particular marketing context.

- Select and justify the use of one or more promotional techniques for a particular marketing context.

- Understand and appreciate the marketing operations process and how it can be delivered through multiple relationships.

- Communicate ideas effectively in a variety of formats; report, article, presentation.

Indicative content and weighting

1.1 The marketing planning process: an overview (15%)

    1.1.1   Conducting a marketing audit:

- Analysis of an organisation's marketing environment Macro: political, legal, economic, socio-cultural, technological Micro: market size/trends, customers, competitors, suppliers, distributors, publics.

- Analysis of organisation's internal capabilities, financial resources, R&D and marketing (strategy, mix, organisation, systems, productivity).

- SWOT analysis and key issues.

    1.1.2   Developing marketing objectives and strategies:

- Marketing objectives as simple goal statements, links to mission statement.

- How marketing strategy defines target markets (from segmentation bases and profiles), differential advantage and desired brand positioning.

- Gap analysis and Ansoff matrix.

    1.1.3   Implementing the marketing plan:

- Implementation barriers.

- Allocation of budgets, tasks, responsibilities.

- Control implications.

- Alternative ways of organising marketing activities: by function, product, region, type of customer, matrix.

- Internal marketing implications, gaining commitment for the plan.

1.2 The marketing mix (50%)

1.2.1   Promotional operations (20%):

- Theories of communication: single step, two step and multi-step communication models, adoption models.

- Advertising techniques: campaign planning, developing creative and media briefs, message content, evaluation.

- Sales promotion techniques: objectives, mechanics (sampling, price-offs, in-pack etc.) evaluation.

- Public relation techniques: establishing publics, press relations, lobbying, crisis management, evaluation.

- Direct and interactive communications: objectives database marketing, direct mail, telemarketing, Internet, evaluation.

- Sponsorship: objectives, types arts, community etc.), evaluation.

- Personal selling techniques (sales force, sales support and sales literature).

1.2.2   Pricing operations (10%):

- The importance of price and its determinants.

- Pricing models for decisions based on cost competition and demand (including basis break-even analysis, marginal costing and pricing elasticity).

- Pricing objectives and methods (cost-plus, perceived-value, competitive parity etc.).

- Adapting the price (discounts, promotions, product-mix etc.).

1.2.3   Product operations (10%):

- The nature of products, components and life cycles.

- Brand management; brand values, brand planning and threats to the brand.

- Product portfolio, product mix (product line breadth and depth).

- New product development (idea .generation, screening, concept development and testing, marketing strategy, business analysis, launch, evaluation and development).

1.2.4   Place operations (10%):

- Distribution channels; consumer and business-to-business, new direct channels of distribution such as the Internet.

- Criteria to select and evaluate alternative channels of distribution.

1.3 Managing marketing relationships (15%)

1.3.1   Relationships with customers:

- Defining the concept, types of relationships, degree of importance.

- The recognition of distributors, intermediaries, agents and franchises as customers.

- Customer retention planning; relationship marketing mix.

- Managing customer relationships.

- Key account management techniques.

1.3.2   Relationships with outside suppliers:

- Briefing, working, control and review of agencies and consultancies (specifying needs/time span/budgets).

- Working with distributors, franchisees and agents; building relationships and controlling performance.

1.3.3   Internal marketing relationships:

- The concept, organisational structures and cultures.

- Effective internal marketing – techniques (recruitment, training, communication, cross-functional team working etc.).

1.3.4   Relationships with the wider public and society:

- ■ The importance of marketing ethics and social responsibility.

- ■ Ethics for marketing executives and within the marketing mix.

- ■ Code of ethics.

- ■ Social responsibility issues: consumer, community, green.

- ■ Proactive, reactive or passive strategies to social responsibility.

1.4 Marketing operations in context

1.4.1   Industrial/business to business marketing applications:

- ■ Distinguishing characteristics of business versus consumer markets.

- ■ Business buyer behaviour, factors affecting buying decisions and buying process.

- ■ Marketing mix differences (service component, bid and negotiated pricing, role of personal selling, use of distributors and agents).

1.4.2   Services marketing:

- ■ Basic characteristics (intangibility, inseparability, perishability, heterogeneity).

- ■ Extended marketing mix (people, process, physical evidence).

- ■ Importance of service quality.

1.4.3   Charity and not for profit marketing:

- ■ Objectives differ from consumer/industrial markets.

- ■ Target markets (donors, volunteers clients).

- ■ Marketing mix differences (product usually ideas and services rather than goods, short distribution channels, approach to pricing, promotion emphasis on PR and face to face fund raising).

- ■ Performance hard to measure.

1.4.4   International marketing:

- Identifying marketing information needs.

- Marketing environment, managing the differences.

- Structure choices; exporting, licensing, joint ventures, trading companies, direct ownership.

- Necessary adaptations to the marketing mix.

Appendix 3

Specimen examination paper

The Chartered
Institute of Marketing

Advanced Certificate in Marketing

Marketing Operations

8.34:   **Marketing Operations**

Time: **09.30-12.30**

Date: **7th December, 2001**

3 Hours Duration

This examination is in two sections.

PART A – Is compulsory and worth 40% of total marks.

PART B – Has **SIX** questions; select **THREE**. Each answer will be worth 20% of the total marks.

DO NOT repeat the question in your answer, but show clearly the number of the question attempted on the appropriate pages of the answer book.

Rough workings should be included in the answer book and ruled through after use.

© The Chartered Institute of Marketing

Advanced Certificate in Marketing

8.34:   Marketing Operations

PART A

The BBC Goes Digital

The British Broadcasting Corporation (BBC) is the UK's main public service broadcaster providing TV, radio and online services to listeners and viewers at home and around the world. A Royal Charter and Agreement governs its constitution, finances and obligations. The Corporation is financed by a licence fee paid by viewers, plus the commercial revenues from its BBC Worldwide operations. The BBC provides a range of domestic broadcast services including BBC 1 and BBC 2 TV channels, and BBC Network Radio Channels 1, 2, 3, 4, and 5 Live. In addition BBC Worldwide is a major international broadcaster which operates the BBC World and Prime Channels and acts as a publishing house for BBC publications of magazines, books, video and audio recordings, and CD-ROMs. The BBC also operates an online channel accessed via the Internet and has a small portfolio of existing digital channels, which includes BBC Choice and BBC Knowledge. The BBC World Service supplies free radio broadcasts to millions of people throughout the world.

As part of its current mission "to meet its public service obligations and operate effectively in a competitive market" the BBC recently announced that it was going to spend more than £300 million on new digital TV and radio channels. Digital represents the latest technology and is regarded as superior to the existing analogue broadcasting systems, enabling better quality sound and vision and the availability of additional channels. As a result of its largest ever public consultation exercise which involved nearly 7,000 responses via its web site and Freepost address, and 1,000 interviews undertaken by the independent research agency BMRB, the Corporation claimed that its plans for the introduction of new digital channels had wide public support.

The BBC made a formal application to the UK Government in January 2001 to replace its existing digital TV channels with four new digital TV services to be launched over the next two years. One of the new TV channels, BBC3, is aimed at 16 to 34 year olds and will focus "exclusively on the young and young at heart". Another channel, BBC4, is aimed at "everyone interested in culture, arts and ideas". A further TV channel (provisionally called Playbox) is aimed at pre-school children and will be mostly educational. The fourth, which has the working title Children's B, is for 6-13 year olds and will have an interactive element. The Corporation also wants to launch five digital radio services including a music station aimed at a young black audience, a speech radio station, an Asian network, a station focusing on music from the 1970s to the 1990s, and a sports network provisionally titled Five Live Sports Plus.

The BBC Director General, Greg Dyke, said viewers and listeners would get "imaginative and distinctive services". The proposal is designed to raise the take-up of digital television and radio. Without a wide choice of free-to-air channels on digital platforms, many viewers may not give up their existing analogue services. The UK Government wants to switch off analogue services between 2006 and 2010, but there are signs that insufficient viewers will have gone over to digital to allow the switch in that period. The BBC's commercial rivals aim to lobby hard against the plans, particularly the proposals for the two children's channels. They believe that the BBC should not spend licence fees on services already provided elsewhere.

PART A

Question 1.

You have been retained as a marketing consultant to advise the UK Government on the proposals presented by the BBC. Present a report which:

a.   Identifies the main challenges in the marketing environment that are likely to affect the BBC and specifies the constraints that it is likely to face as a not-for-profit organisation when implementing its proposals.

(20 marks)

b.   Proposes an approach for developing one of the new channels further and presents an outline plan for its launch in 2002.

(20 marks)
(40 marks in total)

PART B – Answer THREE Questions Only

Question 2.

As a consultant who specialises in advising industrial marketers, you have been approached to write a case history that illustrates excellence in the practice of business to business marketing. Select an example of your choice and provide an outline case history, which should include details of the organisational buyer behaviour of the target market, and the marketing mix employed to meet the specified objectives of the business.

(20 marks)

Question 3.

You are the Brand Manager for a company that markets a range of household cleaning products.

a.   Explore the reasons for the increase in the use of sales promotion in this sector.

(6 marks)

b.   Identify the range of promotional tools available to the company and illustrate their applicability to achieving particular marketing objectives.

(14 marks)
(20 marks in total)

Question 4.

You are the Commercial Director of a book publisher that specialises in producing car repair manuals. You have been asked by the Board of Directors to consider new strategies for growing the business. Produce a report for the Board which identifies options for growth in the short and medium term, and which sets out a process by which these options might be evaluated.

(20 marks)

Question 5.

As the Marketing Operations Manager of a tour operations business that targets package holidays at the 55 and over age group, you have been asked by your Marketing Director to review your distribution strategy.

a.   Outline the various channels of distribution available.

(7 marks)

b.   Identify a set of criteria for their evaluation.

(7 marks)

c.   Recommend an appropriate strategy for your target market.

(6 marks)
(20 marks in total)

Question 6.

Using examples from an industry of your choice, illustrate how new developments in Information Technology may be used in conducting a marketing audit and implementing a marketing plan.

(20 marks)

Question 7.

You have just started your career as a member of the marketing team in a large multiple food and grocery retailer. You have been asked to advise the Chief Executive on the importance of ethics and social responsibility in food retailing. You should consider:

a.   The range of specific ethical and social responsibility issues that might be addressed by the business.

(10 marks)

b.   Ways in which your marketing operations activities might need to change in response to such issues.

(10 marks)
(20 marks in total)

Appendix 4

Feedback to specimen exam paper

The following do not represent full specimen answers to the Examination Paper, but look at:

- The rationale for the question – what the examiner is looking for.

- The best way to structure your answer.

- The key points that you should have included, and expanded upon.

- How marks for the question might have been allocated.

- The main syllabus area that is being assessed.

Note that many of the key points are represented here in the form of bullet point lists. All of these points should be expanded in your answer, unless the examiner **specifically** asks for a bullet point list.

The timings given for each part of each question allow a little time for reading the case study, planning your answers, and choosing which questions you will answer. Remember to follow the instructions on the paper.

Part A

Question 1.

The Case Study for this paper tests your knowledge of factors that affect marketing planning and new product development in a specific non-profit context. Also, note that you are acting in the role of **marketing consultant**, so will be giving an objective, external perspective. We can see that some key marketing issues are highlighted:

- The challenges posed by the **marketing environment**.

- Use of the **PEST** or similar framework to analyse these challenges.

- Use of framework such as **Porter's 5 forces** to look at the industry situation and competitive pressures.

- Constraints posed within the **not-for-profit** sector.

The important thing to remember about approaching the mini case question is that you must apply the **concepts** that the examiner is looking for to the **context** and situation described in the case and/or the question. With every question that is broken up into sections, you also need to consider how marks are spread across the various parts of the question, as this should dictate how much time you allocate to each part.

a.   The examiner in this case has asked you for a **report** which covers part a and part b of the question.

Political factors – government influence, lobbying.
Economic factors – demand for digital technology.
Social/cultural factors – changing viewing habits.
Technological factors – digital technology, Internet, etc.
Competition from large multi national broadcasters who hold financial power.
Indirect competition from other leisure activities.
Customer expectations of better quality viewing.

BBC is presented with an **opportunity** to improve offering to customers through new technology.

General constraints posed by **not-for-profit** context (and recognition that, in the BBC case, it is a **service** and not-for-profit) – potentially conflicting objectives, multiple audiences, governmental influences, etc.

There are 20 marks for this part of the question, so you should spend approximately 30 minutes answering it.

Syllabus –   1.1.1, 1.1.2, 1.4.2, 1.4.3

b.   The second part of your report should consist of a **proposal** and an **outline plan** for the development of one of the new channels and its launch.

Proposal should focus on **NPD process** and include the role of **marketing research** at the appropriate stages of this process. The new channel is a **service**, rather than a tangible product, and your answer should raise the issues associated with services – intangibility, perishability, inseparability and variability.

The plan should include the following stages:

Introduction and background.
Situation analysis and SWOT.
Objectives.
Strategy.

Tactical plan – marketing mix – 7 Ps.
Implementation issues – resourcing, timing and schedule.
Monitoring and control mechanisms.

All of this should be expanded in the context of the launch of the new TV channel.

There are 20 marks for this part of the question, so you should spend approximately 30 minutes answering it.

Syllabus –   1.1.3, 1.2.3, 1.4.2, 1.4.3

Part B

Question 2.

This question is looking for a Case Study about **business-to-business** marketing. If you select this question it gives you a very good opportunity to demonstrate both your understanding of theory and your ability to apply it to a specific context.

You should choose a company with which you are familiar that operates on a business-to-business basis. In your first section you should give the background to the company you have chosen, justifying why you have selected it as an example of **best practice**. You would also need to give some background to business to business marketing in general – for example, **characteristics of business to business markets**, and differences in **buyer behaviour**.

You need to go on to describe the organisation's **target market**, and how the **DMU** is made up. You should also outline the **influences on buying behaviour** in the specific organisational setting. As you write, make sure that you link the **theory** to the **example** in all instances.

Finally, you should outline the **marketing mix**, and refer back to ways in which the particular mix selected has contributed to **organisational objectives**.

There are 20 marks for this question, so you should spend approximately 30 minutes answering it.

Syllabus –   1.4.1, 1.2

Question 3.

This question sets a clear context of **household cleaning products**, and gives you the role of **Brand Manager**. It has two parts, attracting different marks, so you need to pay attention to the depth of content and time spent on each part.

a. The question asks for the **reasons** for the increase of use of **sales promotions** in this sector. Your answer should ideally define sales promotion, and then cover 4-6 relevant points. These might include:

- Increase in specialist agencies in this field.
- Improved measurement of the technique.
- More targetable.
- Used to build brands.
- Used in building relationships with customers.
- Adds to customer's perception of value.
- Supports retailers short-term goals.

There are 6 marks for this part of the question, so you should spend approximately 10 minutes answering it.

Syllabus –   1.2.1

b. This part of the question extends the content to the **other promotional** tools available and useful for **this type of product**.

You should consider both **push and pull** strategies in your answer. Make sure that you link the promotional tools you recommend to appropriate **marketing objectives**.

You might split your answer into these two areas – **consumer and trade**. Suggest what marketing objectives, and then link appropriate promotional tools to each.

Part a of this question tells you that there has been an increase in use of sales promotion in this market – this should be recognised in the emphasis you place on the use of sales promotion in the answer to this second part. You might also want to highlight that different promotional tools are useful at different stages of the **product life cycle**, and in different **buying situations**.

There are 14 marks for this part of the question, so you should spend approximately 20 minutes answering it.

Syllabus –   1.2.1

Question 4.

This question sets a clear context of **book publishing**, and gives you the role of **Commercial Director**. It asks you about **strategies for growth**, which should immediately suggest the use of the **Ansoff** matrix, and also looks at **short and medium term** options, and how they might be **evaluated**. It asks for your answer to be in **report format**, and the format may well attract a couple of marks.

There are two main issues to cover here:

Firstly you should outline Ansoff, producing a **diagram**, but more importantly, applying the matrix to the publisher. Give publishing examples under each of the **four growth options**. You can link this part of your answer to the requirement for **short and medium term options**, by highlighting which strategies could be achieved in the short term, and which would take longer to achieve.

Secondly, it asks for a process for **evaluating the suitability of the options** identified. An ideal framework for this would be the **SWOT analysis**, which highlights **internal and external factors** that will influence strategy selection.

There are 20 marks for this question, so you should spend approximately 30 minutes answering it.

Syllabus –   1.1.2

Question 5.

This question asks you to take on the role of **Marketing Operations Manager** of a **tour operations business** for the **Over 55s**. It focuses on the **distribution** strategy of the firm, and is in three parts.

a.   This first part of the question looks for you to identify the **channels of distribution** available to **tour operators**. You should explain those that would be relevant, and avoid listing all potential channels available.

There are 7 marks for this part of the question, so you should spend approximately 10 minutes answering it.

Syllabus –   1.2.4

b. This next section links to the first part of your answer, and asks you to identify a **list of factors** that you might use to **evaluate the options** available to you. You might use the **4 Cs framework** to illustrate the factors that would impact on the decision – cost, coverage, contribution, control.

Factors might include:

Cost, and impact on profit.
Organisational objectives.
Suitability for target market.
Reputation.
Relationship, or likelihood of being able to build one.
Staff expertise.
Creditworthiness.
Ability to protect/control brand.

There are 7 marks for this part of the question, so you should spend approximately 10 minutes answering it.

Syllabus –   1.2.4

c. The final part of this question asks you for a **recommendation** for an **appropriate strategy** for this **target market**.

The key here is to make sure that you are able to clearly link your recommendation to the target market, in terms of its suitability.

There are 6 marks for this part of the question, so you should spend approximately 8 minutes answering it.

Syllabus –   1.2.4

Question 6.

This question is all about the use of **information technology** to improve various aspects of **marketing planning**. You are asked to use an **example of your choice**. A number of marks will be allocated to your **application of the relevant theory** to this example, so make sure you do not simply record the theory.

No structure is specified for this answer, so ensure you use a logical flow to your answer, using sub-headings to break up your words.

Your **introduction** should highlight the **developments in IT** that are relevant to both the **marketing audit** and the **marketing plan**. These might include the fact that costs of both computer hardware and software are becoming more affordable, speedier, and more user-friendly. Software is being designed to ease such processes and can be customised to your industry or business. Developments in laptops, the Internet, email, mobile phones, etc. can also aid the business.

Give an overview of both the marketing audit and the planning process, linking each stage to relevant developments in IT, and ensuring you use your chosen industry as the example all the way through.

For example, if you use 'banking' as your industry example, you would indicate specific ways that the Internet might be used within the marketing audit to research competitor activity. Under planning, you might highlight the way that databases might be 'mined' to identify segments.

There are 20 marks for this question, so you should spend approximately 30 minutes answering it.

Syllabus –   1.1

Question 7.

This question puts you in the role of a **member of the marketing team** in a large **food retailing** firm, and asks you to advise your **Chief Executive**. The marketing issue is that of **ethics** and **social responsibility**.

a. You might start your answer with a **definition of ethics** and a **definition of social responsibility**. You could classify any activity in terms of impact on consumers, the community and the environment.

You should move on to highlighting specific issues relating to food and grocery retailing – for example, ethics might include treatment of suppliers (fair trading), and social responsibility might include high prices (consumer), too few social goods (community), and pollution through transportation of goods (–). Your list should ideally cover at least one more example of each.

There are 10 marks for this part of the question, so you should spend approximately 15 minutes answering it.

Syllabus –   1.3.4

b. This part of the question asks for ways in which marketing operations might need to change in order to accommodate ethical and social responsibility issues. You might highlight the four strategic approaches – pro-active, defensive, accommodation, and re-active.

The 7 Ps would then offer a suitable structure for the remainder of your answer, highlighting such issues as stocking fair trade products (product), not using price to force small suppliers out of business (price), offering free transport to out-of-town locations (place), sponsoring local community events (promotion), fair pay rates (people), confidentiality of data (process) and not exploiting children by placing sweets at checkouts (physical evidence).

There are 10 marks for this part of the question, so you should spend approximately 15 minutes answering it.

Syllabus –   1.3.4

Appendix 5

Assessment guidance

**There are two methods used for assessment of candidates – Examination
<u>or</u> Continuous Assessment via projects.**

The Chartered Institute of Marketing has traditionally used professional, externally
set examinations as the means of assessment for the Certificate, Advanced
Certificate and Postgraduate Diploma in Marketing. In 1995, at the request of
industry, students and tutors, it introduced a continuously assessed route to two
modules, one at Certificate level, and one at Advanced Certificate. With an
increased emphasis on marketing practice, all modules at Certificate level are now
open to assessment through examination or assessed project.

At Advanced Certificate level, only Management Information for Marketing
Decisions and Effective Management for Marketing are available on a continuously
assessed basis, and at Postgraduate Diploma level, all subjects are examined.

The information in this appendix will:
- Help you prepare for continuous assessment.
- Provide hints and tips to help you prepare for the examination.
- Manage your time effectively in preparing for assessment.

**NB: Your tutor will inform you which method of assessment applies to
your programme.**

Preparing for continuous assessment

If you are being assessed by project you will be given a full brief for the
assignment. This will include what you have to do, how it is to be presented, and
the weighting of marks for each section. **YOU MUST READ THIS BEFORE YOU
START, AND CHECK YOUR UNDERSTANDING WITH YOUR TUTOR.**

The assignment will consist of a number of tasks, each with their own weighting,
so make sure you take account of this in your final presentation of the project.

The size of the project will be identified by a recommended word count. Check
your final word count carefully, but remember quality is more important than
quantity.

The assignment tasks will include a reflective statement. This requires you to
identify what you have learned from the experience of undertaking the module,
and how you have applied that learning to your job.

Questions you might want to consider to help you write this reflective statement included: What was the most difficult part? How did you feel at the start of the exercise and how do you feel at the end? Did you achieve your objectives? If not, why not? What have you learned about yourself as you have worked through the module? How much of your learning have you been able to apply at work? Have you been able to solve any real work problems through work you have done in your assignments?

This statement will be personal to you, and it should look forward to the points you have identified as needing work in the future. We never stop learning. You should keep up this process of Continuous Professional Development as you go through your studies and your career, and hopefully you will have acquired the habit by the time you need to employ it to achieve Chartered Marketer status!

Examinations

Each subject differs slightly from the others, and the style of question will differ between module examinations. All are closed book examinations apart from **Analysis and Decision** (see below).

For all examinations, apart from **Marketing in Practice** (see below), the examination paper consists of two sections:

Part A – Mini case, scenario or article

This section has a mini case, scenario or article with compulsory questions. You are required to make marketing or sales decisions based on the information provided. You will gain credit for the decisions and recommendations you make on the basis of the analysis itself. This is a compulsory section of the paper designed to evaluate your practical marketing skills.

Part B – Examination questions

You will have a choice from a number of questions, and when answering those you select, ensure you understand the context of the question. Rough plans for each answer are strongly recommended.

The examination for **Marketing in Practice** differs in that the compulsory questions and examination questions are all linked to the mini case and additional relevant information given such as memos and reports.

The examination for **Analysis and Decision** is an open book examination and takes the form of a Case Study. This is mailed out 4 weeks before the examination and posted on the CIM student web site (www.cimvirtualinstitute.com) at the same time. Analysis and preparation should be completed during these four weeks. The questions asked in the examination will require strategic marketing decisions and actions. The question paper will also include additional unseen information about the Case Study.

CIM code of conduct for examinations

If being assessed by examination you will receive examination entry details, which will include a leaflet entitled "Rules for Examinations". You should read these carefully, as you will be penalised by CIM if you are in breach of any of these rules.

Most of the rules are common sense. For example, for closed book examinations you are not allowed to take notes or scrap paper into the examination room, and you must use the examination paper supplied to make rough notes and plans for your answer.

If you are taking the **Analysis and Decision** examination ensure that you do take your notes in with you, together with a copy of the Case Study.

Hints and tips

There are a number of places you can access information to help you prepare for your examination, if you are being assessed by this method. Your tutor will give you good advice, and exam hints and tips can also be found on the CIM student web site (www.cimvirtualinstitute.com).

Some fundamental points are listed below.

- Read the question carefully, and think about what is being asked before tackling the answer. The examiners are looking for knowledge, application and context. Refer back to the question to help you put your answer in the appropriate context. Do not just regurgitate theory.

- Consider the presentation style of your answer. For example, if you are asked to write a report, then use a report format with number headings and not an essay style.

- Structure – plan your answer to make it easy for the examiner to see the main points you are making.

- Timing – spread your time in proportion to the marks allocated, and ensure that all required questions are answered.

- Relevant examples – the examiners expect relevant theory to be illustrated by practical examples. These can be drawn from your own experience, reading of current journals and newspapers, or just your own observations. You could visit "Hot Topics" on the CIM student web site to see discussions of topical marketing issues and practice.

Managing your time

What is effective time management? It is using wisely one of your most precious resources, **TIME**, to achieve your key goals. You need to be aware of how you spend your time each day. Set priorities, so you know what's important to you, and what isn't. You need to establish goals for your study, work and family life, and plan how to meet those goals. Through developing these habits you will be better able to achieve the things that are important to you.

When study becomes one of your key goals you may find that, temporarily, something has to be sacrificed in favour of time needed for reading, writing notes, writing up assignments, preparing for group assessment, etc. It will help to "get people on your side". Tell people that you are studying and ask for their support – these include direct family, close friends and colleagues at work.

Time can just slip through your fingers if you don't manage it, and that's wasteful! When you are trying to balance the needs of family, social life, working life and study, there is a temptation to leave assignments until the deadline is nearly upon you. Don't give in to this temptation! Many students complain about the heavy workload towards the end of the course, when, in fact, they have had several months to work on assignments, and they have created this heavy workload themselves.

Knowing how to manage your time wisely can help you:

- Reduce pressure when you're faced with deadlines or a heavy schedule.

- Be more in control of your life by making better decisions about how to use your time.

- Feel better about yourself because you're using your full potential to achieve.

- Have more energy for things you want or need to accomplish.

- Succeed more easily because you know what you want to do and what you need to do to achieve it.

Finally…

Remember to continue to apply your new skills within your job. Study and learning that is not applied just wastes your time, effort and money! Good luck with your studies!

Index

See also the Glossary on page 258.

You may find referring back to the Learning Outcomes and the Summary of Key Points at the beginning and end of each Session will aid effective use of the Index.

Only where subjects are relevantly discussed or defined are they indexed.